D1139075

Desmond Seward

Prince of the Renaissance

The Life of François I

HISTORY BOOK CLUB

This edition published by
The History Book Club
St Giles House
49–50 Poland Street, London W1A 2LG,
by arrangement with Constable & Company Limited

This book was designed and produced by
George Rainbird Limited, Marble Arch House,
44 Edgware Road, London W2

Text set and printed by
Jarrold & Sons Limited, Norwich
Colour plates and jacket originated and printed by
Impact Litho Limited, Tolworth
Bound by Dorstel Press Limited, Harlow

Design by Ronald Clark
Index by Myra Clarke

© Desmond Seward 1973

All rights reserved. No part of this publication
may be reproduced, stored in a retrieval system, or
transmitted, in any form or by any means, electronic,
mechanical, photocopying, recording or otherwise,
without the prior permission of Constable & Company
Limited, 10 Orange Street, London WC2

PRINTED IN GREAT BRITAIN

To my god-daughter, Anna-Rose Phipps

AUTHOR'S ACKNOWLEDGMENTS.
I particularly wish to thank M. Marcel Dufay,
Préfet of Loir-et-Cher, who gave a memorable
reception at Blois for me to meet antiquarians and
château owners of the Loire Valley. I am most
grateful to him for his hospitality and sympathetic
encouragement.

In addition, I would like to thank the following:
The Hon John Jolliffe; Dom Edward Corbould; Mr
Michael Thomas; Mr Christopher Manning, who
read the proofs; Mr Mark Heathcoat Amory; Miss
Caroline Benwell; Mrs Gerard Girkins and Miss
Sandra Girkins; and Major Peter Black, who drew
my attention to du Fouilloux's contemporary work
on hunting in sixteenth-century France.

I also acknowledge a special debt to the recent
exhibitions in Paris—*L'Ecole de Fontainebleau* at the
Grand Palais, and *La Collection de François I*[er]
at the Musée du Louvre.

I must express my gratitude, once more, to Mr
Richard Bancroft, Superintendent of the British
Museum Reading Room, and the members of his
staff for their courteous and patient assistance.

                                                    D.S.

Contents

Colour Plates

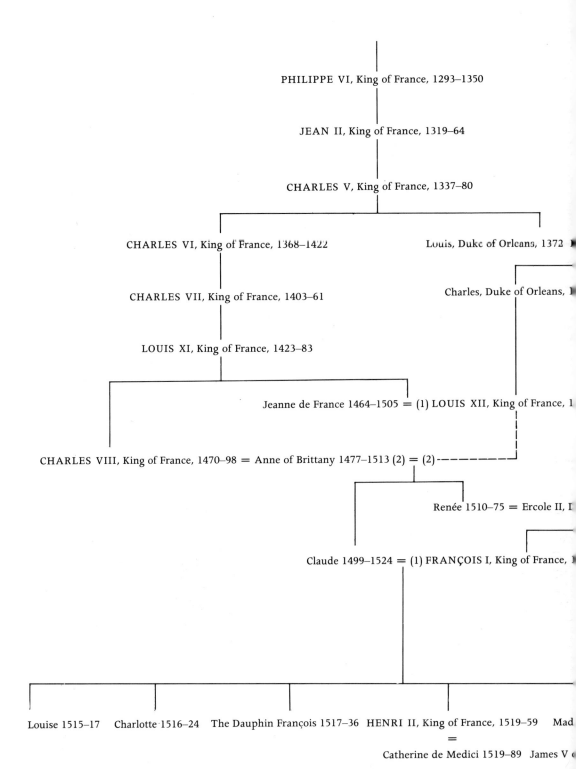

PHILIPPE VI, King of France, 1293–1350

JEAN II, King of France, 1319–64

CHARLES V, King of France, 1337–80

CHARLES VI, King of France, 1368–1422   Louis, Duke of Orleans, 1372

CHARLES VII, King of France, 1403–61   Charles, Duke of Orleans,

LOUIS XI, King of France, 1423–83

Jeanne de France 1464–1505 = (1) LOUIS XII, King of France, 1

CHARLES VIII, King of France, 1470–98 = Anne of Brittany 1477–1513 (2) = (2) ----------

Renée 1510–75 = Ercole II, I

Claude 1499–1524 = (1) FRANÇOIS I, King of France,

Louise 1515–17   Charlotte 1516–24   The Dauphin François 1517–36   HENRI II, King of France, 1519–59   Mad

=

Catherine de Medici 1519–89   James V

The House of Valois

Dates shown are life span
= married

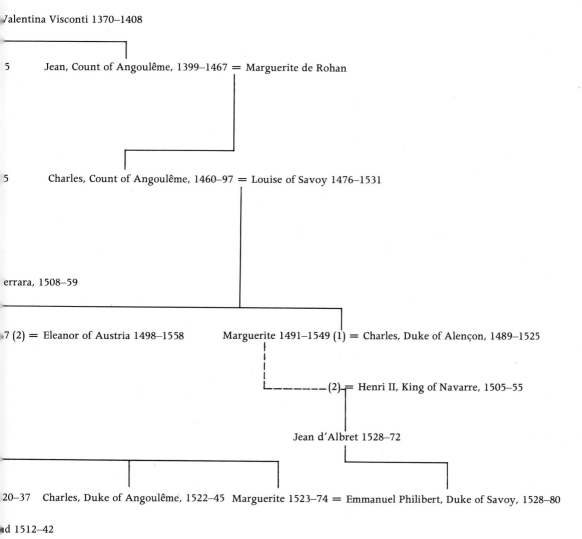

Valentina Visconti 1370–1408

5   Jean, Count of Angoulême, 1399–1467 = Marguerite de Rohan

5   Charles, Count of Angoulême, 1460–97 = Louise of Savoy 1476–1531

errara, 1508–59

7 (2) = Eleanor of Austria 1498–1558   Marguerite 1491–1549 (1) = Charles, Duke of Alençon, 1489–1525

(2) = Henri II, King of Navarre, 1505–55

Jean d'Albret 1528–72

20–37   Charles, Duke of Angoulême, 1522–45 Marguerite 1523–74 = Emmanuel Philibert, Duke of Savoy, 1528–80

d 1512–42

Foreword

If any picture of François I exists in English or American minds, it is one of a French Henry VIII. However, François is not one of France's popular monarchs. He has no cult like Henry IV or Louis XIV. Yet his achievement is staggering; many rulers have dominated their age, few have identified themselves with it completely, as he did. To do this a ruler has to create a superb personal life style like Louis XIV or become a great aesthete like the Medici. François I did both and he personifies the French Renaissance. But he has been outshone by the very brilliance of his own epoch.

François has not attracted biographers; no English life has appeared for forty years. His strange face has a disturbing quality – with its leering eyes, long nose, and Priapic grin it resembles a satyr's mask. In the nineteenth century François I became a bogey of Romantic mythology, the archetypal royal lecher, frivolous and cruel. He was the philanderer-king of Victor Hugo's *Le Roi s'amuse* whom a librettist changed into the Duke of Mantua for *Rigoletto*. Yet once he had been considered a great prince. Brantôme venerated the king of his boyhood, declaring: 'This name of great was given him not so much for his tall stature and stoutness, which indeed were very fine, nor for his most rich and royal majesty, but for grandeur of virtues, brave deeds, noble actions and high merits, just as formerly it was given to Alexander, Pompey and others.'

François was the Sun King of the sixteenth century. His greatness lies in his role as supreme patron of the later Renaissance. When he was born in 1494 France was still Gothic; when he died in 1547 the French Renaissance was near its peak. Nowadays, since private patronage has virtually come to an end, it is beginning to be realized that a patron was often an artist in his own right, and sometimes a very great artist. Europe has learnt to reassess its aesthete kings – as aesthetes. The madness of the Bavarian Ludwig II is accepted in contemplation of his dreamlike palaces. George IV has at last received his due as creator of Carlton House and the Brighton Pavilion, as the inspired employer of Nash and Lawrence. Charles I seems a less tragic figure when one remembers how he had been the patron of Van Dyck and Inigo Jones, and one of the world's outstanding collectors of Dutch and Italian Masters. But François is the supreme royal aesthete. Leonardo da Vinci and Andrea del Sarto were his court painters, Raphael and Titian portrayed him, Benvenuto Cellini was his jeweller. He built palaces which even Versailles could not overshadow. At Fontainebleau he was responsible for the acclimatization of an entire new school of art – Mannerism. He paid no less attention to letters,

François I c1540, an eighteenth-century bronze
cast from a stone bust once at Fontainebleau.

FOREWORD   13

choosing poets and scholars for his gentlemen-in-waiting. It was King François who collected the library which would one day become the Bibliothèque Nationale, and who founded the Collège de France.

The reign of François I is the most radiant, the most creative in French history, a reign in which two brilliant cultures came together, those of Gothic France and Renaissance Italy. Everywhere there was splendour, King François riding, dancing, or promenading in an unending pageant, escorted by glittering nobles, by famous poets, painters, and savants. It was a life of sublime unreality but it was also one of sublime creativity. For François did not merely preside; no ruler since Charlemagne has had a more direct influence upon the civilization of France.

Heir
Presumptive

'François, by God's grace King of France and my own gentle Emperor, had his first experience of this world's light at Cognac about ten o'clock of the afternoon in 1494, on the twelfth day of September.' So wrote his mother, Louise de Savoie, in her Journal. When she penned these words in the triumphant early years of his reign, he seemed like some Phoebus ascending towards the sun by comparison with those who had reigned before him.

Few centuries have a worse name than that into which François I was born. Though its gloom can be exaggerated, the fifteenth century was dark and cruel, a time when northern Europe was ravaged by vicious wars and sapped by economic recession. Men had a fundamentally pessimistic attitude to life. Death had become a cult in itself; charnel-houses drew crowds of avid sightseers, for it was the time of shroud brasses and skeleton effigies, of *Les Trois Vifs* and *Les Trois Morts*, of the *Danse Macabre*. Many suspected that a world so dreadful must soon come to an end.

Certainly there was beauty; manuscripts with gem-like illuminations, the flying buttresses and soaring convolutions of Flamboyant, the celestial music of Machault or Josquin des Prés. The Late Gothic reached its climax at the extraordinary court of the Dukes of Burgundy. In their domains in eastern France and in the Flemish lands, there were such painters as the van Eyck brothers and Hugo van der Goes, architects, goldsmiths, and sculptors, who all contributed to an ornate, fantastic culture. The Dukes themselves were its epitome, at the court, on progress or in the hunting-field, in the joust or at the banquet, where ritual splendour achieved heights which have never been surpassed. They and their courtiers, attended by vast retinues, lived an endless pageant, dressed in costly silks, velvets, and furs, with sleeves which swept the ground, shoes elongated like the beak of a bird, great turbans and jewelled bonnets. Court life was like a modern film spectacular, with heralds and marshals for producers, the Duke as director. This lordly, unreal way of life was not confined to Burgundy; in Provence King René of Anjou held no less splendid court. It was an art form in its own right, but the canvas was disquietingly sombre despite all the rich colours.

For France the fifteenth was a peculiarly dismal century. In the first half English invaders brought massacre and famine – wolves entered Paris to eat the corpses. After the English went there were wars between the Crown and the great lords and the struggle with Burgundy. Significantly, the period's favourite poet was François Villon, a gallows' bard who scurried through the underworld of Paris like a hunted

Left A detail from the *Danse Macabre*, a disturbingly popular theme in fifteenth-century art. *Right* François's mother, Louise of Savoy (1476–1531), from a miniature in a Book of Hours belonging to Catherine de Medici.

rat – the exquisite melancholy of Charles d'Orléans was too gentle. The country's rulers were as grotesque as their age, like Louis XI (1461–83), the Spider King, who broke over-mighty subjects with treachery and torture.

François's father, Charles d'Angoulême, was a great-grandson of King Charles V (1364–80) – 'Le Sage' – whom he strikingly resembled, or so his courtiers judged from portraits which have not survived. Count Charles inherited the King's bookish tastes but not his love of statecraft. He preferred to cultivate books and women at his massive old *château fort* which guarded the prosperous little Gascon town of Cognac. Here, a Prince of the Blood, he held his own miniature court with poets and musicians and an illuminator-painter. He collected both manuscripts and the new printed books.

In 1488, when he was nineteen, Charles married Louise de Savoie, the twelve-year-old daughter of a future Duke of Savoy. Before François was born, she gave her husband a girl in 1492, Marguerite d'Angoulême, destined to be one of the most gifted women of her time. Louise was remarkable enough herself. In appearance she belonged to a classically French type, with a slight, wiry figure, thick dark hair and metallic black eyes. Highly strung, her strength stemmed from nervous energy and an iron will. She was widely read, with a love of books unusual for a lady of her day. But despite this common interest, the Count preferred the company of his mistresses.

For the first few years of François's life the King of France was Charles VIII. The
young King was nightmarish in appearance, with an overlarge head on a tiny,
crippled body. His face was flabby and he spoke haltingly through thick, wet lips.
Yet he had a great heart. In 1494 he led the chivalry of France over the Alps and into
Italy. There, as Bacon put it, Charles VIII 'conquered the realm of Naples, and lost
it again, in a kind of a felicity of a dream'. Despite early triumphs, Spanish intervention
soon drove the French out of the peninsula. But the King and his troops returned
with the Italian Renaissance. Italy had been a dazzling revelation – its sunshine
and sophistication, its learning, its buildings, its painting and statuary, its music,
even its games. Noblemen coming home to dank *châteaux forts* carpeted with filthy
straw and decorated with hunting trophies, realized that something was missing.
Their northern pleasures, jousting and the chase, the splendid ritual of noble life,
no longer sufficed. They were reminded of their poverty by a host of Italian ad-
venturers – soldiers, bankers, clerics, savants, painters. Their own artists and scholars
went to study in Italy, their sons to fight there. The French were obsessed by Italy –
everyone spoke, dressed, sang, and danced *à l'italienne*.

One day in the late winter of 1495, Count Charles became wet through while
travelling, and caught a cold. It soon turned into a fever, then pneumonia. He died
on 1 January 1496. During his illness, which lasted a month, Louise behaved like
the most loving wife imaginable; according to an eyewitness she nursed her husband
throughout, refusing to leave his chamber and insisting on sleeping in the same bed,
'. . . when despite everything my said Lord's malady worsened, it was necessary to
take my said Lady out of the chamber. And indeed there was need to do so. Otherwise,
to speak truth, she would never have left it in this life, and certainly she seemed
more dead than alive.'

She was only nineteen and all her short life had been insecure. Yet she does not
inspire pity. Louise was the sort of mother who dotes on her son for basically selfish
reasons. Discontented and ambitious, she had made a bad marriage. Her position,
as a poor relation hoping for a great inheritance, was bound to exaggerate her posses-
siveness over the son on whom everything depended. Even during Charles VIII's
reign – his children died with miserable regularity – she must have suspected that
François would one day wear the Crown. In 1504, when he was ten, she had a medal
struck with his head on one side and a salamander on the other; the salamander, a
fabulous lizard which thrives amid fire, became François's personal badge. But it
was a truer symbol of Louise.

She was fortunate in the man whom King Charles appointed as François's guardian,
Louis d'Orléans, son of the poet Duke. His life had been a sad one. Louis XI forced
him to marry his crippled daughter, Jeanne de France, whose twisted body so revolted
her own father that whenever she saw him the poor girl hid behind one of her ladies.
Later, the Duke rebelled, to be punished by three years' imprisonment. In 1495 he
was thirty-three, a tall, thin, nervous man with a worried face. Indecisive, of mediocre
intelligence, his sole gift was his extraordinary kindness. The death of Count Charles

François and his sister, Marguerite d'Angoulême. *Opposite* A manuscript illuminated by Robinet Testard shows them playing chess c1504. Their parents' arms are beneath; behind Marguerite is probably Boisy. *Below* Medallions of François aged ten and Marguerite before her marriage.

genuinely distressed him; a courtier wrote: 'As for Monseigneur [d'Orléans] I think no man ever died whom he so mourned. For he loved him with a great and perfect love, above all others, as nearest kinsman of his father's house, truest vassal and most loyal friend.'

As François's governor, Louis chose another cousin, the Maréchal de Gié who was related to the late Count's mother. Pierre de Rohan, Sieur de Gié, was a hero of the Italian Wars, who had saved Charles VIII's life during the retreat. He came of a proud family, whose motto was later said to be:

Roy ne peut	(King I cannot be
Prince ne veut	Prince I would not be
Rohan suy	I am Rohan)

But the haughty Marshal combined tactlessness with a total inability to understand Louise. Like her, he foresaw a brilliant future for François. To a widower of forty-four, Louise, young and personable, seemed a most desirable wife – the role of step-father to the King of France offered glittering prospects. Gié did not realize that his very presence infuriated her.

First, the Marshal dismissed her Chamberlain. Then he tried to remove François from his nurse's chamber – henceforward, said Gié, the boy must sleep in the men's quarters. Louise refused, barricading herself and François in her own room, whereupon a servant broke the door down. Even the Marshal gave way before the storm which ensued. His worst sin came in 1501 when François was six. On a January day 'about two o'clock in the afternoon, my King, my Lord, my Emperor and my son was carried across the fields, near Amboise, on a hackney given him by Marshal Gié, and the danger was such that those present believed there was no hope. Yet God, protector of widows and guardian of orphans, knowing the future did not abandon me, seeing that had cruel fortune taken away my love I should have been too unfortunate.'

Ce liure present fut fait z ordue
principalmt a linstance dung aulf
fait en riine na gueres z de nouel
venu a coruoissance y est intitule
des esches amoureux et des esches da
mes aussi cõe pó declarer aucunes
choses y la riine cõtient y semblēt
estre obscures et estrātes de piinere
face. Et pó ce fut il fait en prose pó
ce y prose est plus clere a entendre
par raison y nest riine lacte donc
y le fist cõmence ainsi son liure z
mect vng tel prologue.

Pour ce que la matere da
mours est dlitaable ẽ soy
et ioyeuse et plaisāt plus
escoutans et par especial aux ieunes
gens du monde ausquelz le fait da
mours aussi est plus appartenant.
pource voult cilz qui fist le liure
des esches amoureux monstrer com
ment il fut amoureux ẽ sa ieunesse
espris et eschicus de lamõ dune riine
damoiselle Et ce voult il signifi
er couuertement par le ieu des eschez
plus y par aultre voye par auēture

On 7 April 1498 Charles VIII who had been watching a game of tennis at his beloved Amboise struck his head against the low doorway of a gallery. The King returned to his game, only to collapse. He was laid on a dirty straw pallet in the same evil-smelling gallery – used as a latrine by the entire court – but died that evening. One of his officials, Commines, wrote of poor simple Charles that 'he was but a little man, both in body and understanding, yet so good natured that it was impossible to meet a better creature'. In his whole life he never spoke a harsh word, not even to his servants. The Duc d'Orléans, who, characteristically, burst into tears when the news reached him at Blois, ascended the throne as Louis XII – and François d'Angoulême became heir presumptive.

However, King Louis was quite strong enough to beget a Dauphin and Pope Alexander VI speedily supplied an annulment. After a humiliating physical examination, in front of twenty-seven witnesses, Jeanne de France was relegated to a convent (the Church made a tardy reparation by canonizing her in 1950). Louis then married Charles's widow, Anne of Brittany – he dared not let her marry anyone else. A delicate cripple with the face of a Gothic Madonna, she was the greatest heiress in Europe. Her Duchy with its partly Celtic-speaking nobility was nearly an independent country, standing in relation to France almost as Scotland did to England. Regal, pious, and gifted, even if a little narrow-minded, Anne was the outstanding French-woman of her day, dominating both husbands and winning all hearts. Brantôme accounted her the most gracious Queen of France since Blanche, the mother of St Louis. One heart which Anne did not win was that of Louise. The coldness was mutual, and the Queen positively detested the ambitious Countess and her children.

The King accepted that François, as senior Prince of the Blood Royal, was heir presumptive. He was made Duc de Valois, though still called Comte d'Angoulême, and given a royal residence. This was to have been Blois, but Louise managed to obtain the far more impressive Amboise. Towering above the Loire and guarding the bridge which was a vital link in the main road to Spain, the château of Amboise was both fortress and palace. Behind the great bastions and curtain walls, the white buildings which crowned the heights were a triumph of the last flowering of Flamboyant Gothic, with candle-snuffer turrets and elegant gables. Here was every comfort; in the tiny, exquisite chapel of St Hubert on the battlements, where the family heard Mass every morning, were two fireplaces, a rare luxury in a church of the time. From gardens and terraces a hundred feet above the courtiers' houses clustered below the walls, the tower of Tours Cathedral could be seen on one side, the royal hunting forests of Blois on the other. It is easy to believe that François passed a joyous boyhood by the wide, placid river with its fresh green banks and constant procession of ships and barges.

Yet if François grew up several days' journey from Paris, he was never more than a few hours away from the effective capital of France. Though the court was sometimes at Paris, royal visits there tended to be brief. The Valois monarchy preferred to progress from château to château, mainly in the Val de Loire where the hunting was

Left Robert de la Marck, Seigneur de Fleurange
(1491–1537) – 'The Young Adventurer'. *Right* Artus
Gouffier, Seigneur de Boisy (1475–1519) –
François's governor at Amboise. From miniatures
c1516 by Jean Clouet. *Opposite* The Chapel of St
Hubert at Amboise, seen from the town.

particularly good. Even the States General were held at Blois or Tours, while great
magnates and officials who had to be near the sovereign built their own splendid
palaces in this rich and lovely valley.

In June 1503 Gié's marriage to the heiress of Vendôme made him a Duke. Already
he had become Louis's trusted servant, the most important man in France after the
Cardinal d'Amboise. When the King fell ill, believing him to be as good as dead,
Gié prepared to seize power. Queen Anne had sent some of her furniture and plate
to Brittany on barges up the Loire. The Marshal impounded them. Quite apart from the
insult, the Queen had her own ideas as to who should be Regent. When Louis recovered,
Gié was accused of *lèse-majesté,* tried, found guilty, stripped of his wealth and offices,
and banished to his estates where he died in 1513. Louise seems to have contributed
in some way to his destruction.

A very different governor came to Blois, Artus Gouffier, Seigneur de Boisy. The
Cardinal's nephew, he was a charming Gascon who had been the King's Chamberlain
and whom even Louise found congenial. With him he brought his brother, Guillaume,
Seigneur de Bonnivet, to join the little court. As a boy François was thoroughly spoilt.
In Michelet's words 'he was born, one might say, between two adoring women, his
mother and his sister, who always remained in their ecstasy of worship and devotion'.
The few Valois who survived infancy had been small and puny but François grew
into a tall, high-spirited, and handsome boy. Marguerite was a gay, slender girl with
blue eyes and golden hair, distinguished even as a child. Later a legend arose that
she was born of a pearl – (*margarita* in Latin) – which her mother had swallowed.
Hence her nickname, 'la perle des Valois', Louise regarded her merely as an ally in
pampering 'my king, my lord, my Emperor, my son'; there are no allusions to any
illness of Marguerite in the journal. However, alarms of a different kind were noted,
as in 1503: 'Anne, Queen of France, at Blois, upon the day of St Agnes, the 21 January,
bore a son; but could not stop the exaltation of my Emperor for he lacked life.'

A boyhood companion wrote: 'I think no prince ever had more pastimes than
did my said Lord or was better instructed, by the provision of my Lady his mother.'
This companion was Robert de la Marck, Seigneur de Fleurange, a future Marshal

Tennis, of the sort played by François at Amboise, from a contemporary Italian painting.

of France. Born in 1491, the younger son of the Duke of Sedan, from a tender age Fleurange called himself 'Le Jeune Adventureux'. About 1500, when only ten, he offered King Louis his sword, asking to serve in Italy. The King, much amused, replied gravely that, while he did not doubt the Adventurer's courage, he did not think he was quite tall enough, and sent him to join the suite of the Duc de Valois. Here he grew to manhood, becoming François's close friend and confidant. Later, in captivity after the Battle of Pavia, Fleurange wrote a chronicle of his life which gives a vivid glimpse of François at Amboise.

There were other young lords besides Fleurange – Philippe Chabot, Montchenu, and Montmorency, the future Constable of France. Tennis was the most popular game. Racquets had recently been introduced, a fringed cord serving as a primitive net, and the courts were enclosed, the ball being played as it rebounded from the walls; the modern method of scoring existed, royal tennis being a far more complicated and cerebral game than today's lawn tennis. The boys also played *la grosse boule* (possibly the Italian *pallone*), they shot at the butts, they hawked and hunted in the forest and trapped deer and other beasts, and they tilted at the quintain. Above all they played at soldiers. 'My said Lord of Angoulême, the Young Adventurer and other young noblemen built towers in which they fought, attacking and defending with strokes of the sword . . . and when my said Lord of Angoulême, the Young

Left Hawking – *Départ pour la chasse* – from a
French tapestry *c*1500. *Right* A tournament.
Jousting was one of François's favourite pastimes.
From an early sixteenth-century miniature.

HEIR PRESUMPTIVE   25

Adventurer and the other young noblemen grew somewhat older, they began to
wear armour and to tilt in every sort of joust and tourney that one can think of. . . .'
Fleurange adds that François excelled in all these exercises.

Nor were the Count's letters neglected, even if he only learnt to read Latin with
assistance. What he really enjoyed were romances of chivalry; Cervantes credits
old tales of this sort with driving Don Quixote out of his mind. The tutor of the
English Queen Elizabeth, Robert Ascham, wrote later of the *Morte d'Arthur* '. . . the
whole pleasure of which book standeth in two special points, in which book they
be counted the noblest knights that do kill most men without any quarrel and commit
foulest adulteries by subtlest shifts.' François also acquired a taste for poetry, and
learnt to write verse. Though not nearly so intelligent as his sister Marguerite, like
her he received from their mother – who claimed to love her books next to her children
– a reverence for art and letters together with a lively intellectual curiosity. This
reverence and curiosity, rather than what he actually studied, were the important
part of François's education.

No age has had more veneration for scholarship than the Renaissance, that endeavour
to rediscover the lost wisdom of Antiquity through a new, closer study of the art
and letters of Greece and Rome. Petrarch, who began the revival of classical studies
in the fourteenth century, wrote, 'After the darkness has been dispelled, our grandsons

will be able to walk back into the pure radiance of the past.' At first its centre was Florence but, later, leadership passed to Rome, the High Renaissance lasting until the sack of the city in 1527. Poets emulated Virgil or Horace, orators cultivated Cicero, historians copied Livy and Thucydides, statesmen and soldiers tried to act like those of Plutarch. Architects like Bramante, painters like Botticelli, sculptors like Donatello, all turned to the ancient world. Fields hitherto impenetrable lay open, besides delicious vistas of guiltless pagan love and hedonism. What gave the Renaissance such force was the sheer intoxication of its message, a euphoria partly due to the Platonist conviction that knowledge is happiness and that man reflects an ideal. Every quality of mind and body was cultivated – not only had a man to master all branches of learning but he must develop his physique to perfection.

The emphasis in northern Europe was slightly different. Instead of seeking the joys of heathen antiquity, scholars hoped to grow closer to Christ through a deeper understanding of the Scriptures. Hebrew was of no less importance to them than Latin or Greek. But the distinction was one of emphasis – there was only one Renaissance. The goal of every 'humanist', northern or southern, was the same, to enlarge man's vision. All sciences were explored. Even the occult was investigated; so devout a Christian as Lefèvre d'Etaples wrote on magic, while alchemists and astrologers abounded. And, with very few exceptions, the most 'pagan' humanists saw religious experience as a widening, not a limitation, of human potentialities.

There is a perennial controversy whether the Renaissance in France was home grown by French humanists or whether it was brought back by Charles VIII's troops. What is beyond dispute is that France had her own Renaissance, a fusion of north and south, of religious zeal and pagan *joie de vivre*. Its most brilliant figure was Guillaume Budé (1467–1540), a lawyer who turned to letters and corresponded with Thomas More, Erasmus, and Rabelais. Best remembered as the restorer of Hellenistic learning in France, Budé wrote on history, mathmatics, law, philology, numismatics, and even hunting. It was Budé who, speaking of the Renaissance concept of 'arms and letters', said that a man without letters (by which he meant a man without knowledge of the Classics) could hardly be accounted a real man; hence no ruler could hope to be a great king unless he cultivated letters. More typical of the French Renaissance as a whole was Jacques Lefèvre d'Etaples (1450–1536), famous for Scriptural studies and his translation of the Bible. Yet in many ways French thought and manners remained medieval – what changed did so gradually and unevenly.

Despite his kindly nature, Louis XII regarded war as a duty. He made nine descents upon Italy. Through his Visconti grandmother he had a claim to Milan; once the Duchy was won he hoped to conquer Naples as well. By 1500 Milan had been conquered, lost, and conquered again; for twelve years it remained part of France. In 1502, in concert with Ferdinand of Aragon, Louis invaded Naples, but was driven out the following year by the treacherous Ferdinand. A decade of war followed, with the Spaniards, the Venetians, and the Pope's mercenaries. The gentle Louis showed he could be ruthless; garrisons were massacred, peasants who supported his enemies hanged in droves. In

Guillaume Budé (1467–1540), the great humanist scholar who was Grand Master of the King's Library, from a portrait c1536 by Jean Clouet.

1509 he nearly smashed his way into Venice. In 1511 he summoned a General Council of the Church to depose the warlike Pope Julius II. Eventually the 'Holy League' drove the French out of Italy while the English invaded northern France and Spain overran the southern provinces of her Navarrese allies. Julius even offered the title of 'Most Christian Majesty' and the throne of France to Henry VIII – if he could conquer it. When France at last made peace in 1514 she had lost all her Italian possessions.

She retained a ruinous heritage of glory and heroism. Every Frenchman remembered the twenty-two-year-old Gaston de Foix, who having beaten the enemy was killed pursuing them with too much eagerness; he was found with fifteen wounds in the face. Nor could France forget Louis leading the attack against the Venetians at Agnadello in 1509, where, shouting '*Mes enfants*, your King is watching you' to his troops, he rode into the enemy cannonade crying that gunfire could not kill a King of France. For François, Louis's wars were a time of frustration. His friends were covering themselves with glory. Gaston de Foix had been a victorious general at less than twenty years of age while Fleurange was carried by his father from the stricken field of Asti with fifty wounds. François had to stay at home.

His hero was Bayard. Pierre du Terrail, Chevalier de Bayard, had been born in 1476 and belonged to the lesser nobility of Dauphiné. During the Italian campaigns he became a legend. Essentially professional in his soldiering and a gifted tactician, at the same time he managed to conduct his life on almost Arthurian principles. An ascetic *dévot* who slept on the ground, winter and summer, he was famed for courtesy to women and contempt for money. When Brescia was stormed by the French in 1512, and 22,000 Brescians were slaughtered, the lady in whose house Bayard installed himself – after being wounded during the assault – expected no mercy. Instead, the Chevalier protected her, her husband, and their two young daughters throughout his convalescence; at his departure he refused the customary ransom and would only accept two cheap presents made by the girls – a purse of crimson satin and a bracelet of gold and silver wire. There were many similar stories about Bayard. Yet despite his piety, the Chevalier possessed a mistress and probably an illegitimate child – and by waging war on fellow Christians he was technically guilty of mortal sin. However, contemporaries insisted that he merited salvation for his alms-giving, his asceticism, his devotions, and his protection of churches when on campaign. It is useful to remember these double standards when trying to understand François.

At home, Louis XII's reign was a time of peace and plenty. In some years he actually reduced the taxes, lightening the hateful *taille* which weighed so heavily upon the peasants. A standing army deterred robber barons. The Grand Conseil ensured that royal edicts were enacted by all regional jurisdictions, the King's writ reaching every corner of France. Everyone, noble, bourgeois, and peasant, prospered. Lyons was a symbol of their good fortune. This city, on the road from France to Italy, was the main channel of Franco-Italian trade – through it flowed all the luxuries of the south. It was also an international money-market. Great nobles built elegant town houses in its crowded streets, for the court was frequently at Lyons. Further, the agrarian recession of the later Middle Ages, which had caused the abandonment of good farmland, was halted. Writing about 1510, Claude de Seyssel declared that since Louis XI's latter years a third more land had come under the plough.

Though François's home was at Amboise, with his mother and sister he spent much time at other châteaux in the region, notably Romorantin and Blois. In 1505 the King fell ill for a second time, so ill it seemed he would not recover; all France – save perhaps

Left King Louis XII (1498–1515), François's predecessor and father-in-law, from his tomb at Saint-Denis. *Right* The betrothal of François and Claude in 1513, from a contemporary manuscript, the *Annales de Louis XII*.

Louise – prayed for his recovery. He survived and when the States General met at Plessis-les-Tours, the following May, its spokesman officially bestowed upon him the title 'Père du Peuple'. He then went on to beseech that little Claude de France should marry '*Monsieur Françoys cy présent qui est tout Françoys*' – the play of words gave his plea particular force. It was a triumph for Louise, a rebuff for Queen Anne who wished her daughter to marry Charles of Habsburg. On 21 May François and Claude, who was only seven, were betrothed by Cardinal d'Amboise in the presence of the King.

France's prosperity was in large part due to Louis's ambitious first minister and friend, Georges d'Amboise, Cardinal Archbishop of Rouen and Papal Legate, who was no less popular than his master. This Prince of the Church bore a certain resemblance to Wolsey. Proud and magnificent and an equally greedy pluralist, Amboise was both more successful and more civilized. A great builder, the patron of Italian architects and painters, he also amassed a fine humanist library. Amboise, not Louis, was the arbiter of French taste. Some historians describe him as the real King of France at this time. Active everywhere, he personally equipped a fleet to fight the English. In any difficulty Louis simply shrugged and said 'Leave it to Georges.' The Cardinal's early death, of gout in 1510, hastened the King's own premature demise.

Since the Councils ended the Great Schism in the fifteenth century, the Gallican

Church had enjoyed considerable freedom from Rome which kept little more than
a primacy of honour. None the less, like every branch of the Church at that period, it
swarmed with abuses. Amboise tried to reform some religious houses but made small
impression. Apart from certain friars and the incorruptible Carthusians, the only
movement for renewal was among the humanists. But the monarchy's concern was to
control the Church, not to reform it. After Louis's excommunication by Julius II in
1512, the Church of France was in schism from Rome.

'On the 3 August 1508 in the reign of King Louis XII my son departed from Amboise
to go and be a courtier', Louise wrote indignantly in her journal. But François was sixteen; it was time for him to mix with the great men of the realm. Nor had her son gone
to some haunt of vice and profligacy. The King lived with such frugality that his very
clothes were poor and shabby – Commines said that Louis, 'often seemed more like
some tradesman or person of low estate than a King'. He ate little save boiled beef and
kept early hours. Expensive fêtes and court ceremonies were abolished. Every sou
was spent carefully. Queen Anne lived with equal simplicity. His subjects jeered at his
parsimony but Louis retorted 'I would much rather they laughed at my meanness
than wept at their poverty.' The poet Mellin de Saint-Gelais wrote 'We never had such
good times under any other King as during his reign.'

Not all Louis's courtiers were sedate. There were war-lords, like la Trémouille or
that battered *condottiere*, Marshal Trivulzio. Among them was 'Richard IV', the
Yorkist Pretender, whom the French called 'Duc de Suffolk dit Blanc Rose'. A nephew
of Richard III, he had fled to France in 1500 with his brother Edmund. Their eldest
brother, the Earl of Lincoln, had been recognized as heir to the throne in 1484. Lincoln
was killed at Stoke in 1487 while Henry VIII judicially murdered Edmund in 1513 – he
was executed when Louis recognized Richard as King of England. This earlier 'King
over the Water' has been forgotten because so little is known about him. Yet European
sovereigns took the Duke of Suffolk quite as seriously as any Stuart Pretender. Sufficient evidence survives to indicate that the White Rose was a colourful prince, fond of
women, horses, fine buildings, war, and the tournament, and no less violent than his
first cousin, Henry VIII.

The setting of Louis's sober court was magnificent. At Blois he rebuilt two wings of
the château, in pleasing red brick and dominated by an equestrian statue of himself.
The King was far from indifferent to Italian refinements. Louis employed both Italian
painters and French artists who had studied in Italy. Jean Perréal painted his portrait –
it was typical of the age that Perréal should also be an expert on alchemy – while Jean
Bourdichon illuminated a Book of Hours for Queen Anne.

Although he was made Captain of 100 men-at-arms in 1511, when Louis formally
recognized him as heir, François's first experience of war did not come until 1512.
Ferdinand of Aragon had long coveted Navarre. Most of this little kingdom, the French
gate through the Pyrenees, lay south-west of the mountains, though its King and Queen,
Jean III and Catherine d'Albret, reigned from the d'Albret estates in France instead of
at their capital of Pamplona. The wily Ferdinand lured Henry VIII into sending an

English expeditionary force; it was only sixty years since England had lost Bordeaux and Henry expected to reconquer Guyenne with Spanish help. On 7 June 1512 10,000 billmen, bowmen, and men-at-arms, commanded by the Marquess of Dorset, landed at Fuentarrabia on the Guipuzcoan coast. Here they waited, drenched by unseasonable rain, drinking bad wine and decimated by dysentery. No Spaniards came. In October the survivors mutinied and sailed home. But they had served Ferdinand's purpose – to block any French attempt to cross the Pyrenees while his own troops were overrunning Navarre. During an abortive campaign François, much to his mother's pride, was Lieutenant-Governor of Guyenne though the only action he saw was the siege of the border town of Saint-Jean-Pied-de-Port.

Henry VIII invaded France in June 1513 with 5,000 troops, joined by 8,000 German *landsknechts*, 'a marvellous fine army' according to Fleurange. They besieged and captured Thérouanne, the first French town gained by English arms since the days of Jeanne d'Arc. Then they laid siege to Tournai, 'the richest city north of Paris'. King Louis's army came to relieve it but the English surprised and routed the French cavalry; they fled so swiftly that the skirmish was named 'the Battle of the Spurs' because they used them more than their swords. Many lords were taken prisoner, including Bayard. François was not among them – he had been caught without his armour, bathing, and ran for it. Louis, helpless in his litter, despaired. Tournai fell, but fortunately Henry went home in October. Shortly after, news came that the Earl of Surrey had defeated and slain James IV with most of the Scots nobility at Flodden Field. France acquired a respect for Henry VIII which was scarcely justified. Once his father's money had been spent, Henry – effective master of half an island – would be of little more account than the King of Scots.

By this time François was six foot tall and broadly built, with luxuriant hair of that peculiarly French hue, light chestnut, which he wore long, like a Raphael page. He was clean-shaven. His face was ugly by most standards, pale, with too long a nose and a thick-lipped mouth, redeemed to some extent by large eyes of the same colour as his hair. Yet contemporaries described him as handsome. If not actually good looking, he certainly gave the impression of being so – what in a woman is called *belle laide*. He made up for his strange face not only by a magnificent physique and presence, and the gorgeous clothes of the Renaissance, but by high spirits, superb manners, and unusual gifts as a conversationalist; the latter, enhanced by a pleasing voice, charmed everyone who met him.

He and his contemporaries were noticeably different from their elders. Hitherto a great nobleman had been essentially a soldier and a hunting man. Now he had to acquire a veneer of culture. The blueprint was Baldassare Castiglione's *Book of the Courtier*. It taught how to 'join learning with comely exercises', arms and letters being necessary partners, and such new virtues as appreciation of the arts and a certain self-effacement in manners. The author, who met François before his accession, wrote that he 'seemed unto me beside the handsomeness of person and beauty of visage, to have in his countenance so great a majesty, accompanied nevertheless with a certain lovely courtesy, that the realm of France should ever seem unto him a small matter'. Castiglione added how François 'highly loved and esteemed letters, and had in very great reputation all learned men'.

For François knew that humanists could give a prince 'immortal glory' – the classical revival had popularized the classical cult of immortality. Further, a ruler's edicts and diplomacy took on force and stature when couched in elegant language. Never was such importance attached to the written word. Humanists wielded enormous power. They constituted a new, mandarin class of dons, secretaries, poets, and historians, who received the adulation nowadays given to famous scientists and technocrats. They could – and did – look down on illiterate nobles as barbarians; like Socrates they held ignorance to be worse than sin.

By 1509 François was already pursuing his first sexual adventures. (The story that his mother's lady, Jeanne de Polignac, seduced him at the age of ten has no foundation.) Marguerite tells us of her brother's first love-affair in the *Heptaméron* – in the forty-second tale, which is headed 'The continuance of a young Maid against the obstinate and amorous Suit of one of the greatest Lords of France, and the happy success which the Damsel did obtain.' Until he was fifteen François preferred 'to ride and to hunt than to behold the beauty of ladies'. Then, in church one day, he saw a brown-haired girl of sixteen with a clear complexion and 'a carriage that did transcend her state for she seemed rather a princess than the daughter of a citizen'. François found 'an unaccustomed heat' in his heart. Her name was Françoise and she was the sister-in-law of his butler with whom she lodged. François wrote to her but she would not reply. He contrived to fall from his horse in front of the butler's house, into which he was taken to be dusted down and bandaged. Even there, despite frantic pleas, the girl refused to become his mistress. A gentleman-in-waiting suggested money. The Duke had some difficulty in obtaining any – Louise managed his finances – but found 500 crowns which he offered her, to be again refused. Blandishments and threats, bribing the butler and countless other ruses could not overcome the girl's virtue. At last François despaired. He was good natured enough to let her marry a member of his household and continued to give the couple presents for many years.

Future adventures were not so platonic. By 1512 his mother was writing of a disease in her son's secret parts – fortunately soon cured. His heart was seldom engaged. He enjoyed a woman in two ways. First, with a simple, uncomplicated sensuality. Second, on an aesthetic level. Quite apart from his sexual appetites, François regarded pretty women as works of art, like some modern master of *haute couture* – he loved to see them beautifully dressed against beautiful backgrounds.

For François, till the day he died, his sister was his ideal of what a woman should be – lovely, adoring, and uncritical. He may well have learnt his own charm and grace from her. Marguerite was a fascinating creature – later, Marot would address her as '*corps feminin, cœur d'homme et tête d'ange*'. At eighteen she was forced to marry Charles, Duc d'Alençon. The wedding, in December 1509, was very splendid, attended by King Louis and the entire royal family. Louise was pleased – Alençon was a Prince of the Blood if personally contemptible – though the tearful bride was deeply in love with that dashing young general, Gaston de Foix. (She escaped a far more grisly fate – there had been an attempt to espouse her to Henry VIII.) When Gaston was killed at Novara, three years later, she turned to books and religion. Throughout an eccentric, passionate life her brother remained her idol.

In his youth François had only one enemy – Queen Anne. She was determined to thwart Mme d'Angoulême by giving King Louis a Dauphin. But throughout 1513 she grew increasingly ill. On 11 January 1514 Anne died; she was only thirty-seven. Fleurange observed that, while the Queen's death saddened many, 'he who had much ease by it was Monsieur d'Angoulême, for she was ever contrary to him in his business; there was never a moment when the two families were not at odds with one another'. Fleurange pitied Anne for having to spend her last years in the company of Louise, 'that proud princess, that upstart'. The King was prostrate – gazing on the Queen's coffin, he cried he would join her within the year. Putting on black, he 'turned all the fiddlers, comedians, jugglers and buffoons out of the court' and shut himself in his closet where he wept for a whole week.

François at once strengthened his position by marrying Claude de France. Brantôme believed that had Queen Anne lived she would never have allowed the marriage 'because she mortally hated Mme d'Angoulême' and 'foresaw the ill treatment that she (Claude) would receive'. Claude, who had been born in 1499, was now Duchess of Brittany in her own right. She was 'very small and strangely fat', walking with a pronounced limp. Her face was round and she had a marked squint. They were married in the chapel at Saint-Germain-en-Laye which, says Fleurange, was 'a very fine château five leagues from Paris, with a fine park in a fine hunting forest'. Though the court was in mourning and Louis in a state of collapse, the Adventurer thought 'the nuptials were the richest I have ever seen because there were 10,000 men there dressed as richly as the King or Monsieur d'Angoulême who was the bridegroom; and for love of the late Queen everyone was in black and neither man nor woman changed it for the said marriage'.

Next day François went hunting. He took little interest in his bride save as a mother for his children. Brantôme comments, 'And my Lady, her mother-in-law, found much fault with her but she fortified herself, with her sweet nature, patience and goodness, to bear with such hardships.' Louise wrote in her journal how Anne had 'left me in charge of her goods, her fortune and her daughters, including Madame Claude, Queen of France and wife to my son; which I have honourably and kindly discharged; everyone knows it, truth is aware of it, experience proves it and it is public knowledge'. Louise protests too much.

François was the hero of the younger nobility who despised the King's bourgeois tastes and were bored with the unaccustomed peace which had begun in March 1514. M. d'Angoulême set the fashion – he squandered so prodigally that King Louis sighed, with tears in his eyes, 'Ah, we toil in vain – this great boy will spoil everything.' Cloaked and masked, the heir to the throne went nightly through the streets of Paris to assignations with his mistresses. He boasted of what he would one day do in Italy. Then, suddenly, it seemed that he had lost the succession.

By 1514 France had been fought to a standstill. She had lost everything in Italy, her ally, Navarre, had almost ceased to exist, while the English were capturing French towns for the first time since the Hundred Years War. The 'Father of the People' had even been forced to raise the taxes. Louis was burnt out, physically and mentally, an old man at fifty-two. In England, Archbishop Thomas Wolsey was anxious for peace. A treaty was signed in August. Louis did his duty – he was betrothed to Henry VIII's sister. 'For many reasons he had no need to marry nor had he any wish to, but because he saw himself beset on all sides by wars he could not wage without sorely afflicting his people, he sacrificed himself, like the Pelican'[1], wrote Bayard's squire.

Mary of York was only eighteen, perhaps the loveliest princess in English history. Very tall, slim, and fine boned, with perfect features and wide blue eyes, she was famous for the golden hair which grew down to her waist. Intelligent, sweet natured, she excelled in all courtly graces, especially conversation and dancing. A Venetian called her 'Paradise'. Henry VIII was fond of Mary but had few qualms at sacrificing her to a husband generally considered a dotard. She can hardly have been reassured when Louis, with his 'decayed complexion', sent her the portrait of himself by Perréal, who had not exactly stooped to flattery.

Mme Louise was furious. Her journal records how on 22 September 1514 'King Louis XII, very ancient and feeble, set forth from Paris to present himself to his young wife, the Queen Mary'. The bride had had a wretched crossing during a storm in which an escort vessel sank and her own ship ran aground off Boulogne; a gentleman carried her ashore through the shallows. In the rain she rode on a white palfrey with a gold bridle to Abbeville, accompanied by 2,000 English courtiers. They were joined by François who wore a coat of cloth of gold and silver. Mary herself was wearing a dress of cloth of gold on crimson and 'a shaggy hat of crimson silk cocked over her left eye'; she looked rather pale though the Venetian who gives these details believed it was due to 'the tossing of the sea and her fright'. The King, riding a hack to make it seem that he was out hawking, met her as if by chance before Abbeville. As they entered the town, it rained heavily – in the evening a fire broke out, thirteen houses being burnt to the ground. It was hardly a good omen.

They were married on 9 October, another day of pouring rain. Louise wrote viciously that on this day took place 'the amorous nuptials of Louis XII, King of France, and Mary of England'. The morning after, Louis boasted that he had 'done marvels'. But François knew better, from some spy who had watched the King's dismal performance. 'Adventurer, I am happier and easier in my mind than for twenty years past,' he confided to Fleurange, 'as I am sure, unless someone has lied to me, that it is not possible for the King and Queen to beget children.' On 5 November 1514 Mary was

---

[1] The young of the pelican feed straight from the mother's beak, giving rise to the medieval idea that they drank her life-blood.

Louis XII by Jean Perréal. This was the portrait
which he sent to Henry VIII in 1514 when he was
seeking the hand of Mary Tudor.

crowned Queen of France at Saint-Denis. François carried her crown, an honour not
without irony. Next day she entered Paris whose citizens were enchanted by her. For
the rest of the month, despite November wind and rain, the capital was *en fête* with
banquets and jousting.

A jousting 'course' consisted of two mounted combatants in special armour charging
each other with wooden lances along opposite sides of a stout fence; the object was to
'break a lance' on the other man. More dangerous was the 'combat at the barrier' in
which champions tried to batter each other into submission with swords, axes, maces,
falchions, battle hammers, or morning stars. It was a trial of strength rather than skill
during which tempers grew heated – marshals often had to separate enraged combatants. Tilting armours were superb, of blue and brown steel, gilded, silvered, and
damascened, or painted black or in bright colours. François was celebrated for his
prowess in these sports.

A great tournament was held between the French and the English. Mary stood in the
royal stand, 'so that all men might see her and wonder at her beauty', but Louis was ill
and lay on a day-bed. The French dazzled their guests with their wardrobes. François
and his gentlemen rode to the tilt-yard in cloth of gold, cloth of silver and crimson
velvet, with horses similarly caparisoned. One day they would be in silver and gold,
another day in crimson and yellow, another in white and green. The Duc de Bourbon
and his men were clad in 'tawny velvet and cloth of silver cloudy', the Comte de Saint
Pol in purple velvet slashed with purple satin, the Duc de Vendôme in cloth of gold
and gold velvet, Count Galeazzo de San Severino and his horse in blue satin. The English
were more plainly dressed, says Hall (a contemporary English chronicler) somewhat
sourly, every man wearing the cross of St George 'to be known for love of their
country'.

The tournament proved disastrous for the French. Veterans of the Italian Wars were
knocked off their horses or beaten into the ground by brawny Englishmen with
embarrassing frequency. The Duke of Suffolk – whose crest, very fittingly, was a bull's
head – and the Marquess of Dorset held the lists against all comers. As Dorset wrote to
Wolsey, 'There was divers times both horse and man overthrown, horses slain and one
Frenchman hurt that he is not like to live . . . the Dolphin himself having a little hurt in
the hand.' Most unsportingly, François introduced an enormous German in disguise
but Suffolk seized him by the neck and bludgeoned him till blood poured from his
nose and he beat a hasty retreat. Dorset boasted how the Queen told him that King
Louis had said, 'My Lord of Suffolk and I did shame all France.' This heroic performance increased Mary's already warm admiration for Suffolk.

Charles Brandon, Duke of Suffolk, was the son of Henry VII's Standard-Bearer who
had been killed at Bosworth Field by Richard III. Like some Edwardian rowing blue,
Suffolk owed his advancement to sporting prowess and good-fellowship. In the words
of the late Professor Pollard: 'A bluff Englishman after the King's own heart, he shared,
as none else did, in Henry's love of the joust and tourney, in his skill with the lance and
the sword; he was the Hector of combat, on foot and on horse, to Henry's Achilles.'

This red-headed, almost illiterate giant had a shrewd eye to the main chance. In 1514 he was considered the most influential man in England after Wolsey. Henry made him a Duke although, as Fleurange notes contemptuously, he was only of 'petite maison'. The King had enough trust in his abilities to send him to France as Ambassador.

A true Englishwoman, Queen Mary cast wistful eyes on Suffolk's splendid physique and bluff manner, which made such a contrast to her husband and all those wiry little Frenchmen with their irritating compliments. Her admiration piqued François. A seventeenth-century historian says 'The young Duke of Valois, who was all fire and flame for the ladies, did not want some sparks for this new Queen' until it was pointed out that if he or Brandon managed to cuckold the King they might beget a bastard who would succeed to the throne. At this, François 'weaned himself of his folly' and had Suffolk closely watched. Brantôme has a far more exciting story – that Mary encouraged him. He related how an old courtier, M. de Grignaux, warned François, 'Don't you see, she's a cunning, crafty woman who wants to lead you on till you make her pregnant? And if she does have a child, you'll stay plain Comte d'Angoulême and never be King of France.' When he took no notice, M. de Grignaux told Louise who was so angry that François dared not continue the flirtation. But the only man Mary ever loved was Brandon.

She did not enjoy being Queen of France. She wrote disconsolately to her brother that, on the morning after her marriage, her English gentlemen had been dismissed together with 'my mother Guildford' and all her ladies-in-waiting. King Louis did his best to cheer her, showering her with the French crown jewels. There was an unending series of fêtes, banquets, and balls, of an extravagance unheard of in the late Queen's time. Bayard's squire remembered how, to please Mary, Louis 'changed his whole way of life. Where once he had been accustomed to dine at eight o'clock, now it suited him to dine at midday; where he had once gone to bed at six o'clock, now he often retired at midnight.'

By Christmas 1514 Louis XII knew he was dying. Mary tried to comfort him but he joked he was going to give her his best present yet – his death. He summoned François to Paris, to the palace of Tournelles, telling him to prepare for his accession. During a storm on the night of 1 January 1515 – 'the most horrible weather ever seen' according to Fleurange – a fit of vomiting seized the King which brought him so low that he died of it, 'a kindly prince'. Louise wrote in her journal, 'On the first day of January I lost my husband and on the first day of January my son was King of France.'

Le Roi Chevalier

For France, this splendid King, tall and charming, was a delightful novelty after so many sickly, shabby monarchs. Brantôme, writing of François's accession, says that he was '*beau prince*, young and gallant, affable, full of grace and majesty, so much that everyone began to love him'. However, a Venetian envoy was less enthusiastic. He reported, on 19 January 1515, that 'the King attended Mass for the obsequies of the late King attired in a purple mantle with a long train. He resembled the Devil.'

After Louis XII had been buried, François commissioned the brothers Antonio and Giovanni Giusti to erect a magnificent tomb at Saint-Denis. The statue of the old King is

oddly touching, with its sad, worn face. Anne of Brittany, not Mary Tudor, kneels by his side (*see* p. 53). Underneath, Louis and Anne are again represented, as corpses, with a realism which depicts even the stitches of the embalmer.

Mary had been immured in the Hôtel de Cluny. It was now that she became known as 'the White Queen' – custom required a royal widow of France to lie in bed for six weeks in a darkened room, lighted only by candles, and dressed in white. This was because a posthumous Dauphin had once succeeded to the throne (Jean I, in 1316, though he had only lived and reigned for ten days). Brantôme says Mary was still determined to rule France as Queen Mother and padded herself out with linen cloths, intending to smuggle a child into her bed, but old Mme d'Angoulême, 'a shrewd Savoyard who knew very well what it is to have babies', had her watched by midwives who discovered the padding. The story is a monstrous libel. None the less, before his coronation François went to Mary to ask 'if he might consider himself King because he knew not if she were with child'. Mary answered, 'He might and that she knew of no other King.'

At Rheims Cathedral on 25 January 1515 François I was anointed fifty-seventh King of France by the Archbishop, Robert de Lenoncourt. After the King had donned the great crown of rubies, emeralds, and sapphires, the robes of hyacinth-blue, the red boots and the gold spurs, and brandished the sword of Charlemagne, he swore on the Gospels to give his people peace, to guard them from greed and iniquity, to give them justice and mercy, and to extirpate heresy. When the congregation had shouted 'Vivat in aeternum' and the choir had sung *Te Deum*, Pontifical Mass was celebrated during which the King, wearing his crown, communicated in both kinds. Later he banqueted with the twelve peers of France, six spiritual on one side of the board, six lay on the other. A notable absentee was the fifteen-year-old Count of Flanders – the future Emperor Charles V – for whom M. de Vendôme did proxy.

The *joyeuse entrée* into Paris on 15 February was said to be the most gorgeous ever seen; 1,200 princes, dukes, counts, and noblemen of the sword took part. Amid the dazzling procession stalked a great warhorse caparisoned in crimson velvet, bearing on its back the King's Seal in a coffer of blue velvet sewn with fleurs-de-lis and with a gold lock. François himself, clad in white and cloth of silver with a white velvet bonnet, rode on a white Arab stallion beneath a white canopy, while heralds threw gold and silver coins to the crowd. His gentlemen, also in white, bore the salamander on their livery. Accompanied by the Marshals of France and the great lords and dignitaries of the realm, each one in furs and velvet, in cloth of gold and of silver, he went to give thanks to God and Our Lady at Notre-Dame.

The anointing had transformed François. Henceforward, he could never forget the mystic grandeur of his office. He was a priest King who touched for the Evil, who embodied the nation in his own person – he *was* France. Something of the magic is conveyed in a famous passage on the French monarchy by Hilaire Belloc:

Its dim origins stretched out and lost themselves in Rome; it had already learnt to speak and recognize its own nature when the vaults of the Thermae echoed heavily to the slow

François riding through Saint-Denis on his
joyeuse entrée into Paris in 1515. *Below* The
sceptre of Charles V of France (1338–80), which
François held during his ceremonial anointing at
Rheims Cathedral.

footsteps of the Merovingian kings. Look up that vast valley of dead men crowned, and you may see the gigantic figure of Charlemagne, his brows level and his long white beard tangled like an undergrowth, having in his left hand the globe and in his right the hilt of an unconquerable sword. There also are the short, strong horsemen of the Robertian house, half hidden by their leather shields, and their sons before them growing in vestment and majesty, and taking on the pomp of the Middle Ages; Louis VII, all covered with iron; Philip the Conqueror; Louis IX, who alone is surrounded with light: they stand in a widening interminable procession, this great crowd of kings; they loose their armour, they take their ermine on, they are accompanied by their captains and their marshals; at last, in their attitude and their magnificence they sum up in themselves the pride and the achievement of the French nation.[1]

Louise had entered into her promised land, Queen Mother in substance if not in name. She was created Duchess of Angoulême and of Anjou. The Duchy of Armagnac went to Marguerite and her husband. Artus Gouffier, François's tutor, became Grand Master of the Household while Bonnivet was made Admiral. Antoine Duprat, who also had been involved in the King's education, became Chancellor and Garde des Sceaux (Great Seal) – law lord of France. Florimond Robertet became Treasurer. These two were old allies of Louise. She herself wielded enormous power – François respected her advice more than that of anyone else.

There remained the problem of the nineteen-year-old Queen Dowager. The Emperor Maximilian hoped to procure her for the Archduke Charles, a marriage which would undermine the Anglo-French alliance. The French, hoping she would marry someone more friendly, did not want her to leave France. François visited her each evening, 'importunate with her in divers manners not to her honour', though addressing her as 'mother-in-law' – after all, she was his wife's stepmother. Mary became still more of a problem when the Duke of Suffolk returned to France at the beginning of February 1515 to congratulate François on his succession and to renew the treaty of the previous year. François told him plainly: 'My Lord of Suffolk, there is a rumour you have come to marry the Queen, your master's sister.' However, he promised to intercede with King Henry. It was a shrewd means of averting the Habsburg marriage.

Mary, as she wrote to her brother Henry, had 'always been of good mind to My Lord of Suffolk because of his great virtue'. In fact, she was wildly in love with him. She confessed as much to François. Charles Brandon, imperturbable on the battlefield or in the tilt-yard, was terrified. Certainly he was ambitious and had once aspired to the hand of the Emperor's daughter. Nor was he particularly scrupulous having already repudiated two wives on grounds of doubtful legality. Indeed, a Friar Langley and another English priest visited Mary at Paris to warn her against the Duke, whom they accused of trafficking with the Devil and casting spells. What frightened Suffolk was that before leaving England he had promised Henry not to marry Mary.

Mary, already suffering from toothache and hysteria, grew desperate. When marriage with the Archduke was suggested, she shrieked, 'I would rather be torn in

[1] *Danton* (1899)

pieces!' She had only agreed to take Louis XII on the understanding she might choose her second husband herself. Mary told Suffolk he must wed her within four days. An hysterical Tudor must have been a daunting spectacle – the Duke wrote to Archbishop Wolsey, 'Sir, I never saw woman so weep.' He surrendered. A secret wedding took place in the Hôtel de Cluny, probably on 3 March 1515. The Duke wrote to Wolsey, 'And the Queen would never let me rest till I had granted her to be married; and so, to be plain with you I have married her heartily, and has lain with her, in so much I fear me lest that she be with child.' The ill-spelt letter is full of excuses – he deserves death for his treachery. Wolsey replied that the King had taken the news very badly – 'grievously and displeasantly' – while councillors were clamouring for the Duke's blood. He warns Suffolk, 'You are in the greatest danger that ever man was in.' The French too were displeased at a Queen of France taking as husband 'a man of low condition'. Moreover, Mary had irritated François by sending her brother, as a placatory gift, the great diamond known as 'the Mirror of Naples' together with eighteen superb pearls, all part of the French crown jewels. In April 1515, the uneasy lovers set out from Paris. Nothing had been heard from Henry. At Calais, nearly mobbed by an angry crowd, Mary wrote to her brother that she would never leave France until he wrote to her, that she would become a nun if she could not marry Suffolk.

On 15 May 1515, Mary Tudor and Charles Brandon were married for a second time, at Greenwich in the presence of Henry and his court. The marriage was unpopular. However, the chronicler Hall notes that 'whatsoever the rude people said, the Duke behaved himself so that he had both the favour of the King and of the people, his wit and demeanour was such.' Just as in the old days Henry and Suffolk rode together in a tournament. Wolsey, anxious to reduce the Duke's influence, may well have exaggerated the King's displeasure. Henry merely asked to be reimbursed for the expense of Mary's marriage to Louis, Suffolk entering into a bond to pay him £24,000 over twelve years. Soon the Duke was once again being given valuable grants of land. Mary bore him several children, but died young in 1533. Till the end she styled herself Queen and as late as 1530 sent a letter to François in which she addressed him as son-in-law – 'mon beau-fils'. Suffolk lived on until 1545, one of the few friends who never lost Henry's affection. The granddaughter and heir of Mary Tudor and Charles Brandon was Lady Jane Grey.

François was leading a life of extravagant pleasure. Bayard's squire remembered how the King continued jousting from the time of his entry into Paris in mid February until after Easter. A Venetian, Marc'Antonio Contarini, who saw him when he received the ambassadors of the Serene Republic at the end of March, writes, 'The King is most handsome, so much so that it's impossible to convey. And generous too – in two months he has given away 300,000 crowns, including pensions of 60,000. . . .' Messer Contarini continues, 'The King's way of life is as follows. He rises at eleven o'clock, hears Mass, dines, spends two or three hours with his mother, then goes whoring or hunting, and finally wanders here and there throughout the night, so one can never have an audience with him by day.'

Mary Tudor (1496–1533), Queen of France, with her second husband, Charles Brandon, Duke of Suffolk (1484–1545). The inscription beneath reads as shown opposite:

Cloath of Gold doe not despise
Tho' thou art matcht to Cloath of Frize,
Cloath of Frize be not too bold
Tho' thou art matcht to Cloath of Gold.

Marguerite gives a strong hint where François went during the night, in the twenty-fifth tale of the *Heptaméron*. This tells of Jeanne le Coq who was his principal mistress in 1515. A Parisian, eighteen or nineteen, with a lovely face and skin and a most attractive figure, she was the wife of an elderly lawyer, Maître Disomme (or Dix-hommes). The King's visits were discreet. He entered her house through the garden of a neighbouring monastery; coming into Matins, the monks frequently saw him kneeling in their church and thought him a very holy young man. On the one occasion when he was caught, François explained to the flattered advocate that he had come to see such a famous member of the Paris Parlement.

Gossip-mongers were less easily deceived. A popular poet, a priest named Cruches, staged what he called a morality play in the Place Maubert. The *Journal d'un Bourgeois de Paris* reports, 'there was a hen feeding underneath a salamander (i.e. François), the which hen was carrying something which would have killed ten men (*Dix hommes*)'. Shortly after, a party of the King's gentlemen went to sup at the Taverne du Chasteau in the rue de la Juiverie. They invited the poet to perform his play. He arrived when it was dark, by torchlight. No sooner had he begun than he was set on, stripped, and beaten until the blood flowed. A sack was waiting in which the gentlemen were going to throw him out of the window and then into the Seine. Cruches saved himself only by deafening howls and by pointing to his priest's tonsure.

When he came to the throne, François had assumed the title of Duke of Milan. At the end of March he promised the Venetian ambassadors he would soon come to the aid of their Republic, which had been attacked by Spain. As a Florentine statesman wrote – in that book which Edmund Spenser calls 'Guicciardine's silver Historie' – 'François was goaded to this undertaking not only by his inclination but also by all the youth of the French nobility, the glory of Gaston de Foix, and the memory of so many victories which had been won by recent Kings in Italy.' By the spring munitions were being collected at Lyons, which was the campaign's forming-up point. Troops and supplies came from all over France, while every old captain of Louis XII's wars received a summons.

At the end of April 1515 François and his court left Paris. On 26 June he attended the wedding of the Duke of Lorraine at Amboise. As an entertainment, the courtyard of the château was turned into an arena in which a wild boar was let loose. Not content with charging straw-filled dummies, the infuriated animal broke through the barriers and rushed at the terrified spectators. The King stepped forward, drew his sword, and killed it with a single thrust. Then he set out for Lyons where he made yet another *joyeuse entrée*, on 12 July, during which the streets flowed with wine. But François's mind was on his great enterprise.

Historians sometimes ask why, during this period, France did not attack the vulnerable Low Countries instead of wasting men and money in Italy. Ultimately Spain was bound to win a Mediterranean war. The answer lies partly in the fact that the Valois Kings saw Italy in the same way that the Plantagenets had seen France during the Hundred Years War – like Henry V, François I convinced himself he was recovering his rightful inheritance. But the chief reason was that the Renaissance had made Italy the centre of the civilized world.

Bayard's squire says of François, 'There was never a King in France in whom the nobility took such joy.' *Noblesse* has no exact translation. It included nearly everyone with a coat of arms, from the Duc de Bourbon, with a household 1,000 strong, to the hedge squire who was only to be distinguished from a peasant by the sword over his fireplace and the gloves he wore when pushing the plough. A nobleman possessed valuable privileges and was exempt from taxation. But if he could not live on the income of his estate and did not wish to enter the Church, the only careers open to him were soldiering or service in the household of some great lord. The traditional 'nobility of the sword' was now being joined by a new 'nobility of the robe' – lawyers who acquired nobility through holding Crown offices. Naturally, the old *noblesse de l'épée* looked down on this parvenu *noblesse de la robe*, although, however blue his blood, the standing of some little squire of the sword was infinitely lower than that of a magnate of the Parlements. In 1515 every nobleman in France thirsted for Italian plunder.

François's troops were mainly paid soldiers of the 'companies of array' (*compagnies d'ordonnance*). Most of his 2,500 men-at-arms came from the companies, heavy cavalry in full armour, equipped with sword and lance, who charged in line. This was still the age of full armour, not the three-quarters or half armour of the later sixteenth century, but the suit of plate *cap-à-pied* with visored helmet. Some field armours were no less works of art than those of the tilt-yard though most *gens d'armes* had to be content with plainer suits. By the side of the companies rode the King's bodyguard, composed of gentlemen pensioners – they were paid twenty crowns a month – and archers, the latter including the famous Scots. Nowadays there was little distinction between archers and men-at-arms, the former having long since discarded their bows. There were also a number of noblemen serving at their own expense. François's light cavalry consisted of 1,500 *stradiots*, mounted skirmishers who wore half armour and often carried a crossbow as well as a lance; some of them may have come from the Balkans.

In 1512, in his *Description of the affairs of France*, Machiavelli had noticed that the French Gascon infantry were of poor quality: 'Wherefore the King of France makes use of Swiss and lance-knights (*landsknechts*) because his men-at-arms dare not rely upon his Gascoigns in time of service.' François's most valued foot-soldiers were 9,000 German *landsknechts* under the Duke of Gueldres, many belonging to the Bandes Noires, veteran companies in which they had fought together for twenty years. They wore little body armour and wielded the great Swiss pike, an eighteen-foot ash stave with a steel head ten inches long; a few carried arquebuses – clumsy, unreliable matchlocks. The French foot numbered 10,000, 6,000 being Gascon and Basque crossbowmen led by a Spanish renegade, Count Pedro de Navarro, who was a famous siege engineer. There were also Italian contingents. Finally, there was an impressive artillery train of 70 great cannon and 300 smaller pieces, directed by Jacques Galiot de Genouillac. His guns, cast in bronze and drawn by horses, with trunnions to alter the trajectory, and firing shot instead of stones, constituted a real field-artillery. French gunners were noted for their rapid reloading.

The whole army amounted to something like 30,000 men. Its captains were as good as any France has known – the Constable de Bourbon, and the Marshals, Trivulzio, Lautrec, la Trémouille, and la Palice. They were supported by the Dukes of Vendôme and Alençon with the Duke of Lorraine. There were also Bayard and younger men like Fleurange and Bonnivet.

Politically the moment was opportune. The Venetians were fighting Spain and the Pope, while Genoa was threatened by the Sforza Duke of Milan; both republics begged François to come to their aid. In Flanders, Archduke Charles, influenced by an anti-Spanish Minister – his old governor Chièvres, who had fought in Italy at the side of Charles VIII and Louis XII – agreed not to help his grandfather, King Ferdinand; he pledged himself to marry Louis's younger daughter, Renée of France. Duke Massimiliano Sforza's allies, Spain and the Papacy, were too busy waging war on the Serene Republic to give him much assistance. As for England, although Henry VIII was no friend to France, he could do nothing without allies.

Henry was consumed with envy when he heard of François's expedition. From the beginning he had been highly inquisitive about his fellow monarch, whom he referred to as 'this youth' – François was twenty-one, Henry twenty-three. In the spring the Tudor interrogated Silvestro Pasqualigo, the Italian Bishop of Worcester: 'The King of France, is he as tall as I am?' When the Bishop said there was little difference, Henry asked, 'Is he as stout?' Pasqualigo answered no, at which the King inquired about François's legs. The Bishop replying that these were 'spare', Henry proceeded to display his own massive thigh, adding 'and I also have a good calf'. The King continued that he was really very fond of François. By the summer, however, he was complaining to the Venetian Ambassador that he had been kept in the dark over the Italian expedition; Messer Giustiniani discerned an intense spirit of competition. When François was about to leave Lyons with his army, an English envoy came to ask him not to disturb the peace of Christendom by invading Italy. Indeed, Henry had declared, 'If I choose he will cross the Alps, and if I choose he will not cross.' Guicciardini comments, 'Most of all, the English King was moved by rivalry and envy of François's glory which he felt would greatly increase if he should achieve victory over the state of Milan.' But Henry was also very angry with François for sending the Duke of Albany to Scotland. This Gallicized Stuart, who was heir presumptive to the infant James V, had quickly established a strong pro-French party.

François took with him not only the realm's great soldiers but also its high officials. He left France in the custody of its shrewdest politician, Louise, whom he appointed Regent. She chose her advisers well. As Garde des Sceaux in place of Duprat, she appointed the President of the Parlement of Paris. The Parlement, arrogant and opinionated, was flattered by her tactful gesture. In addition, Semblançay, her financial adviser, managed to borrow 300,000 crowns from the Lyons money-market, a useful asset for any administration. The King left Lyons on 31 July, accompanied by seven

Princes of the Blood. On 12 August he and his army, horse, foot, guns, and munition wagons marched out from Embrun to disappear into the Alps.

The Swiss were François's real adversaries. It was only two years since they had cut to pieces a numerically superior French army at Novara, a spectacular triumph which made them masters of Milan. Though Massimiliano had been restored, part of his Duchy was annexed by the Confederation – later it would become the Canton of Ticino – while Swiss garrisons were installed in his strongholds. The Duke – the 'usurper', as the French called him – was young, feckless, and little more than a puppet. The Swiss imposed crushing taxes which made him dangerously unpopular with the Milanese.

In those days the 'Switzers' were no less renowned as soldiers than they are now as hôteliers and bankers. Guicciardini describes them as 'a race of men naturally valiant, warlike and rude'. Machiavelli calls them 'brutal, arrogant and victorious'. Even in war they were hard-headed tradesmen, exploiting the demand for pikemen. They had little time for uncommercial sentiments like honour or glory. 'Point d'argent, point de Suisses' – 'No money, no Swiss' – ran the saying and they frequently sprang wildcat strikes on their employers for arrears of pay or double wages. Recruited by cantons, Swiss troops were organized on a remarkably democratic basis. They had few officers – some cantons elected their own – and no generals, campaigns being directed by a council of captains. Each company was commanded by a *Hauptman* (captain), assisted by a *Venner* (standard bearer) and a staff of less than a dozen, with no under officers. In practice, this organization was rather like a soldiers' trade union. They fought in huge phalanxes, pike-points held at shoulder-level. By this date they were usually supported by a handful of arquebusiers though their cannon were very sparse. Swiss cavalry were unknown. But their hedgehogs of pikemen could repulse the most determined cavalry charge, while their own charge, at the double, three columns one behind the other in echelon, could roll up the strongest enemy formation. No prisoners were taken and discipline was ferocious, the company *Scharfrichter* (executioner) beheading any man who panicked. After their destruction of Charles the Bold of Burgundy in 1476, these unarmoured 'Alpine cowherds' had acquired the reputation of being the best troops in Christendom. Beneath the banners of their cantons they marched confidently to fifes and drums, the first European troops to march in step to music.

The Swiss believed there were only two Alpine passes through which the French could come, those of Mont-Cenis and Mont-Genèvre. Both could be commanded from Suza where 10,000 troops were concentrated. However, old Marshal Trivulzio, together with Lautrec and Pedro de Navarro, explored Dauphiné for another way into Italy. Shepherds and chamois-hunters told them of a little-known series of defiles, hardly a pass, which would bring them over the mountains and behind the enemy. Count Pedro went ahead with a thousand pioneers, blasting rocks and clearing boulders to make the dizzy tracks over the crags into something like roads on which carts and cannon might travel – slowly and dangerously. Chasms and crevasses were bridged with wood, cannon hoisted across on ropes.

It was a frightening passage. Jean Barrillon, the Chancellor's secretary, says that there was only room for one horse at a time, that if a horse fell it fell 'half a league', that torrents swollen by melting snows ran so fast that no horse could keep its footing in them, that coming down the valleys the slopes were almost too steep for the horses. The 'Moine san froc' – a renegade cleric and early journalist who rashly accompanied the expedition – thought the transporting of the artillery was as miraculous 'as if done by angels'. A Venetian diplomat complained that for three days he had to eat bread and cheese and sleep on the cold mountainside. Each man had to carry his own provisions – for two days the King himself went without wine. He wrote to his mother:

> Madame, we are in the strangest country that any man of this company has ever seen. But tomorrow I hope to be in the plain of Piedmont with the troops I command, which will please us all as it is troublesome wearing armour in these mountains because most of the time we have to go on foot and lead our horses by the bridle. Those who do not see it will not believe that anyone could bring over horsemen and heavy artillery in the way we are doing. Certainly, Madame, it has not been without difficulty; if I had not come, our heavy guns would have stayed behind.

The guides had led them high up, towards the snow. François's letter seems to have been written on the fourth day, when the French had passed over the Col d'Argentière which is 6,545 feet above sea-level. The big guns went by a slightly different route, over Mont-Genèvre. Next day the French came down into the plain of Saluzzo. Francois's passage of the Alps was an heroic achievement which contemporaries compared to that of Hannibal.

Meanwhile 300 picked men-at-arms, led by la Palice, Imbrecourt, and Bayard, had gone ahead, taking a third, even higher route – over the Col d'Agnello. Descending from Monte Viso, they played hide-and-seek with the Papal cavalry. The latter's elderly but formidable commander, Prospero Colonna, was sitting down to dinner in Villafranca when the French suddenly galloped into the little walled town and seized him at table. At one stroke the Swiss had lost 700 irreplaceable men-at-arms – the greater part of their cavalry – and an excellent general. The news, followed by the bewildering arrival of the main French army on their left, warned them that their entire position had been reversed. Hastily they withdrew into Milan. Following, the French advanced within striking distance of the city and pitched camp. Part were at Melignano (known to history as Marignano) ten miles away while the King and most of his army lay at Santa Brigida a little nearer. Other troops guarded the approaches to Milan.

François then demonstrated the strange double standards of Renaissance knighthood. Most unchivalrously, he offered the Swiss an enormous bribe. He would give them the balance of an indemnity pledged by the defeated French commander in 1513 with an additional sum – 700,000 gold crowns in all – besides an annual subsidy to each canton. (At this date the *écu-au-soleil* was worth about four Tudor shillings.) In return the Swiss were to withdraw immediately from Milan, the King promising that Duke Massimiliano would receive a pension and a comfortable home in France. To

The Battle of Marignano, 13–14 September 1515.
The Swiss pikemen fought without armour, often
bareheaded and sometimes barefooted as well.
From a contemporary French miniature.

prove his sincerity François sent every piece of money and plate in the French camp, amounting to 150,000 crowns, to the Swiss envoys. An eyewitness records that this patriotic sacrifice 'left each nobleman no more than enough money to keep him for a week'.

What followed shows the inadequacy of the Swiss command structure. The envoys reported François's offer to a Council of Captains, grizzled and opinionated veterans, who argued interminably. One, Albrecht vom Stein, who was already in François's pay, persuaded the captains of Berne, Fribourg, Solthum, and the Valais, to accept the offer. But the men of the eastern cantons, suspicious of the arrogant Bernese, claimed it was dishonest to do so. None the less, 12,000 Swiss went home after signing a treaty at Galarate on 8 September. Cardinal Matthaus Schinner, Bishop of Sion in the Valais and commonly called 'the Cardinal of the Swiss', was an old enemy of the French and as loyal a supporter of Pope Leo X as he had been of Julius II. Feverishly he strove to rally his countrymen to Massimiliano, claiming that to abandon the Duke was to abandon the Vicar of Christ. After a clash between French and Milanese scouts, he persuaded those Swiss who remained that King François meant to destroy them.

On the morning of Thursday, 13 September the Cardinal preached in front of Milan Cathedral, declaiming, 'I want to wash my hands and swim in French blood'. His sermon had the desired effect. The Swiss agreed they would take no prisoners save the King. Proudly they marched out, along a causeway through the rice-fields, towards Marignano, perhaps 15,000 men, cantonal banners flying and Alpine horns blaring.

'Most were without bonnets or shoes or armour,' says Barillon, who was watching. The men of Zürich – among them the chaplain Huldrych Zwingli – Glarus, Appenzel, and St Gall would form the right wing, those of the 'Old Cantons' – Uri, Schwytz, Zug, Unterwalden, and the Grisons – the centre, and those of Basle, Schaffhausen, and Lucerne the left. For cavalry they had only Duke Massimiliano and his retinue, perhaps 400 men-at-arms, and no more than ten cannon. Yet the Swiss were supremely self-confident – quite sure they could beat a better armed force twice their number. Jean Barrillon could see from the swagger with which they marched that they expected to win. Schinner rode at their head, side-saddle in his scarlet robes, the great processional cross of a Papal Legate borne before him. They hoped to take the French by surprise. But the day was extraordinarily hot 'with the most dust ever seen', and the clouds raised by the marching men warned look-outs that an attack was imminent. It was about one o'clock in the afternoon.

The French were not expecting an assault. By a lucky accident they were ready with a defence in depth, formations posted one behind the other – Bourbon's advance guard, the centre under the King, and the rearguard under Alençon. The light horse, commanded by Fleurange, was well out in front, the heavy cavalry on roads down which it would charge, and the artillery, guarded by *landsknechts*, placed at the front where it had a clear field of fire. The treeless plain before Marignano, intersected by canals and covered with rice-fields, was ill suited to offensive tactics.

The only strategy possible for the Swiss was a headlong frontal attack. They determined to take the French guns at the outset. Forming up into their usual three columns, the left moving to the front, they immediately launched their loping charge, driving the French light cavalry back into its own infantry. Though slowed down by a ditch, the Swiss crashed into the *landsknechts*, hurling them back. They captured fifteen of the foremost guns. One company of Germans began to falter. Bourbon held on, praying for help.

As soon as his cavalry were driven in, Fleurange galloped furiously back to warn François. He found him in his chamber at Santa Brigida admiring himself in a new German armour for fighting on foot – 'marvellously made and very cunningly, so that one could not pierce it, even with a pin or a needle'. Fleurange sounded the call to arms himself, on a trumpet. The Swiss were only two miles away. Hastily the King dispatched the Venetian General, Bartolomeo de Alviano, to bring his troops from Lodi. Then he led the vanguard to Bourbon's rescue.

The panic among the Germans was the most dangerous moment of the day. Sixteenth-century battles were settled by pikemen even if guns and cavalry tilted the balance. And the Swiss were accustomed to winning battles in the first few minutes, as at Novara. Here, the clash between Germans and Swiss was like two porcupines colliding – with the impact of battering-rams – but once their pikeshafts were crossed a trial of strength ensued. Each side tried to heave the other back 'at push of pike' – *landsknechts* gripping their weapons low down the shaft, the Swiss higher up. If the Germans weakened only a little more, the Swiss would punch widening holes in their front until

Anne of Brittany, Queen of both Charles VIII and
Louis XII, from her tomb at Saint-Denis. She was
François's first enemy.

the entire column disintegrated. Frontal attacks could not halt the mountaineers – most of Fleurange's cavalry had had their horses killed beneath them. But they could be slowed down by a charge in flank.

The *landsknechts* rallied. They had seen François coming up with the main body of the army. The King was unmistakable, in steel from head to foot and mounted on a huge warhorse with a saddle-cloth of blue velvet powdered with gold fleurs-de-lis and crowned F's. He rode beside the Bandes Noires who escorted the guns.

He was just in time. The second column of the Swiss had launched another battering-ram attack. They were checked, by a flanking charge. Throughout the day the Swiss continued to come on as grimly as ever, time and again. Both front lines reeled backwards and forwards, staggering at the shock of each collision, summoning up barely enough strength to mount or meet a fresh assault. François said that he and his household made no less than thirty charges. Brantôme heard years later that the King 'was an excellent man-at-arms and could handle a lance very well'. In the brief lulls French cannon fired steadily into the dour mountaineers re-forming their columns.

Dismounted cavalrymen joined the *landsknechts* to hack at the Swiss pikeheads with halberds, swords, and axes. They fought in a fog of black powder smoke. Above the roar of cannon – often blowing up or backfiring – and the hiss of crossbow quarrels could be heard the enemy's fifes and drums, sounding the charge and the retreat. Noblemen boiled like lobsters in their armour beneath the sun, their close helmets clogged with dust.

Night fell but fighting went on in the moonlight. Dust made it impossible to see – no one knew where they were, Swiss, French, and *landsknechts* being inextricably mingled. At one point the King saved his artillery by charging with only twenty-five men – the Swiss were only a few paces off so he ordered a nearby fire to be put out lest it give away the guns. A pike thrust went through his armour, despite Fleurange's good opinion. The latter, who had his horse shot beneath him, writes, 'I swear on my faith that he (the King) was one of the finest captains in the whole army and never left his artillery, rallying as many men as he could.' Bayard's squire tells us that even the Chevalier came to grief in the gloom. Attacking some Swiss, their pikes cut the bridle of his horse which promptly bolted. Pulled up short by some vine stakes, Bayard dismounted, knowing 'he would be dead for certain if he fell into the enemy's hands'. Throwing away his helmet – to see better – and his leg armour, he crawled on all fours along ditches towards shouts of 'France, France!' He was lucky enough to find the Duke of Lorraine who gave him another helmet and a fresh horse with which he was able to plunge back into the fight. The mêlée only came to an end when both sides were too exhausted to continue. Men crept back to where they thought their lines were. It was nearly midnight.

The night was so dark that 'French and Swiss slept beside one another, some of our men in their camp and some of theirs in ours'. François, still in his armour, could only lean against a gun. He wrote afterwards, 'We stayed by our horses, helmeted, lance in hand, all night long, the *landsknechts* drawn up in battle order.' Someone brought him a

François at Marignano in 1516. The armour is
contemporary, but the King was in fact clean
shaven until 1519.

LE ROI CHEVALIER   55

drink of water in a helmet but so full of mud and blood it made him ill. Noticing the
Swiss had lit camp-fires, he ordered his artillery to bombard them, inflicting heavy
casualties.

Morning broke. It was Friday, 14 September, the Feast of the Holy Cross. Each
army re-formed, the sharp notes of the French trumpets contrasting with the mournful
lowing of the great Alpine horns used by the Swiss – the Bull of Uri and the Cow of
Unterwalden. The French formation was now in breadth instead of depth – Bourbon
on the right, the King in the centre, Alençon on the left. The Swiss *schwerpunkt* was at
the centre where they massed 8,000 men and mounted two cannon.

The Swiss charged even more fiercely than on the day before, pushing on towards
the French guns which never ceased firing into them. Led by the men of Zürich, they
hurled themselves forward. Bayard's squire thought 'no men ever fought better'.
Their own cannon, firing point-blank, made François duck his head. This time he too
was fighting on foot, pike in hand. But the Germans held – the one Swiss who reached
the French guns was cut down as he did so. On the right, Bourbon and Trivulzio
attacked the Swiss flank with some success. However, on the left, Alençon, without
artillery, was driven back – some of his men fled to Marignano, shouting that all was
lost.

Then, about eight o'clock, shouts of 'Marco, Marco!' announced the arrival of
the Venetian light horse. Bartolomeo de Alviano had spent nearly twenty hours in
the saddle. By eleven, clouds of dust heralded the approach of his heavy cavalry
and infantry, 12,000 men.

The Swiss knew the battle was lost but had no intention of running. Four hundred
Zürichers were left to hold back the enemy; after severely mauling a detachment of
Venetian horse, they took refuge in a farm where they were wiped out by cannon-fire.
Their gallant stand enabled their comrades to gather up the wounded and beat an
unhurried retreat into Milan. Neither French nor Venetians cared to pursue them.

A typical piece of Renaissance play-acting now took place. François asked Bayard
to knight him. The Chevalier replied that the King of France and the Church's Eldest
Son hardly needed the honour of knighthood. François insisted, telling him to hurry
up. Whereupon Bayard knighted his kneeling sovereign, with various graceful
references to Charlemagne's paladins and Godefroy de Bouillon. Those present,
deeply moved, thought that the Chevalier acted with great dignity. They were even
more touched by François's humility. It was not a time to remember that most un-
chivalrous bribing of the Swiss.

The same day, the King wrote to his Regent. So breathless are his words that they
read as though written on a gun-carriage. He claims, 'There has not been seen so
fierce and cruel a battle these last 2,000 years.' He tells his mother that no one can
ever again call his men-at-arms 'hares in armour' – a reference to the Battle of the
Spurs – and boasts that it was they who had won the victory. He laughs at a suggestion
that it was due to the artillery. In fact, despite François's boasts and the claims of
the gunners, the Swiss had been defeated by the combination of cavalry, infantry,

and artillery in what was basically a straightforward slogging match. No one realized it but the Swiss were out of date – against all arms, properly handled, unsupported pikemen were bound to lose. The French thought they had killed 14,000 Swiss; it is more likely that each side lost about 5,000 men. None the less, Marignano was a famous victory. Old Trivulzio, 'a captain of great trial and experience of things, affirmed that this battle was fought by giants and not by men and that eighteen battles wherein he had been an executioner, were but combats of little children in comparison of this'. And if many noblemen had fallen – including the Royal Standard Bearer and Fleurange's brother – relatively few of them had been François's close friends. That night, he celebrated his victory in the arms of a beautiful Milanese.

Meanwhile the Swiss had reached Milan whose inhabitants went out to meet them with bandages and with food and wine. But those strange men, as venal as they were brave, at once asked Duke Massimiliano for three months' pay. When he replied he had no money, they told him that their contract was broken. On

Saturday, 15 September, the day after the battle, they marched back to their valleys. Cardinal Schinner had already fled, to take refuge with the Emperor. The Duke retreated to the *castello* with his supporters and a few honest Swiss who together amounted to less than 2,000 men. The Constable de Bourbon speedily invested the *castello* and on 4 October Pedro de Navarro began to dig trenches and to site batteries. Massimiliano knew that although his citadel was considered impregnable he had little hope of being relieved. He accepted the terms which François had offered earlier, at Galarate – an indemnity of 94,000 crowns, an annual pension of 36,000 crowns, and a suitably palatial residence in France. In return he surrendered any claim to the Duchy. Massimiliano then retired to France where he lived quietly but happily for many years. The poor Sforza commented, 'I count myself the most fortunate member of my family. When I was called Duke I was really only a slave, the Swiss being my masters who did whatever they liked with me.'

Milan was once again part of France. In a single, brilliant campaign François had

'François I, King of the French and tamer of the Swiss' – the medal struck c1515 to commemorate Marignano.

recovered everything for which Louis XII had struggled so fruitlessly for so long. No doubt the Milanese were less pleased. Guicciardini's sad lament is particularly applicable: 'Thus by civil disorders which so long hath blinded the princes of Italy, to the great dishonour and scorn of the men of war of that nation, and common danger and ignominy of every region of the same, was transferred one of the most goodly and mighty parts of Italy and of the empire of Italy, to an empire and government of a nation beyond the mountains.'

François stayed at Pavia until the surrender was complete. He dined at the beautiful Charterhouse whose architecture he much admired; here he displayed his exquisite manners, refusing to eat in the refectory because Carthusians never take meat. On 16 October he made his *joyeuse entrée* into Milan, 'wonderfully fine and triumphant'. Sword in hand, the youthful conqueror, clad in blue velvet sewn with golden fleurs-de-lis, rode in at the head of his men-at-arms to give thanks in the Cathedral. There followed the usual feasting, dancing, and jousting. The fickle Milanese seemed genuinely delighted with François. 'There was never prince in Italy who was better feasted by lords and ladies.' News came from Claude that she had borne him his first child, a daughter, Louise. Then the Doge of Genoa surrendered his Republic. François's cup overflowed.

Marignano was immediately recognized as one of the great victories of French history. A medal was struck with the legend 'François I, King of the French and tamer of the Swiss'. It shows him in profile, wearing a plumed hat. He looks even younger than his twenty-two years and, despite that long nose, surprisingly handsome. Clément Jannequin, later to be Master of the Royal Music, wrote one of the first military marches, the *Chanson de Marignane*, whose metallic word-play echoes fifes and drums. France resounded with the envoi:

> *Victoire au noble roi François!*
> *Victoire au gentil de Valois!*
> *Victoire au noble roi François!*

Like Charlemagne, François had gone over the Alps and like Charlemagne he had conquered. Now he had to show that he could hold what he had won, that he was a second Charlemagne in peace as well as war.

François I as Charlemagne, from the fresco in the Vatican *The Coronation of Charlemagne* by Raphael (and pupils)

A Second Charlemagne

Early in 1516 Raphael and his pupils, Giovan Francesco Penni and Giulio Romano, painted a great fresco in the Vatican, the *Coronation of Charlemagne*. It is in that chamber in the Borgo which is named after his mural of a fire – the Stanza dell' incendio. The faces of the Pope and the Emperor are those of Leo X and François I, for their meeting at Bologna was fresh in the Master's mind. Amid rows of coped and mitred prelates, François, in armour, kneels before a glamorized Leo. Behind the King, as his page, is Ippolito de' Medici, who holds the royal crown.

All the Great Powers had been taken by surprise. With Machiavelli they had believed that 'the French cannot stand against the Switzers'. The Spanish Viceroy in

Naples, Don Ramon de Cardona, had a formidable army while there was a large Papal force at Piacenza, but both were busy fighting the Venetians. Old King Ferdinand of Spain, 'apoplectic and tremulous', formed another 'Holy League' with the Pope and Emperor Maximilian. However, the League was still-born. In part this was due to the action of the Pope.

Leo X had begun his reign with the intention of continuing the policy of the warlike Julius II, of keeping the French out of Italy. Always vacillating, he now decided that the policy was impracticable. As both Supreme Pontiff and a Medici, Leo had much at stake. If a shrewd politician he was none the less timid and also something of a gambler. He decided on a complete volte-face. It was arranged that François should visit him at Bologna, in Papal territory, where he himself arrived on 8 December 1515.

On the morning of Tuesday, 11 December François entered Bologna. The streets were garlanded, tapestries and rich carpets hanging from the balconies, and packed with the cardinals' gentlemen in violet liveries. As usual the King was splendidly dressed, in a black velvet robe embroidered with silver, though an eyewitness – the Bishop of Worcester – was disappointed by his bodyguard, 300 French archers 'who looked like bargees with greasy, threadbare coats'. He was escorted to his apartments in the Papal palace by two cardinals. Although the Bishop thought the entrance made little more stir than that of a city magistrate, he nevertheless expected to be trampled to death in the cheering crowd which surged backwards and forwards 'like the waves of the sea'. However, he was more impressed when later he saw François on his way to his first audience with Leo. He describes the King as 'tall in stature, broad shouldered, oval and handsome in face, very slender in the legs and much inclined to corpulence'. (In a portrait attributed to 1515 François looks more Gallic than handsome with a noticeably blue chin, although he seems to have stayed clean-shaven for some years yet.) We know from Barrillon that by now the King had changed into a robe of figured cloth of gold lined with sable. It was nine o'clock at night.

In the candlelight Pope Leo, sitting in Consistory amid his Cardinals, outshone them all. He tottered beneath the weight of the Papal tiara and a golden cope so heavy that, huge and unwieldy as he was, he could barely walk. After François had made three genuflections he kissed the Pope's toe, much to the emotion of the crowd, whereupon the delighted Leo embraced him and kissed him on the mouth. When he left his throne François gave him his arm lest he fall under the weight of his vestments. Years later, long after Leo had betrayed them and was dead, Fleurange recalled bitterly how the Pope 'really looked like a truly good and honest man . . . he gave the King wonderfully good cheer and they lodged together under the same roof'.

Next day, Wednesday, Leo sang Mass 'with the greatest pomp and triumph that ever Pope sang it'. François sat with the Cardinals, as was his right as Eldest Son of the Church, and took Communion from the Pope's own hands. The twenty-two-year-old King and the forty-year-old Pope were charmed with each other, spending

the next few days together in long and secret discussions. Leo was less formidable than might be expected from the bull-necked, triple-jowled prelate of his portraits. Affable, elegant, witty, and a patron of poetry, painting, music, drama, and indeed of all the arts, he had much in common with François. He even shared his fondness for hunting. Nevertheless, there were awkward moments. When, with careful symbolism, Leo presented François with a diamond reliquary, containing a fragment of the True Cross, which had once belonged to the Sforzas, the King asked for the *Laocoön* instead. This masterpiece of antique sculpture, in which the Trojan priest and his sons writhe in eternal agony beneath the serpents' coils, was the jewel of the Papal collection. Taken aback, Leo agreed. It was rumoured that he asked Leonardo to counterfeit his pagan treasure but Leonardo seems to have declined. When the Pope returned to Rome François was sent a poor copy. But meanwhile nothing was allowed to disturb their friendship. Leo gave the King a banner inscribed *In hoc signo vinceris*, offering him the Empire of the East if he would expel the Turk from Constantinople. As a final compliment François was asked to touch for the King's Evil (scrofula) in the Papal chapel and exercise a sacramental power which not even Popes possessed. When he left Bologna on 15 December it was agreed that the meeting had been an unqualified success.

In temporal matters François offered two things very dear to Leo's heart. He would help the Pope's brother, Giuliano de' Medici, hold Florence and assist in establishing his nephew Lorenzo, Captain of the Papal Army, as Duke of Urbino. The delighted Pope was only too willing to recognize the undisputed master of northern Italy as Duke of Milan. Leo also surrendered Parma and Piacenza (called Plaisance by the French) which had been wrested from the Milanese. The anti-French League had been smashed before it had properly come into existence.

A Concordat was also agreed. This was more than a mere annulment of Louis XII's schism with Rome. Since 1438 the Pragmatic Sanction of Bourges had given the French Church independence from both Crown and Papacy. The Gallican clergy elected their own bishops and did not pay annates to Rome. Both Leo and François were anxious to reach an agreement before the Lateran Council met at the end of 1516 – the Pope wanted French recognition of Papal supremacy while the King wished for control over the Church in France of the sort possessed by Spanish monarchs. For three months before François's visit to Bologna diplomats of the Curia and French Ministers – the latter led by Duprat – had been haggling over terms. Finally it was agreed that the King would reject the doctrine of the Council of Basle (that General Councils could overrule Popes) and enforce the payment of annates. In return French Kings obtained the right of nomination to ten archbishoprics, eighty-two bishoprics, over 500 abbeys, and countless priories and canonries. The acquisition of this vast reservoir of patronage meant that François had bridled the clergy as Louis XI had the nobility.

The King left Milan for France on 8 January 1516. Behind him he left Bourbon, with 700 men-at-arms and 10,000 foot, for the unpredictable Emperor Maximilian might attack at any moment. Louise, who thought she had received a mystical intimation of victory on the very day of Marignano, was reunited to her son on 13 January 1516 at Sisteron in Provence, on the banks of the Durance, 'towards six o'clock in the evening'. She wrote in her journal: 'God knows how I, a poor mother, was comforted to see my son safe and sound after all the hardship he had suffered and endured for the common good.' She was accompanied by Marguerite and Queen Claude. Together the four set out on a pilgrimage to Sainte-Baume. They prayed in the damp forest cave where, according to legend, Mary Magdalene, Martha, and Lazarus had spent their last years.

There began a triumphal progress through Provence and up the Rhône. On his way to Marseilles François passed through Aix and Saint-Maximin. There is a story that at the little town of Manosque his attentions were so unwelcome to the daughter of its leading citizen that she disfigured her face with a chafing-dish. His entry into Marseilles was as splendid as any, 4,000 men-at-arms and 2,000 children clad in white preceding him. The magistrates presented their King, who was dressed in silver velvet and riding a grey horse, with the keys of the city while cannon boomed salutes. There were pageants and then dancing which lasted all through the night. Next day there was a battle of oranges in which François joined enthusiastically. On the third day he sailed out to intercept a Portugese vessel carrying a gift to the Pope from King Manoel, a wonderful beast called *reynoceron* – alas, the poor rhinoceros perished soon after in a shipwreck and only its hide reached Rome. François continued his progress through Provence, visiting the little town of Tarascon. In February he was welcomed at Papal Avignon by the Cardinal Legate. Then he journeyed up the Rhône to Lyons which pleased him so much that he stayed there for three months, apart from joyful visits to Grenoble and Chambéry. Only in the autumn did he at last go home, reaching Amboise on 21 August, after another splendid entry into Tours.

Meanwhile, even the unromantic Swiss had accepted that François's star was in the ascendant. A treaty negotiated in November 1515 was confirmed as a 'Perpetual Peace' at Fribourg in 1516. In return for a million gold crowns and a pension of 2,000 francs for each canton, they agreed that the King of France should levy troops among them whenever he wanted. But, to ensure technical neutrality, they must never be asked to declare war on the Emperor.

Henry VIII simply refused to believe the news of François's victory. Finally, a French envoy, M. Bapaume, delivered two letters to Greenwich in François's own hand which had been brought by Guyenne Herald. Bapaume wrote, with relish, that Henry did not enjoy reading them – 'It seemed tears would flow from his eyes, so red were they with the pain he suffered on hearing of the King's good tidings and success.'

The pivot of the English diplomatic campaign which ensued was the Emperor Maximilian, a frivolous, fantastic monarch. Pope Julius II had dismissed him as 'light and inconstant, always begging for other men's money which he wastes in chamois-hunting'. Poverty – often he was unable to pay for his own dinner – reduced

him to the most ignominious shifts. In 1513 he had actually served as a private soldier for 100 crowns a day, in the English army in France. Now, approaching sixty, charming, totally without scruple, and hounded by creditors, Maximilian was ready to do anything – or seem to do anything – for ready money. The English offensive often approached high comedy. Money sent to subsidize a Swiss invasion somehow passed into the Emperor's hands *en route*. When, in March 1516, he advanced on Milan it was only to come within striking distance and then, inexplicably, beat a hasty retreat back to the Tyrol. English ambassadors led a nerve-racking life at Maximilian's court – one was even held to ransom by Imperial troops as security for their pay. It was impossible to believe anything he said. He proposed creating Henry Duke of Milan, after which he would abdicate for Henry to take his place as Emperor. The English recognized a gigantic swindle. But Maximilian was their only ally.

Henry also turned to Ferdinand of Aragon – who had tricked him so cruelly in 1512 – but the old King, now ailing, partly through his fondness for hawking in wet weather, died in January 1516. Rumour ascribed his death to 'dropsy occasioned by a beverage which Germaine, his wife, had given him, to enable him to beget children'. His grandson, Archduke Charles, became King of Spain. In July 1516, at the Treaty of Noyon, Charles betrothed himself to François's daughter, Louise; she was to have Naples for a dowry and he would return southern Navarre to the d'Albret dynasty.

Worse still, as the English envoys said, 'The Pope is French and everything from Rome to Calais.' In 1517 Raphael and his pupils completed another fresco in the Vatican, the *Oath of Leo III*. The Carolingian Pope is shown vindicating himself through his piety – his face is that of Leo X while a youthful figure behind him, carrying a crown, is François. The fresco symbolized the Pontiff's determination to be faithful to France.

Maximilian, Charles's other grandfather, made a fine show of rage when he heard what had taken place at Noyon. He announced his intention of punishing the Archduke's advisers. Again, Henry gave the Emperor money and he advanced on Flanders. Once there, he accepted 75,000 French crowns and in March 1517, at Cambrai, signed a treaty of alliance with François. In the amiable Habsburg's own words to his grandson, 'You're going to fool the French and I'm going to fool the English.' As Professor J. J. Scarisbrick puts it, Maximilian 'had tricked and humiliated the King of England and made him the laughing stock of Europe'.[1] Many other European rulers concluded peace treaties with France in 1517, from the Duke of Urbino to James V of Scotland.

At last, in October 1518, Cardinal Wolsey achieved his grand design, a general peace signed by more than twenty States, with Pope Leo's blessing. The infant Dauphin was betrothed to the four-year-old Princess Mary at Greenwich, with much pomp; Bonnivet, acting as proxy, placed a diamond ring on her finger. That

[1] *Henry VIII* (1968)

excellent civil servant, Jean Barrillon, comments that, 'the Kingdom of France enjoyed great peace and tranquillity and there was no whisper or rumour of war, faction or party. Merchants traded in complete safety, both by sea and land, and business was done peaceably between Frenchmen, Englishmen, Spaniards, Germans and all the other nations of Christendom, which was truly God's mercy upon his Christian people.'

François, young and victorious, was the most admired ruler in Christendom. He had astonished Europe by giving the Swiss their first real beating; everyone remembered how, only two years before, they had cut the French to ribbons at Novara. François's moderation – a businesslike approach to the Swiss, tactful treatment of the Pope – made him seem more statesmanlike than he really was. The splendour of his court created an impression of boundless wealth. He had no rivals. Charles of Habsburg had not yet entered into his inheritance while, internationally, Henry VIII cut a poor figure. François himself, full of dazzling optimism, had no misgivings. His good fortune seemed complete when, in 1518, Claude presented him with the Dauphin François and then, in 1519, with the future Henri II.

As François matured, he put on weight and his face became fat. He retained his fair complexion. It was probably during these years that Marguerite wrote:

> De sa beauté, il est blanc et vermeil
> Les cheveux bruns, de grande et belle taille.

Antonio de' Beatis, who met François at Rouen in August 1517, considered that although he had a very fine appearance his legs were too thin for such a big body and that his nose was too long. However, he thought that the King had a kind face and a most cheerful and agreeable nature. François's hair darkened. In 1519 he grew a beard, which with his nose – Frenchmen spoke of 'le roi grand-nez' – made him look like an amiable satyr. He was always smiling, always laughing and joking. He bewildered the excellent Beatis by pretending that he dared not visit Brittany because its inhabitants were so ferocious – no doubt this was to tease Queen Claude. Michelet writes of the 'hilarité menteuse' of his expression, but this is unfair, even if there was a hint of slyness in his watchful eyes.

A small circle stood very close to the King. Closest was Guillaume Gouffier, Sieur de Bonnivet and Grand Admiral of France, to whom François had been attached since their boyhood at Amboise. Six years older than the King, this swaggering, rather stupid Gascon, handsome if coarse-featured, was no less pugnacious a jouster and relentless a womanizer. Their friendship resembled that of Brandon and Henry VIII. Bonnivet even tried to seduce the King's sister. One attempt amounted almost to rape – he entered Marguerite's bedroom through a trapdoor but fled after being badly scratched. None the less, his unwilling victim wrote, 'His grandeur, beauty and good grace surpassed those of all his companions.' His ambitions were epitomized by his great château of Bonnivet at Neuville, which he began in 1513; Rabelais thought it as impressive as Chambord. It was near the old-fashioned fortress of the Duc de Bourbon at Châtelherault. François asked the Duke if he admired it. Bourbon

Left Guillaume Gouffier, Seigneur de Bonnivet (1482–1525); *middle* Jacques Galiot, Seigneur de Genouillac (1465–1546); *right* Françoise de Foix, Dame de Châteaubriant (1495–1537).

replied, 'The cage is too big for the bird.' Bonnivet was also a Marshal of France. His functions and influence gave him the power of a modern Minister of War.

Next in the King's affections came Anne de Montmorency, a future Constable of France, intelligent but brutal and overbearing to all save his master. His wife was the daughter of François's bastard uncle, René of Savoy. In 1520 Montmorency was made First Valet of the Bedchamber, in 1522 a Marshal of France. Then there was the amiable Fleurange, still the Young Adventurer, a simple soldier, genuinely devoted to his King; he was Captain of the Swiss Guard. Other friends from Amboise were Martin de Montchenu and the greedy Philippe Chabot. All grew beards in the fashion set by the King.

In addition, there were trusted elder statesmen like Bonnivet's brother Boisy, the Bastard of Savoy (who was Louise's half-brother), and that formidable warrior, Galiot de Genouillac, who in 1518 was made Master-General of the Artillery — the second highest military office in France. With them may be numbered the indispensable Chancellor, Duprat, and the Treasurer, Florimond Robertet, though they stood aloof from Semblançay, the Superintendent of Finances. On the periphery of this charmed circle were Alençon, Marguerite's ineffectual husband, and the haughty Duc de Bourbon.

Early in 1518, François acquired the first of his great mistresses, Françoise de Foix, Dame de Châteaubriant. Her brother, Odet de Lautrec, had been with François at Amboise. Now about twenty-three years old, she had been married when very young in 1509 to Jean de Laval, Sire de Châteaubriant. She was a big, strong, dark woman

Left Marie de Langeac, Dame de Lestrange (1508–1588); *middle* Marie de Macy, Dame de Montchenu (1515–60); *right* Marie d'Assigny, Dame de Canaples (1502–58).

A SECOND CHARLEMAGNE 69

with a forceful if rather shallow personality who was both demanding and promiscuous. The relationship was stormy, a passionate saga of jealousy and reconciliation. She slept with Bonnivet and told the King how much she enjoyed his Admiral's company. In calmer moods François and Françoise exchanged portraits and verses. One of her poems warns him not to trust a certain blonde beauty and stresses her own swarthy charms. Mme de Châteaubriant's influence was not altogether beneficial. She extorted rich presents for her husband, while her three brothers – Odet de Lautrec, Thomas de Lescun, and André de Lesparre – were promoted to commands beyond their ability.

The affair did not stop François from sleeping with other ladies. A modern biographer has written that he was 'as amorous as a cat, amorous and inconstant'.[1] '*La petite bande*', as the King's seraglio was called, included Marie de Langeac, Mme de Montchenu, his friend's wife, and the charming Mme de Canaples. Jean Clouet's delightful painting of Marie de Canaples is in the National Gallery of Scotland – like most of François's loves, she was a brunette with a rounded figure and sparkling eyes. Brantôme has some colourful stories. 'On one occasion King François wished to sleep with a lady of the court with whom he was in love, but found her husband waiting with his sword, ready to kill him. But the King pointed his own sword at the gentleman's throat and commanded him, on his life, to do her no harm, adding that if the gentleman hurt her at all he himself would kill him or have somebody else

[1] Charles Terrasse, *François 1, le Roi et le Règne* (1948)

The Field of Cloth of Gold, 1520. The painting
from which this detail is taken shows only the
English camp.

cut his head off, and for that night he sent the gentleman outside and took his place.' Another time, going to sleep with Mme de Châteaubriant, he almost caught her in bed with Bonnivet. The Admiral had time to hide in the fireplace, which, as it was summer, was filled with green boughs. Unwittingly, François revenged himself before leaving, by relieving himself in the fireplace and drenching poor Bonnivet to the skin. The King was always curious to hear full details of his courtiers' love-affairs and would roar with laughter when told. Nevertheless, as Brantôme puts it: 'King François, who was very fond of the ladies (although . . . he was convinced that they are most changeable and fickle) never would have any slandering of them at his court, but insisted on their being accorded great honour and respect.'

Brantôme alleges that the ignoble role of procurer to the King was filled by 'that very great, very magnificent and very great-hearted nobleman, the Cardinal of Lorraine'. Born in 1495, Jean de Lorraine had been Bishop of Metz since the age of ten; in 1518 he was made Papal Legate in his brother's Duchy. Extremely dissolute, he held his own court at the Hôtel de Cluny in Paris. He could behave like a dissipated layman and in 1522 was taking a prominent part in all-night revels with François and his ladies. 'Rarely or never did any maid or wife leave that court chaste' says Brantôme of the Cardinal's pimping. 'You would have found their coffers and their wardrobes more full of gowns and petticoats of cloth of gold or silver, and of silk, than those of our Queens and great princesses today.'

In Paris François behaved just as he had before his accession, wandering nightly, cloaked and masked, through the city's narrow streets to an assignation in some high-gabled, half-timbered house. This could have been dangerous. The capital already contained 400,000 inhabitants and its unlit thoroughfares were infested with footpads; after nightfall, wise men stayed behind barred and bolted doors. In 1519 some English courtiers who had returned from France were criticized for riding with the French King 'daily disguised through Paris, throwing eggs, stones and other foolish trifles at the people'.

The King had grown fond of his long-suffering Queen. The sweetness of Claude's expression, with its hint of melancholy, gave her plain face the look of a rustic Madonna. She had a charming manner besides a most agreeable way of speaking and her unfailing kindness made her popular with everyone. She was an excellent mother to the little Princesses of France, Mmes Louise and Charlotte. Claude adored her magnificent husband, bearing his infidelities with resignation. On 10 May 1517 she was consecrated and crowned Queen of France at Saint-Denis. She had spent the previous evening praying at her parents' tomb. On the day itself, the Cathedral bore the arms of Brittany as well as of France, for she was still the reigning Duchess. Over a silver robe, with a coif of white satin and cloth of gold and a surcoat of ermine, Claude wore a mantle of royal blue lined and bordered with ermine. Her ladies were Marguerite and the Duchess de Vendôme. After her anointing, three Dukes held the crown of Charlemagne over her head. Next day, she made her own *joyeuse entrée* into Paris, accompanied by sixteen Princesses clad in gold with gold hats fashioned like crowns. In the evening

Henry VIII, by Joos van Cleve who also painted
François. The two Kings had a genuine regard for
each other.

A SECOND CHARLEMAGNE   73

she presided over a banquet, wearing a new crown which bore her name and which sparkled with diamonds, rubies, emeralds, and pearls.

Like its English namesake, the Parlement of Paris – which included the Peers of France – had developed from the old Curia Regis. But, instead of becoming a representative assembly, it had developed into the central judicature – it was both the High Court and a corporation of great lawyers. Provincial Parlements were smaller versions of the Parlement of Paris. New laws had to be registered by the Parlements – frequently they would criticize or refuse to enact them. The Paris Parlement had political ambitions, seeing itself as a Roman Senate. Its first big clash with François was over the Concordat of Bologna. The Parlement declared that only a General Council of the Church, in which the Gallican Church was fully represented, could legislate on such matters. On 5 February 1517 the King told the Parlement to register the Concordat – the lawyers asked for time to consider. In June, he ordered them by letter to register it but they refused. In January 1518, two councillors arrived at Amboise with a remonstrance of 116 articles. A fortnight later, an enraged François shouted at them, 'There will be only one King in France. What was done in Italy shall not be undone in France – I will take good care that there is no Senate in France as there is in Venice!' He ended 'Get out! Leave tomorrow – make no mistake about it – leave first thing in the morning!' They begged to stay a little longer as the Loire was in flood, whereupon François threatened to throw them into a pit. On 15 March a royal messenger told the Parlement that the King 'was marvellously angry at the delays and dissimulations of the said court, for it is his right to command them as his subjects, and their duty to obey.' He added that François had said, 'If the court is at fault again . . . I will make it regret it.' At last, on 22 March 1518, the Parlement of Paris registered the Concordat, noting that it was done 'by the order and command of the King and not by the court'.

In 1518, on Sunday, 28 February at Amboise, Queen Claude gave birth to a son whom François described as 'a beautiful Dauphin who is the most beautiful and puissant child one could imagine and who will be the easiest to bring up'. 'Tell the King that he is even more beautiful than himself,' said Claude. The christening took place at Amboise on 25 April. The château courtyard was filled by pavilions, its walls hung with tapestries depicting tales from antiquity – the Sack of Troy, the Labours of Hercules, the Destruction of Jerusalem. Outside it was a wild night but the rain could not penetrate the tents which were lit by a thousand candles. Leonardo had designed the decorations. From the Dauphin's chamber to the church, there was a lofty bridge, lined with Turkey carpets – it had a roof ornamented with dolphins, and at every pillar stood a great torch of white wax on a gold plate. Drums announced the procession to the church down this bridge, Heralds and Kings-at-Arms – Dauphiné and Normandy, Brittany and Savoy – with the Chevaliers of Saint-Michel, the high officers of the household carrying their batons, and a glittering host of lords and ladies. The focus of this splendour was borne by his godfather Lorenzo de' Medici, Duke of Urbino and the Pope's nephew, the four corners of the Dauphin's mantle of cloth of silver furred with ermine being held by the Prince of Orange, the Marquis of Mantua,

the Comte de Guise, and the Scots Duke of Albany. Louise de Savoie followed proudly, her train carried by the Bastard's wife; another of Mme Louise's ambitions had been achieved – her dynasty's future was secure. The clergy, including three Cardinals, were waiting in the nave of the church which was hung with cloth of gold and silver. Even the font was draped in cloth of gold; over it a canopy had been erected, 'a sky of honour' supported by four pillars like trees of gold, round which stood the Chevaliers of Saint-Michel in their crimson hoods. Duke Lorenzo held the child while Bonnivet's brother, the Cardinal de Boisy, christened him François. When the baptism was over, the Kings-at-Arms cried three times *'Vive Monseigneur le Dauphin!'* and fanfares were sounded. There followed a sumptuous banquet, with dancing, music, and masquerades. Finally, Bayard knighted what must have been an exhausted baby.

However, 1518 was not a year without sorrow. During it, François's eldest daughter, Louise, died – she was only three. Speaking of her death, Brantôme shows an unaccustomed delicacy: 'Thus are pretty rosebuds carried off by the wind as well as flowers full blown, and children snatched away are mourned a hundred times more than the old who die.'

Despite fatherhood and a *maîtresse en titre*, the two chief influences in François's life remained his mother and his sister. They still seemed 'a single heart in three bodies'. Marguerite, childless and unhappy in her marriage, continued to worship her royal brother. Now in her mid-twenties, she was growing plump and her nose was too long. But she was still blue-eyed and fair-haired and kept her fascination. Her device was a sunflower, to indicate that she lived by the light of her brother's brilliance. A poet and a dreamer, already Marguerite had become, in Rabelais's words 'a rapt, ecstatic spirit'. This 'princess of very great mind and abilities' occupied herself in learning Greek, Hebrew, German, Spanish, and Italian. A lover of Petrarch, she also admired Dante. (The latter was hated by François for perpetuating the legend that a butcher's son founded the Capetian dynasty.) Above all, Marguerite enjoyed Boccaccio and had the *Decameron* translated by her secretary. Her humour was an odd mixture of earthiness and courtliness, of obscenity and piety, half Gallic, half Italian – a peculiarly Valois mixture. Everyone agreed that she was 'a princess worthy of a great empire, besides being very kind, gentle, gracious, charitable, a great alms-giver and disdaining none'.

Mme Louise, only forty in 1516, held court at her châteaux of Cognac, Romorantin, and Angoulême, but, like Marguerite, also spent much time with her son. Indeed, it has been said that King François was nothing but a splendid automaton and that his mother and Antoine Duprat were the true rulers of France. This is untrue, even if François relied more on his mother's advice than on that of anyone else. And though Duprat was the mainspring of the administration, he was often overruled by the King.

Duprat undoubtedly resented François's appointment of Semblançay to the entirely new post of 'Superintendent of Finances Ordinary and Extraordinary' in 1518. Originally a merchant banker and a former Mayor of Tours, Jacques de Beaune, Baron de Semblançay, had been Anne of Brittany's Treasurer. From 1515 he had administered the estates of Mme Louise. He was sixty when he became financial overlord of France. 'Ordinary' revenues came from the royal domains, 'Extraordinary' from taxation, direct and indirect. Direct taxation meant the *taille*, a heavy poll-tax levied on those who worked the land. Indirect taxation consisted of the *gabelle*, a levy on salt, of *aides* which were duties on certain commodities and commercial transactions, and of *traites*, the last being tolls and customs duties on external and internal trade. In theory, the clergy and the nobility were exempt, but in practice the King frequently extracted forced loans and tithes from them. Taxes varied widely from region to region. Fiscal machinery was inextricably complicated. There were a whole host of minor officials and tax-farmers, with ill-defined and often conflicting functions. It was impossible to control them, to regulate taxation, or even to know what was in the Royal Treasury. Extravagance, inefficiency, and plain robbery were bringing the Kingdom to the verge of bankruptcy. In the circumstances, Semblançay's feat in staving off financial collapse for three years was something of an achievement. In addition, he had to face the enmity of the court, who resented him as a bourgeois upstart, and administer the estates of Mme Louise who was bent on amassing a vast fortune.

The Emperor Charles V (1519–58), a bust by Conrad
Meit.

On 12 January 1519 the Emperor Maximilian I died. In his last ailing years, he had produced the most fantastic of all his eccentric schemes; he would abdicate, be elected Pope, and then canonized – he told his daughter that one day she would pray to him. Having attempted to sell his crown to Henry VIII as late as 1517, at the end Maximilian had been trying to procure the election of his grandson Charles as King of the Romans and his official successor as Holy Roman Emperor. But at the Reichstag, at Augsburg in 1518, the Imperial Electors had voted inconclusively. The English reported to their jealous master that François 'goeth about covertly and layeth many baits to attain the empire'.

Charles, the Most Catholic King of Spain, heir to both the Habsburgs and the Dukes of Burgundy, bore little resemblance to the warrior Emperor of Titian's equestrian portrait. In 1519 he was a cold, phlegmatic youth, who seldom spoke or smiled, with a thin face framed by lank, tow-coloured hair. His mouth hung open, and a deformed Habsburg jaw made it difficult to understand what he said. Brought up in Flanders by the Francophil Chièvres, French was his first language; he spoke very little German, indeed he was rumoured to speak it only to his horse. A devout confessor, Adrian Florisse of Utrecht, had taught him the piety of Thomas à Kempis. Otherwise he was poorly educated. So far, his only real interest was in the deeds of his great Burgundian forebears; he dreamt of recovering their lost lands in eastern France. He was obsessed by Burgundian court ceremony, which in Flanders became known as 'la nouvelle religion'. Later Charles introduced it into Austria and Spain where it survived until the present century. The Spaniards regarded their foreign King with distaste. Many would have preferred his brother Ferdinand, who had been brought up in Spain. Others considered their true ruler to be Charles's co-sovereign, his mother, 'Juana la Loca' – although she was so mad that people said she ran up curtains like a cat. This sickly, callow young man was going to mature into François's lifelong rival.

The 'Holy Roman Empire of the German Nation' was, as the saying goes, neither holy nor Roman. Though most of the lands which lay within it were German, it also included the Low Countries, eastern Burgundy, Savoy, and much of northern Italy. Its Electors, dukes, princes, margraves, counts, barons, were all independent rulers together with many abbots and bishops and free towns – even Imperial knights were independent, though their domain might be no bigger than a manor-house. The Reichstag, or Imperial Diet, was supposed to meet annually, while there was an Imperial court of justice, the recently instituted Reichskammergericht, but Maximilian's dream of reasserting Imperial authority had not materialized. Yet in a curious way every German regarded the Emperor as his sovereign – in theory he was Lord of all Christendom.

Charles ruled the Austrian Archduchies, and the Habsburgs had occupied the Imperial throne for three generations. He had considerable support as German candidate. However, the seven Electors were open to bribery. At first the Margrave Joachim of Brandenburg – whom some called 'the father of all greediness' – with his brother, Albrecht von Hohenzollern, Archbishop of Cologne, favoured the French

King. So did the Count Palatine. Another Elector, Archbishop Richard von Greiffen-klau zu Wolratz of Trier, canvassed openly for François. Pope Leo was his staunch supporter.

On 21 February 1519, François attended a Requiem for Emperor Maximilian at Notre-Dame. The throne of Charlemagne had fired his imagination. Telling Sir Thomas Boleyn to lean out of the window with him, so they would not be overheard, he promised, 'I will spend three million of gold but be Emperor.' At the same time he wrote gracefully to Charles that though both were in love with the same girl, they must stay good friends, whoever won her. Charles brought in the Fuggers of Augsburg, the greatest bankers of the day, to fend off this takeover; they refused to service French bills and advanced Charles half a million florins. When the Margrave of Brandenburg was offered the Queen Dowager of Spain as additional bait, François promised him Louis XII's daughter, Renée, at which Charles went higher still and offered his own sister. Then in May Artus de Boisy, that wise and charming old preceptor, died – he had been François's most able negotiator. His brother and Fleurange set off to take his place. Bonnivet, disguised as a German *landsknecht*, Captain Jacob, hoped to secure the votes of the Margrave and the Duke of Saxony – he even spied on the English Am-bassador from behind the Margrave's tapestry. But the French cause was doomed. Despite greedy waverings by the Electors, Charles was elected Emperor at Frankfurt on 28 June 1519. It had cost him 850,000 florins. François commented, a little sourly, 'I am well pleased not to have the Empire's cares', and went hunting at Fontainebleau. In fact, he was deeply hurt by his rejection.

There had been a third competitor, Henry VIII. That long-suffering diplomat, Richard Pace, Dean of St Paul's, had been sent to Germany in May; his mission was to effect a deadlock between Charles and François, to solve which the Electors would turn to Henry. The Archbishop of Trier, always open to a good offer, said the English King had an excellent chance. Pace also heard hopeful rumours about the Margrave of Brandenburg and the Archbishops of Mainz and Cologne. But the English had entered the contest too diffidently and too late and with too little money.

In a sense, the competition for the Empire continued for nearly thirty years. As Bacon says: 'During that triumvirate of Kings, King Henry VIII of England, François I, King of France, and Charles V, Emperor, there was such a watch kept, that none of the three could win a palm of ground, but the other two would straightways balance it, either by confederation, or, if need were, by war; and would not in any wise take up peace at interest.'[1]

The strength and the weakness of the new Emperor can be seen in his titles: 'King of the Romans; Emperor Elect; Semper Augustus; King of Spain, Sicily, Jerusalem, the Balearic Islands, the Canary Islands, the Indies and the Mainland on the Far Side of the Atlantic; Archduke of Austria; Duke of Burgundy, Brabant, Styria, Carinthia, Carniola, Luxemburg, Limburg, Athens and Patras; Count of Habsburg, Flanders and Tyrol;

[1] Francis Bacon, 'Of Empire', *Essays* (1597)

Count Palatine of Burgundy, Hainault, Pfiart, Roussillon; Landgrave of Alsace; Count of Swabia; Lord of Asia and Africa.' Jerusalem, Athens, and Patras had fallen to the Turk, Africa was only a string of coastal forts, Asia a fiction, while Cortes and Pizarro had not yet conquered Mexico and Peru. None the less, no Christian ruler since Roman times had held so wide a sway, not even Charlemagne. Spain and Germany coupled were a monstrous power, whose menacing jaws might close on France at any time.

Already Charles had declined to return southern Navarre to King Henri II d'Albret. But the Emperor could not attack in Italy if Henry VIII cut the sea lines between Spain and the Low Countries; the French occupation of Milan had cut the land lines between the Low Countries and Naples. For exactly opposite reasons, François was ready to pay a heavy price for an English alliance.

The treaty of 1518 had stressed the desirability of Henry visiting France, because 'the said serene princes of England and France be like in force corporal, beauty, and gifts of nature right expert, and having knowledge in the art militant, right chivalrous in arms, and in the flower and vigour of youth'. Hearing that François had grown a beard, Henry swore he would not shave until they had met. Queen Catherine objected to the beard and he went back to his razor. This caused alarm in diplomatic circles until it was pointed out that the new affection between the Kings was 'not in the beards but in the hearts'.

On 31 May 1520 Henry VIII and his Queen set sail from Dover, probably in the

Katherine Pleasaunce and not in the *Great Harry* as is sometimes said. Their suite, who sailed in the fleet which accompanied them, numbered 5,000, the flower of England's lords, gentry, and great ladies, with most of her prelates and high officers of State. The armada landed safely in Calais the same evening. This was still English soil. The Pale, or lands round the port, included the small town of Guines, six miles away. The meeting was to take place near here in a valley known as the Val Doré.

François was waiting, with 5,000 courtiers and nearly 3,000 horses. The French camp was outside Ardres, a small, decayed town not far from Calais. François's principal tent was a huge pavilion, perhaps sixty feet high, supported by great masts. It was covered in cloth of gold, with three horizontal stripes of royal blue velvet, each stripe sewn with golden lilies of France. The cloth-of-gold cover was fastened to the tent canvas by broad strips of violet taffetas. It was crowned by a wooden statue, six feet high, of St Michael trampling on the dragon, which had been painted by Jean Bourdichon. The Archangel wore a blue mantle sewn with gold lilies and held a lance and a shield bearing the royal arms of France. Inside, the pavilion was lined with royal blue velvet sewn with fleurs-de-lis and had a ceiling fringed with gold. It was divided into rooms, some of which were hung with black velvet. In addition, there were three smaller pavilions to serve as chapel, dressing-room, and council chamber. There was also a 'house of solace and sport' or banqueting hall, which was a round pavilion of blue velvet.

Queen Claude's tents were of *toile d'or, toile d'argent* and violet satin, sewn with the gold lilies of France and the silver ermines of Brittany. The pavilion of Mme Louise, which was of purple velvet and crimson satin, sported the silver crosses of Savoy. Many of the banners had been painted by Jean Clouet. Fleurange remembered how these tents, with their devices and their gold apples, 'when they were in the sunlight, were wonderfully fine to look upon'. There were nearly 400 of them, an entire town of silver and gold, of silk and velvet, of floating tapestries.

Henry VIII was determined to outdo his splendid rival. His banners were painted by Holbein. Near Guines, a prefabricated castle had been built, of wood and canvas painted to look like brick and stone. Its four walls were crenellated and embattled, with four tall corner towers, and had great windows of diamond-paned glass. The imposing gatehouse was flanked by redbrick towers and decorated with Tudor roses and statues – St Michael was a tactful inclusion among the latter. In front of the gatehouse were two fountains. One was of blue and gold and crowned with the statue of 'the old God of wine called Bacchus' pouring out the wine; from it were conduits which 'ran to all people plenteously with red, white and claret wine'. The other fountain, 'of ancient Roman work', bore a statue of Cupid and also dispensed wine in limitless quantity. Both fountains had silver cups. The effect was marred by the crowds who came for the free drink; according to Hall, vagabonds, ploughmen, labourers, waggoners, and beggars lay in drunken heaps.

Inside the castle was a whole range of apartments on three stories. Their hangings, besides the ubiquitous cloth of gold and silver, were also of silk, in Henry's personal colours of green and white. They were furnished with chairs of estate and Turkish cushions. Here lodged not only the King and Queen Catherine but also Mary Tudor, Duchess of Suffolk, who still styled herself 'Queen Dowager of France', together with her husband, and also that proud prelate, Wolsey. Mary's hangings were of gold, silver, and crimson velvet, embroidered with M's and L's and porcupines, a souvenir from her days in France. The Cardinal's sheets and pillows were of gold cloth, his bedposts gilded, and his bed-curtains of crimson velvet. The most important part of this pasteboard castle was the hall. Its ceiling was of soft green silk studded with gold roses, its floor of taffetas patterned white and yellow and spotted with red roses. Behind was the chapel with a choir hung in gold and silver and altar-frontals of cloth of gold sewn with pearls; on the high altar were a great crucifix, ten candlesticks, and statues of the Twelve Apostles, all of massive gold. Of this palace it was said, by a Venetian, that it excelled any invention of the great Leonardo. The covered way between it and Guines was compared to the garden of Morgan le Fay.

Next to the palace was a great golden pavilion, supported by many smaller tents. However, while the great lords were sumptuously housed, many courtiers endured considerable discomfort. There was no accommodation at all for sightseers. Edward Hall, a London lawyer who was present, says that 'both knights and ladies that were come to see the nobleness, were fain to lie in hay and straw'.

It was a full week before the Kings met. Wolsey, who was anxious to secure the peace which he had won in 1518, went ahead to negotiate. Tournai, captured in 1513, had already been returned to the French. Most important was the marriage contract between the infant Dauphin and the Princess Mary who had been betrothed in 1518. All these matters were settled reassuringly by the Cardinal, who with much pomp, visited François in his lodging at Ardres. The new treaty contained an interesting clause; any problems of Anglo-Scottish relations were to be solved by Wolsey and Mme Louise. They dined together on at least two occasions during the coming festivities.

François and Henry met in the late afternoon of Thursday, 7 June, the Feast of Corpus Christi. Another gold pavilion had been erected, in the Val Doré, with rich hangings and Turkey carpets; chairs were placed beneath a canopy for the two Kings. There was a good deal of suspicion on either side and both monarchs were accompanied to the meeting-place by a large contingent of infantry. Among the French troops, the Swiss Guard stood out, in striped uniforms of black and white and tawny, with tall plumes, and shouldering long pikes. Fleurange rode at their head. The English Yeomen of the Guard were in red and gold, with the crowned Tudor rose on their breasts, and carried bills and bows. There were also archers in white and green.

François's doublet was of cloth of silver slashed with cloth of gold, embroidered with diamonds, pearls, rubies, and emeralds, over which he wore a cloak, fastened at the shoulder, of gold satin shot with purple. Round his neck he wore the plain gold collar of the Saint-Michel. His long boots were white, his bonnet black, with black feathers and sparkling with jewels. Even his great bay horse – called Dappled Duke –

was caparisoned with gold and jewels. Hall, an eyewitness, gives a fascinating vignette. He remembered King François as: 'a goodly prince, stately of countenance, merry of cheer, brown coloured, great eyes, high nosed, big lipped, fair breasted and shouldered, small legs and long feet'.

The King was accompanied by the Duc de Bourbon in cloth of gold and silver, carrying the Constable's sword, by Galeazzo de San Severino, the Grand Esquire, in cloth of gold lined with sable and carrying the Sword of State, and by Bonnivet in silver and gold who wore an Admiral's whistle set with pearls. Beside them rode the French Kings-at-Arms – Mountjoy, Normandy, and Brittany. François's personal escort, limited to thirty-nine men of note, was 'all the rufflers and gallants of the French court'. It included another King – Henri II of Navarre – three more Dukes, three Princes, four Cardinals, one Archbishop, ten Bishops, all the great officers of State and of the household; among them were the indispensable Duprat, Robertet, and three Marshals of France. Guillaume Budé was in this privileged band, an honour which may have over-awed even that sour pedant.

Henry VIII was also in silver, ribbed with gold and studded with jewels, and he wore a hat similar to François's, black with black feathers. Round his neck was the jewelled collar of the Garter from which hung a great George, round his waist a massive gold belt. He too rode a bay; it was trapped with gold bells which jingled melodiously. The French were impressed by his thick red beard and regal but gentle manner. They thought him rather fat. Of the two Kings, he had the more feminine face, in the opinion of a Venetian observer. Next to Henry rode Wolsey, in crimson figured velvet, on his mule which was caparisoned in red and gold, the Marquess of Dorset, who carried the Sword of State, Sir Richard Wingfield, who was dressed in a brocade suit which had been given to him by King François, and the Master of the Horse, Sir Henry Guildford, in cloth of gold. The other English notables included the Dukes of Buckingham and Suffolk, the Archbishop of Canterbury, seven Bishops, the Prior of the Knights of St John, ten Earls, and twenty Barons, with one Irish Earl, Garret Óg Fitzgerald of Kildare. The Venetians were struck by the massiveness of the English lords' collars. But they were more impressed by the elegance of the French.

Both sides halted; each suspected that the other had hidden troops within call. They mastered their nervousness and advanced to the appointed place, to wait. Trumpets blew. Alone, save for two running footmen, Henry and François galloped up to each other, and, doffing their hats but still in the saddle, embraced in front of the great gold tent. They dismounted, to embrace for a second time. Then, followed by the company, they walked arm in arm into the tent. Wine and hippocras – a spiced wine cup – were served. The great nobles were presented. The toast was 'English and French – good friends!'

François had made a deep impression on Henry. Fleurange says that when an English herald, reading a proclamation, began 'I, Henry, King of France . . .' the Tudor stopped him, saying to François, 'I cannot be while you are here, for I would be a liar.' He told the herald to say instead, 'I, Henry, King of England.' It is quite possible that

The meeting of François I and Henry VIII at the Field of Cloth of Gold on 7 June 1520. From a relief in the Hôtel Bourgtheroulde at Rouen.

the Welshman felt genuinely inferior. Less than a hundred years ago, his family had been little hedge squires – François came from a line of Kings which had reigned in France since the tenth century.

Jousting commenced on Saturday, 5 June. Fleurange says that 300 gentlemen took part. However, these were only the preliminaries. On Sunday François dined with Queen Catherine, in the wooden castle at Guines, while Henry dined with Queen Claude at Ardres. The French King arrived on a mule; his pearl buttons were much admired. During the banquet he was entertained with music from the Gentlemen of the Chapel Royal. Afterwards, he went into the hall where he found 130 ladies dining; taking off his bonnet, François proceeded to kiss them all, 'saving four or five that were old and not fair, standing together'. Dancing followed though Queen Catherine did not take part. François's partner was the beautiful Miss Anne Browne, to whom he took a great fancy. Before leaving, the King again kissed all the ladies.

Jousting continued happily for the next ten days, despite several storms of wind and rain. Claude, who was expecting her fifth child, rode to the scene in a litter of cloth of silver; she wore, among other dresses, a cloth-of-silver gown over a gold petticoat. Queen Catherine's litter was of crimson satin picked out in gold. The Mantuan Ambassador considered the Englishwomen neither pretty nor well dressed – he also thought they drank too much. François broke spears like reeds and never missed his opponent. Henry too distinguished himself, smashing the Seigneur de Grandville's helmet. On some days the Kings did not take part. On Wednesday there was a wrestling match between the Yeomen of the Guard and some Bretons, no doubt in the Cornish style. Henry asked François to wrestle with him. The Valois threw the Tudor, with a *tour de Bretagne*, giving him 'a wonderful fall'; Henry demanded another bout but François declined. On Friday, the French King, riding against the Earl of Devon,

Left Queen Claude(?) from a drawing by Jean Clouet. *Right* Queen Catherine of Aragon (1485–1536).

A SECOND CHARLEMAGNE   85

received a black eye and possibly a broken nose; he had to put on a black patch. Meanwhile, the King of England jousted with such vigour that he killed one of his best horses.

On Sunday, 17 June, François and Claude entertained the English King and Queen. At dinner Claude sat next to Mary Tudor, Queen and Queen Dowager both wearing magnificent pearls, and afterwards masques were performed by Henry and his courtiers. Early on the same morning when Henry was still asleep, François had appeared at Guines, with only two gentlemen, demanding to see the King. He insisted on acting as Henry's valet, helping him on with his shirt. Henry was delighted. 'Brother,' he said, 'you have played me the best trick ever played, and shown me the trust I should have given you. From now on I am your prisoner.' He then gave him a collar of rubies worth 30,000 Venetian gold ducats. François reciprocated with a bracelet worth twice as much but would not stay for breakfast. François's lords told him plainly that he was mad to do what he had done. Discussing the incident, Fleurange calls the King 'the least suspicious of men', meaning the most foolhardy. However, François had taken a calculated risk which was intended to reassure Henry, that most distrustful of men. He succeeded. Some days later, the English King paid a similar visit to Ardres and stayed for dinner.

During the second week, jousting was replaced by tilting – competitors fought in pairs instead of singly. The peacock changes of costume by the two Kings almost beggar description. They far outshone their Queens. François was fond of a combination of purple satin and cloth of gold, Henry of gold and silver or russet velvet with cloth of silver. The French lords were nearly as splendid, 'all clinquant, all in gold, like heathen gods'; while Hall boasted about 'the riches of apparel that was amongst the lords and gentlemen of England, cloth of gold, cloth of silver, tinsins [tinsels], satins

embroidered and crimson satin', and the solidity of their gold chains and baldrics. Banquets, dancing, and masquing went on with unflagging enthusiasm. It was noticed that King François invariably danced with Anne Browne. So lavish were the servings of food – heron, swan, peacock, and other rare delicacies – that some choked. Wolsey gave dinner-parties of his own – his table was famed for delicious fare.

The climax came on Saturday, 23 June, St John's Eve. At noon Wolsey celebrated Pontifical High Mass at an outdoor chapel built next to the tilt-yard. It was rumoured he had not said Mass for several years. There were five Cardinals at the altar, with more than twenty other prelates. An Englishman described the singing as 'a heavenly hearing'. At the *Agnus Dei* when the *Pax* – a consecrated Host encased in crystal – was passed among the congregation for them to kiss, the pious Queens embraced each other. After the service there was a banquet in the open air, Henry and François eating together beneath a gold canopy. There followed the 'combat at the barrier', on foot, the most brutal and dangerous of all chivalric sports.

The next day, Sunday, 24 June, was the last. François spent it at Guines with Queen Catherine. He wore mulberry-coloured brocade, with emeralds sewn on his sleeves and yellow and mulberry feathers in his hat. After the final banquet, with gay dancing and mumming – François took part – prizes for the jousting were presented by Queen Catherine; the King received a ruby and diamond ring. Then, after kissing all the ladies for the last time, he said good-bye and left for Abbeville. King Henry spent a similar day at Ardres with Queen Claude. There was great giving of presents. Notable among them were the English King's gifts to Mme de Châteaubriant and to Bonnivet, a rich crucifix and a jewel from his own hat. Wolsey gave Mme Louise a fragment of the True Cross enshrined in gems while she gave him a jewelled cross of great price. Henry returned to Catherine and then retired to Calais for another meeting with the Emperor.

Henry and François had acquired a genuine regard for each other which they never quite lost. But, as an attempt to persuade England to commit herself to France during the coming struggle with Charles V, the Field was a failure. Aesthetically, it was more successful. As a modern chronicler has written, 'The Field of Cloth of Gold has become a household word among the nations. It stands for any superlative luxury or splendour, with no need of justification or thought of cost. Perhaps on this level alone it deserves remembrance. It is a last gay and amiable incident in the history of Christendom undivided.'[1]

[1] Joycelyne G. Russell, *The Field of Cloth of Gold* (1969)

Left Leonardo da Vinci (1452–1519), a self-portrait *c*1512. *Right* The *manoir* of Cloux at Amboise which François gave to Leonardo.

87

The Humanist Prince

François was determined to make his court a centre of art and learning. For his models he had Papal Rome and Medici Florence. At the same time, he mounted a presentation of the monarchy which owed much to Ducal Burgundy, a presentation whose ceremonies were no less works of art than the paintings and statuary. These last fulfilled his role as a new man, an *uomo universale*, while the impressive ceremonial expressed that side of him which was the *roi chevalier*.

Significantly, he appointed many poets, painters, and scholars as gentlemen-in-waiting. Guillaume Budé was among these and frequently employed as a diplomat. The King was most anxious to enhance France's reputation for learning. In 1517, through Budé, he invited Erasmus to become chancellor of a college for the study of Greek, Latin, and Hebrew, which he intended to found in Paris. Erasmus declined and the project was shelved, though only for the time being. In 1520 François established a short-lived Greek college in Milan for which Johannes Lascaris, a Byzantine exile, was engaged to recruit professors and pupils. Later measures would bear more fruit.

In Italy he had seen the wonders of the High Renaissance with his own eyes. He was overwhelmed by Leonardo da Vinci's *Last Supper*, in the Friary of Santa Maria delle

The Virgin, Jesus and St Anne by Leonardo da Vinci. Leonardo brought it with him to France where François acquired it when he died.

Grazie at Milan. According to Vasari, the sixteenth-century art historian, the King 'tried all he could to find architects to make cross-stays of wood and iron with which the painting could be protected and brought safely to France, without any regard for expense, so great was his desire to have it. But as the painting was done on a wall His Majesty failed to have his way and it remained in the possession of the Milanese'. Instead, François acquired the Master himself. By this time Leonardo was ageing, his energies impaired. It is probable that the King met him at Pavia. He asked him 'to devise some unusual entertainment, and so he constructed a lion which after walking a few steps opened its breast to reveal a cluster of lilies'. No doubt the lilies were the gold fleurs-de-lis of France. Far from demanding great works, like the Pope, François, who addressed him as 'mon père', simply offered him a post in France. Vasari, in his near-contemporary *Lives of the Painters*, tells us that 'Leonardo for a long time put him off with more words.' Only when the Pope showed what Leonardo considered excessive preference for his rival Michelangelo did he accept.

'The divinely endowed Leonardo' was now over sixty, bald and venerably bearded. He made the wearisome journey over the Alps, accompanied by his favourite pupil, Francesco Melzi, whom he treated as a son, and a faithful servant, Battista de Villanis, to arrive in France in 1516. His baggage included drawings and notebooks, together with some of the greatest paintings in the world – amongst them the *Mona Lisa*.

François revered him. He said that 'no one in the world knows so much as Leonardo', and appointed him 'First Painter, Engineer, and Architect to the King'. He also gave him an annuity of 700 gold crowns and a pleasant little house of white stone and red brick at Amboise, the *manoir* of Cloux – a tunnel connected it with the château. Though this rustic retreat was a haven after the fevered competition of Rome, and though the Loire air is clear, even luminous, the old man, feebler every day, must have missed the Italian sun. In October 1517, the Cardinal of Aragon visited 'Messer Leonardo Vinci, the Florentine, a greybeard of more than seventy years'. The Cardinal's secretary Antonio de' Beatis, noted, 'Since he has been struck with a certain paralysis of the right hand, no more masterpieces can be expected.' Leonardo was not too ill to continue teaching his beloved Melzi, and he designed a canal to link the Loire with the Sâone. In 1518 he could still sketch the towers and battlements of his master's palace, as they appeared from Cloux. François paid him affectionate visits. His last appearance at court was probably during the celebrations in 1518 for the wedding of Lorenzo de' Medici – father of a future Queen of France – to Madeleine de la Tour d'Auvergne. He may well have designed the entertainments (which seem to have been a repetition of his pageant for Bernardo Bellinzoni's *Il Paradiso*, first performed at the Milanese court in 1490).

On 2 May 1519, Leonardo da Vinci died at Cloux, lamenting that he had not made better use of his wonderful gifts. He was sixty-seven. There is a moving passage in Vasari which purports to describe his last hours: 'to show him favour and to soothe his pain, the King held his head. Conscious of the great honour being done to him, the inspired Leonardo breathed his last in the arms of the King.' Alas, on the day Leonardo

Caritas by Andrea del Sarto. This was painted in
France in 1518 when Andrea was François's
resident court painter.

THE HUMANIST PRINCE 91

died, François was at Saint-Germain-en-Laye, celebrating the birth of a second son.

If his 'First Painter' had produced almost nothing during his stay in France, the King none the less obtained the masterpieces which Leonardo had brought from Italy. He now possessed the *Virgin of the Rocks,* the *Virgin and Child with St Anne*, the *Mona Lisa*, and the strange, hermaphroditic *St John*. Undoubtedly François acquired other works by Leonardo. It is probable that he possessed one of two portraits of Isabella d'Este which have since disappeared. He may also have had another lost painting, *Leda and the Swan*. He certainly possessed a cut-down portrait of a girl – *La Belle Ferronière*, sometimes thought to be Lucrezia Grivelli, a mistress of one of the Sforza Dukes – which is still in the Louvre. However, this may have been by Leonardo's pupil, Melzi. Unfortunately, no one knows just what François's collection contained, while no dates have been established for most of his acquisitions.

In 1516 the King purchased two paintings from the dealer Gian Battista della Palla. These were a Madonna and the *Dead Christ mourned by Angels*, from the brush of a young Florentine Master, Andrea del Sarto (the former is now in the Louvre but the latter has been lost). François sent to Florence to see if Andrea would enter his service. Desperate for money to pay the bills of an extravagant wife, he accepted. He arrived in France in the spring of 1518. François gave him 300 gold crowns to paint the Dauphin François, who had just been born. He then painted the *Caritas* which is now in the Louvre. However, while Andrea was painting *St Jerome* for Mme Louise, disturbing letters arrived from his wife who asked him to come home. He begged the King for leave to visit Florence, swearing on the Gospels that he would return. François granted it, commissioning him to buy works of art. Unfortunately, Andrea, passionate and unstable, squandered the money on his wife and dared not go back to France. The King was so angry that he could not bear to look at any Florentine paintings. He promised to punish the truant Master if ever he came within reach. But Andrea del Sarto stayed in Florence, where he died of the plague in 1530.

François invited Michelangelo to come and work for him, but the invitation was declined. Fra Bartolommeo also refused; the King had to content himself with a single picture – the *Annunciation* – by this artist. François also employed at this time Nicolas Bellini of Modena and the Giusti brothers – the latter were working on the Tomb of King Louis which was not completed until 1531.

François's agents were scouring Italy for paintings, sculpture, precious stones and rare manuscripts. Often he was given pictures. In about 1516–17 Lorenzo de' Medici, acting on behalf of Pope Leo, commissioned Raphael to paint *St Michael* (*see* p. 112) and *The Holy Family* for the French King; in 1518 one of his pupils brought the two works, on muleback, over the Alps, to François. Cardinal Bibbiena gave him the famous portrait of the beautiful Joanna of Aragon, by Raphael's pupil, Giulio Romano (*see* p. 119). In addition, François acquired Raphael's *St Margaret* and *La Belle Jardinière* – the former may have been painted for Marguerite. Raphael also designed for him a strange incense-burner.

In the general Renaissance passion for building, new châteaux, *manoirs*, and hôtels

Paintings from François's collection: *opposite The Virgin of the Rocks* by Leonardo; *top left St John* by Leonardo; *top right The Madonna* by del Sarto; *below left The Visitation* by del Piombo; *below right La Grande Sainte Famille de François I* by Raphael

had been springing up all over France, and especially in the Loire Valley. François, of course, shared this enthusiasm. Even before the Italian expedition, in June 1515, he ordered repairs and improvements to his wife's palace at Blois; work continued until 1524. It is the first great monument of François's reign but, sadly, there is no record of the architect's name.

The work at Blois was confined to one wing, where the walls of the old *château fort* were encased by a façade of white stone. Looking down from its sharp cliff on to the town, the new wing has undeniable elegance, with galleries and arcaded *loggie* which may have been inspired by Bramante's Vatican. But it relies on the decoration rather than on the essential forms of Italian architecture, and has an oddly hybrid appearance. La Fontaine, who visited Blois in 1663, wrote that 'the part built by François I pleased me best. There are many little galleries, little windows, little balconies and little ornaments without any sort of regularity or order; together, they make a truly great and pleasing whole.'

Inside the château courtyard was the new wing's open, octagonal staircase. It belongs both to the Renaissance and to Gothic France which, during the fifteenth century, had built many spiral staircases. But the staircase at Blois is peerless. On each level there is a platform where François's guard paraded in tiers, in their striped uniforms of blue, red, and white, holding halberds – and torches at night – to salute him when he rode in. Opposite, in the Gothic south wing built by Charles d'Orléans, was the *perche des Bretons* where the Queen's guard paraded. The white stone of the great staircase is beautifully carved and fretted, emblazoned with salamanders and ermines and with crowned F's and C's (*See* pp. 99, 102.)

Small, massive-walled, with narrow doorways and tiny, diamond-paned windows, the new wing's apartments seem like dark tunnels in huge blocks of masonry. The atmosphere was that of the Middle Ages rather than of the Renaissance. The rich hangings, the carved and gilded panelling, the low plasterwork ceilings, and the great fireplaces crowned by the salamander must have combined to produce a feeling almost of claustrophobia. However, relief might be obtained by gazing from the little windows on to wide terraces and formal gardens in the Italian style – dotted with fountains, pavilions, and orangeries, and reaching far down into the town.

Even these gardens benefited from François's careful attention. In 1516 Fra Pacello de Mercogliano, an Italian gardener whom Charles VIII had brought to France, was paid several hundred gold crowns for a year's work on them. They lacked nothing save a menagerie (like that at Amboise, where the King kept bears and leopards – on one occasion he made a bull fight three lions in the moat). Pierre Belon brought the rare greengage tree from Palestine and planted it at Blois; today its fruit is still called a 'Reine Claude'.

Blois was pre-eminently the Queen's home, where she brought up the Children of France. The King wanted his own palace. He found a lonely manor-house in the Sologne, on the banks of a river on the outskirts of the Forest of Chambord. The woods were haunted by a phantom huntsman, Thibaud le Tricheur, and his ghostly hounds.

Chambord with its moat, as it appeared at the end of François's reign. From *Les Plus Excellents Bastiments de France* by Jacques Androuet du Cerceau.

THE HUMANIST PRINCE   95

Here, beneath venerable oaks and surrounded by melancholy meres and marshes, roamed many noble stags, while above wheeled the red kite – the *milan royal* – most sought-after quarry of the falconers. On 6 September 1519 François gave orders for work to begin, replacing the old manor of the Counts of Blois by 'a beautiful and sumptuous edifice'.

The original architect was almost certainly Bernabei Domenico da Cortona, called 'the Boccador', who prepared a wooden *pourtraict* or model. The master builder was a Frenchman, Pierre Nepveu. Basically, Chambord is a medieval French château of the sort which gleams from the miniatures in the *Très Riches Heures* of the Duc de Berry. It consists of a square keep, flanked by corner towers, at one end of an enceinte. There was even a moat. What makes the design so unusual is the room plan, which is centred on a Greek cross running through the keep and dividing it into four separate blocks. Such an arrangement had been employed by Cortona's master, Giuliano da Sangallo, in a villa which he had built in 1496 for Lorenzo de' Medici.

The entire character of Cortona's design was altered by three remarkable additions. The first was an extraordinary roof whose appearance has been compared to an over-crowded chessboard, so many are its turrets, dormers, gables, and chimneys – though

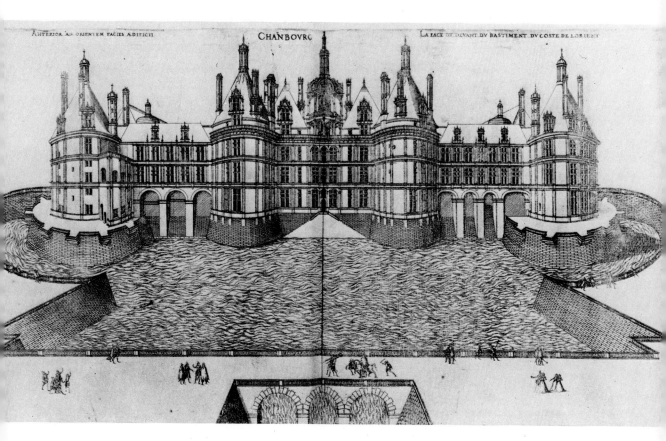

An exterior view of Chambord and *left* its staircase.
Of the château, Brantôme thought, 'one could have
numbered it among the world's miracles'.   THE HUMANIST PRINCE   97

the detail is Italian, the over-all effect is that of some fantastic production of the Late
Gothic. It might be called the first penthouse roof, since it could be reached from doors
in the turrets. The towers supporting this strange canopy are so massive that their
rooms seem hewn out of a mountain. Second, at the centre of the Greek cross, a great
staircase was inserted, a double spiral, rising from floor to roof and constructed in
such a way that someone ascending sees others descending without meeting them. The
third addition was that of long, flying galleries to join the keep with the great flanking
towers – from them the ladies of the court could witness the ritual of the hunt's return.

It is possible, though there is no proof, that Leonardo suggested these additions to
the original plan. He certainly designed a château for François to build for his mother
at Romorantin, though nothing came of the project. Also, at about this time, he drew a
similar spiral staircase.

Chambord has 218 rooms, great and small, the gem of which is the King's *Cabinet de
Travail*, with its barrel-vaulted ceiling studded with salamanders. Yet the château was
only inhabited when François went hunting in the Sologne. Building continued fitfully
throughout his reign, and it was not completed until long after the King was dead.
Brantôme thought that had Chambord been finished 'one could have numbered it
among the world's miracles'. Indeed, the great hunting-box was a work of magic, the
Neuschwanstein of the Valois. The Venetian Lippomano, who saw it at the end of
François's reign, wrote: 'I have seen many magnificent buildings in my life but never

The octagonal staircase of François's new wing at
Blois, begun c1515–16. *Overleaf* The roof of
Chambord, François's great hunting-box in the
Loire Valley. From it the ladies of the court
watched the royal hunt.

one so beautiful or so rich as this.' Louis XIV fell in love with it, paying several long
visits. In the eighteenth century, the moat was filled in and the palace lost something
of its magic. In its heyday, a guest approaching Chambord through the trees would
have seen the great white château soaring out of the water like some enchanted castle.

The medieval châteaux in which François was brought up were much more comfortable and more cheerful than might be thought from the bare, chilly walls one sees today.
Their rooms were hung with bright tapestries or painted cloth, the air between stone
and fabric serving as insulation against the cold. Curtains, screens, and canopies kept
off the draughts. The great chimney-pieces were painted in gay colours and gilded – in
summer, fireplaces were filled with greenery. Though furniture was sparse, consisting
principally of chests, tables, benches and the occasional cabinet, it was supplemented
by many cushions, as well as carpets – which often served as table-cloths. Prized
possessions were set out on the tables. These included gold and silver plate – great
salts and standing cups and platters – with caskets, mazers of wood or coconut
mounted in silver, and even books and reliquaries. Panel-pictures were rare, their
place on the wall being filled by weapons and hunting trophies. There were flowers
everywhere.

Yet even the floors of François's early châteaux were sometimes of marble or
parquet, covered by carpets instead of rushes. His pictures, in great gold frames, took
the place of boarspears and antlers. His tables were covered by table-cloths of gold.
The rich plate which stood on them was flanked by Venetian glass, by dishes of majol-
ica and enamel, by cups, bowls, and ewers of agate and crystal, of lapis lazuli and amber,
of sardonyx, of red, white, and green jade and jasper. The rooms were lit by flaming
torches in burnished gold or silver sconces, by candles in holders of crystal, and by
scented logs – juniper, apple, and pear – burning in the great hearths beneath the
salamander.

Beautiful women were an integral part of the decoration. François said more than
once that a court without ladies was a spring without roses. 'King François believed
that the entire ornament of a court lay in its ladies, and wished that his should have
more of them than had hitherto been the case. For truly a court without ladies is a
garden without beautiful flowers, like that of a Satrap or a Turk, where one never sees
any ladies at all.' Brantôme continues, 'I myself have seen chests and wardrobes,
belonging to old ladies of those days, filled with dresses which the King had given
them, for fêtes and great occasions, which were worth a fortune.' The Venetian Cavalli
says that François spent 300,000 gold crowns each year on presents for ladies.

One wonders if Anne Boleyn was given a dress. She probably came to France in
1519, when she was twelve, with her father, Sir Thomas, who was the English Ambassador. No doubt she remained at the French court until his return to England at the end
of 1521. Her elder sister, Mary, had acquired such a bad reputation during an earlier
visit that for years afterwards François remembered her as 'the hackney'. However,
Anne became 'one of Queen Claude's women', which should have proved an edifying
experience. The Queen and her own little court retained the sober, pious ways of

Anne of Brittany, most of their time being taken up by needlework and devotional reading.

The King took no less care of his own appearance. His clothes were habitually splendid, sewn with pearls and diamonds, fastened by gold buttons and buckles. His shirts were kept in cases of scented Russia leather. Sometimes his cloaks were lined with egrets' feathers. His scabbard was of white velvet. He loved jewellery and wore rings, bracelets, chains, and collars of gold which were studded with precious stones. Everything about King François flashed and sparkled. His writing case or desk was of agate and cornelian set in gold, his looking-glass of crystal surrounded by rubies, topaz, and emeralds. His books were bound in velvet – crimson or green, or white, black, and tawny – clasped with silver. Even his rebeck (a sort of fiddle) was of silver.

Restless by nature, the King seldom stayed in any one place for more than three months. Like some magnificent nomadic tribe, he and his court ceaselessly travelled the roads of France, white with dust in summer, black with mud in winter. As many as 18,000 people followed him, 12,000 of them on horseback. The cortège included the great magnates and officials of the realm, 3,000 troops, many merchants and, of course, ladies. The latter usually travelled in carts or in litters. Sometimes Queen Claude, exhausted by pregnancies, went by river on barges with specially built cabins. A vast baggage-train followed in the wake of the court, carrying food and wine, plate, furniture and tapestries, and every luxury necessary to a Sybaritic existence. Lesser folk may not have fared too well. Benvenuto Cellini, writing of 1540 says: 'We sometimes danced attendance in places where there were hardly two houses, were often under the necessity of pitching inconvenient tents, and lived like gipsies.' But, according to Brantôme, whose elder brother had been a royal page, it was a far from uncomfortable life. The great lords' tables 'were very well supplied and lacked nothing. What was so unusual was that, whether in a village or in the forest, the assembly was served as well as if one had been in Paris.'

François visited many parts of his kingdom in this way; in 1517 Normandy and Picardy, in 1518 Anjou and Brittany, in 1519–20 Cognac, Charenté, and Angoulême. There were also visits to Paris, where he stayed at the palace of Tournelles, near the Bastille, rather than use the gloomy Louvre; he sometimes held court in the great hall of the Parlement (the modern Palais de Justice). The King made a *joyeuse entrée* into city after city, always with banquets and jousting. But on the whole, during the first part of the reign, the royal wanderings tended to centre on the Loire Valley. His glittering court performed a Rabelaisian pilgrimage along the gentle river, from château to château, from forest to forest, picnicking beneath the trees at tables set for thousands.

The royal household, the *maison-du-roy*, had a carefully ordered hierarchy. First came the Grand Master, with a staff of six *maîtres d'hôtel* and seven private secretaries; this was Boisy, who in 1519 was succeeded by the Bastard of Savoy. Then there were the Grand Chamberlain, Louis de la Trémouille, in charge of the Bedchamber, and the Grand Esquire of France or Master of the Horse; until 1525 the latter was Galeazzo de San Severino, a Neapolitan *condottiere* who was reputed to be the best horseman in

Left A great French lord at dinner in the early sixteenth century. *Right* A sixteenth-century Venetian glass vase with griffin handles, from the collection of the Kings of France.

Europe and whose manners had been admired by Castiglione. Next came the Grand Huntsman and the Grand Falconer, whose functions are described below. Finally, there was the Grand Almoner, in charge of the royal chaplains; the post was occupied by the third Gouffier brother – Adrien, Cardinal de Boisy. These six great officers possessed their own budgets and staffs of gentlemen-in-waiting who performed many functions which nowadays are carried out by Government departments. François's court cost him over a million and a half gold crowns a year. He has been criticized for treating the Kingdom as his personal property. But at that date no distinction was drawn between the expenses of the royal government and of the royal household. And by attracting the great nobles, he kept them away from their provinces and out of mischief. In this, as in so many things, he anticipated Louis XIV.

When he was not on a royal progress, François's day followed a fixed routine, each detail of which was performed with elaborate ritual. He liked to rise at ten o'clock, scandalously late – Henry VIII often rose between five and six in the morning. After hearing Mass, the King dined by himself, at about eleven o'clock. Seated beneath a canopy, he ate a simple but lengthy meal, talking to his courtiers or playing with his marmoset. He enjoyed conversation, not only with his lords but also with scholars and artists. Brantôme says that 'the King's table was a real school as he discussed every subject, not just war (there were always great captains to talk about that) but also the sciences, high and low'. Martin du Bellay, who had taken part in these conversations, claims that although François had not had too much education, he could speak on any branch of knowledge because of his wonderful memory – 'Many learned men who had

been much in his company admitted that they learnt more from him than he did from them.'

A lengthy reading followed the meal, from whatever book took François's fancy. In 1518 the Dominican friar, Guillaume Petit, who was Librarian at Blois, listed 'the books which the King commonly carries with him'. These were the favourite volumes which accompanied him everywhere, even on progress or on hunting expeditions. Some he may have acquired during his boyhood at Amboise. Predictably, there were three romances of chivalry, among them *Le Romaunt de la Rose*, together with a work on falconry. Chronicles included two of Clovis and the Kings of France, one a manuscript, besides *La destruction de Troye la grant* and a history of the Machabees. Contemporary history was represented by an account of Charles VIII's descent upon Italy. More scholarly were works by Appian, Diodorus the Sicilian, and 'Thucidides Athénien', all three French translations in manuscript. The *Triomphes de Petrarque*, a manuscript, has a fashionable ring, as does an Italian comedy. But perhaps the most significant was a French translation of Justinian – a knowledge of Roman law was essential for any King who hoped to rule France.

When reading was over, François went hunting. On his return, if not too tired, he might play a game of tennis. After supper there was dancing – jigs, pavanes, galliards, and country reels. There might be a concert of music from viols, spinets, flutes, and hautboys, or of songs accompanied by a lute. Occasionally a rather primitive farce would be performed. Sometimes there were elaborate masques, in which he himself took part. And throughout the day there was an unending performance by one of the royal jesters – the most famous was Triboulet. Towards midnight, François retired to his great curtained and canopied bed.

The sixteenth century found court ceremony both beautiful and moving. The rites of chivalry were an important part of the pageant. The greatest French Order of Knighthood was that of Saint-Michel, which had been founded by Louis XI. Membership of this earliest Légion d'Honneur was limited to thirty-six. Each wore a collar of gold scallop shells from which hung an oval medallion depicting the Archangel Michael thrusting the dragon down to hell. The robes were a long mantle of white damask, bordered with gold scallops and lined with ermine, a gold-embroidered cape, and a hood of crimson velvet. Each Michaelmas the King and the Chevaliers attended services in honour of their patron in their chapel at Bois-de-Vincennes and dined together. Henry VIII was made a Chevalier of Saint-Michel in 1527 and his letter of acceptance – in which he promised to wear the collar and mantle – was read out to the Chevaliers assembled in Chapter. François habitually wore the collar himself. His pride in the Order is reflected in his collection of paintings of St Michael.

There were other rituals which were less solemn. A select group of prostitutes followed the court under an official Madam, 'la dame des filles de joie'. Every first day of January, François gave these ladies gifts, and each May day, by ancient custom, they presented the King with a bouquet of flowers.

Much of François's time was spent hunting. Such importance was attached to this that the Grand Huntsman of France was a great officer of State – the Duc de Vendôme, a Prince of the Blood, held the post for many years. The King even commanded the foremost scholar in France, Guillaume Budé, to prepare a Treatise on Venery. A massive establishment was kept. François never hunted with less than twenty-five couple of 'lime hounds' and six harbourers to find his quarry or with less than twenty-five couple of hounds and six whips to hunt it; in addition, he always had twelve skilled huntsmen at his side. There were also scores of grooms and running footmen. The Grand Huntsman's staff included a Captain of the Nets who was assisted by 100 archers. The Captain's function was to drive game into an area enclosed by nets, for the King to shoot at with a crossbow or an arquebus. The equipment for this was carried in fifty carts. Servants who were injured or bitten by hounds, were sent to the Ardennes in hope of a cure, on pilgrimage to a shrine of St Hubert, patron saint of hunting. At the end of the reign, the Venetian, Marino Cavalli, stated that the royal hunt cost 150,000 gold crowns each year.

François hunted in the royal forests of Blois and Fontainebleau and in the Sologne. The last is densely wooded country with dank pools and marshes and possessing a strange, dreamlike quality (it is the setting of Alain-Fournier's *Le Grand Meaulnes*). There were deer – red, fallow, and roe – and boar, besides wolves and beech martens, otters, and hares. In François's time, as nowadays, French hunting was a slow, stately ritual conducted with military pomp and music. Along the woodland rides, noblemen gravely caracoled their horses in response to melodious signals from great brass horns. At the climax, when the animal had been brought to bay, the lord who dispatched it, amid the whoops of the *hallali*, did so with a gilded sword or boar-spear, after which the *mort* was blown. Even then the pageant was not over. When the hunt came home at dusk, another concert of braying horn music took place in a château courtyard lit by hissing flambeaux before huntsmen drawn up in ranks like soldiers, during which the hunt was re-enacted, and hounds devoured the quarry's head.

The King had such a passion for the chase that he hunted all the year round. Always impetuous, he refused to keep to the rides, galloping straight into the forest. In his treatise, Budé pictures François crashing through trees, brushwood, and thickets with only an arm held in front of his face to guard him from the branches. Sometimes the King lost his way – one winter night, he had to shelter in a cave where he nearly froze to death before he was found. A contemporary authority on hunting, Fouilloux, called François 'the Father of Venery'.

The Grand Falconer, another great officer of State, was the aged René de Cossé Brissac, who had married Boisy's daughter. He was assisted by fifty gentlemen-in-waiting and fifty professional falconers. In the mews at Blois they kept 300 gerfalcons, peregrines, sakers, lanners, falconets, merlins, and hobbies. It took much skill to persuade a gerfalcon to stoop on a kite or to fly peregrines at herons – sometimes one of the latter would impale its pursuer, by raising its beak at the last moment. Flying merlins at skylarks was less dramatic sport.

The King had time for gentler recreations, including verse. His court contained

François I hunting in the forest of Fontainebleau with his huntsman Perot in 1519. From a miniature by Godefroy le Batave in *Commentaires de la Guerre Gallique.*

Left Bonnivet, Admiral of France and *right* Anne de Montmorency, Constable of France, from miniatures c1516 by Jean Clouet.

many amateur poets, among them François himself, his mother, his sister, and his mistress. Save for Marguerite, their verse was mediocre though not without charm. The King could write:

> *Où êtes vous allez, mes belles amourettes?*
> *Changerez-vous de lieu tous les jours?*
> *A qui dirai-je mon tourment*
> *Mon tourment et ma peine?*
> *Les arbres sont secrets, muets, et sourds.*

He is also supposed to have composed the music for his little song. One is reminded of Henry VIII who wrote similar trifles.

In 1519 Marguerite took into her service a young, silky bearded, brown-eyed gentleman-in-waiting from the Midi. This was Clément Marot, who up till then had been working as a clerk in the office of the King's Financial Secretary. Clément had been born in Cahors in 1496, the son of Jean Marot who was Valet of the Wardrobe to King François. The elder Marot was a *rhétoriqueur* in the manner of the late Middle Ages, a versifier rather than a poet. His son was too much of an individualist and too much a man of fashion to remain a *rhétoriqueur*. As a courtier poet, he has some superficial resemblance to the English Sir Thomas Wyatt. Gay, feckless, but always polished and supremely French, Clément Marot was to become to the court what Villon had been to the underworld.

François did not employ only Italian artists. Of French artists, he retained the services of the illuminator-painters, Jean Perréal and Jean Bourdichon. The latter, who died in 1521, is known to have painted portraits, as is Perréal who died in 1530, but both were essentially illuminators.

Some time before 1519, the King commissioned a Flemish illuminator, Godefroy le Batave, to illuminate the *Commentaires de la Guerre Gallique*, a dialogue between François and Julius Caesar in which the two heroes modestly discussed their triumphs. The manuscript is written in a fine Italian hand – much easier to read than the period's black-letter print – and illuminated in blue, grisaille, and gold. There is a delightful miniature by Godefroy of the King hunting in the Forest of Fontainebleau, hard on

Joanna of Aragon, wife of the Viceroy of Naples,
by Giulio Romano. The portrait was given to
François in 1519 by Cardinal Bibbiena.

the heels of a stag – his huntsman 'Perot' rides beside him and is blowing a great horn.

The manuscript also contains portraits of François – beardless and fuller faced than usual – and of his comrades at Marignano. The latter include Fleurange, Boisy, Bonnivet, and Montmorency – like their King, they too are all clean-shaven beneath their flat bonnets. However, these miniatures were painted not by Godefroy but by another Fleming, Jean Clouet. It is possible that his tiny portraits in their roundel frames were the prototype for the miniatures of Hans Holbein and Nicholas Hilliard.

For 300 years Jean Clouet (or 'Janet') was completely forgotten, his works being attributed to his son, François. Then, in 1850, Count Laborde discovered a document which referred to him. Gradually, research has uncovered sufficient details to reconstruct the outline of his life and to attribute works to him with some degree of certainty. He was born in Flanders between 1485 and 1490, and settled in France at Tours, where he married a local girl. King François engaged him, probably in 1515, not as an illuminator-painter like Bourdichon or Perréal, but as a portrait artist. He remained in the King's employment until about 1540, leaving an extraordinary record of François's court, in miniatures, drawings, and paintings. The King is portrayed many times over, together with his family, his mistresses, his friends, his ministers, and even his enemies.

The drawings are the most numerous. For these, Clouet used red and black chalk on white paper, employing an Italian method of shading – diagonal cross-hatching. Holbein, who visited Paris in 1524, may have borrowed this method from him. The drawings were copied in large numbers. Some were sent by the sitters to friends or relatives, rather like photographs today or like miniatures in the eighteenth century. They would have been popular with those who could not afford paintings. Clouet attended sitters in their own houses. His studio also produced albums of fifty or sixty drawings of François and his circle, which were bought by members of the court. These portraits often show remarkable psychological insight. Underneath each an epigram was inscribed which contained the sitter's identity. Thus, Marie de Canaples, now Mme d'Assigny, was *'Assigny, la mieux faict'* – 'Assigny, the best done'. Mary Tudor was *'plus fole que royne'* – 'more madwoman than queen'. Legend says that these epigrams were written by François himself, and that he and the *petite bande* amused themselves by trying to guess the sitter.

Jean Clouet also painted portraits. The most famous is that of François, now in the Louvre, the best-known likeness of the King (*see* p. 144). He is shown against a red background, wearing a doublet of gold satin and black and gold brocade. Surprisingly, his fingers are ringless. It is a peculiarly convincing portrait – the royal features are as curious as ever yet the sitter is undoubtedly a handsome man. Clouet's paintings of François's children are particularly appealing. There are other powerful portraits, like the morose study of Guillaume Budé (p. 27) – one can well believe that the great scholar suffered from migraine and melancholy.

Though François did not give him the respect which he paid to great courtier

painters like Leonardo, he rewarded Clouet well enough for him to live in considerable comfort. Like Bourdichon and Perréal, he was made a gentleman-in-waiting. The King showed great discernment in his patronage of this major artist, who, combining Flemish and Italian methods, founded a native French school of portraiture. François also deserves credit for encouraging the vogue for the popular portrait which was a complete novelty. It is not too much to claim that the King discovered for himself an artist who ranks as the French Holbein.

However, despite the wonderful works which he had acquired and despite his châteaux, these early years were not the most fruitful of François's patronage. The High Renaissance was only just coming to an end. Mannerism had yet to establish its dominance. Even in Italy it was a time of transition. In France, French and Italian ideas remained distinct while existing side by side – they had yet to coalesce. None the less, François I had gone far in his conscious striving to be a great creative patron whose influence would bring into existence a new style of painting and design.

All is Lost Save Honour

No one present at the Field of the Cloth of Gold can have foreseen the ruin of François I. Yet within a year, Charles V was to challenge him, beginning a rivalry which would become the great matter of both their lives. The wars in Italy began again, 'only to make a burial ground for a world of brave and valiant Frenchmen'. They would also lead to the worst humiliation of François's entire life. For France, the 1520s were 'the time of tears and sorrows', of crushing taxation, of war, of invasion.

They were fallow years for the arts – all the money was needed for troops and munitions. Admittedly, Clouet was busy but then he was inexpensive. One hears little of great Italian painters working for François, or of superb acquisitions. The College of Greek at Milan came to an end in 1522 when the Duchy was lost. No new palaces were begun. Work at Chambord stopped in 1524.

On 14 July 1520, a month after the Field of the Cloth of Gold, Henry VIII signed a treaty with Charles V, promising not to make any alliance with France for two years. He abandoned a proposed marriage between the Dauphin and Princess Mary, and there was talk of her marrying the Emperor. In Italy, Pope Leo was preparing to betray François. At the end of 1520 he sent Charles a white hackney – a traditional gesture of Papal recognition. Charles promised to give Parma and Piacenza to the Medici. On 8 May 1521, the day that Martin Luther was condemned at Worms, Leo X entered into a secret league with the Emperor.

There were shadows at home, too. In 1519 Sebastiano Giustiniani had written to the Venetian Signory: 'King François and his mother the Duchess are very unpopular all over France. The Duchess is believed to have amassed monies throughout the country with the object, people say, of helping the King in any sudden need.' The situation was much worse in 1520. It took a decade to pay for the Field of the Cloth of Gold alone.

In April 1521 the Sorbonne condemned Luther. His books were pouring into France, and were greeted with delight. The French already had their own Reformers. They were mainly restricted to a circle of humanists gathered round Cardinal Guillaume Briçonnet, in his diocese of Meaux. The circle's intellectual leader was Jacques Lefèvre of Etaples, who in 1512 had published a commentary on the Epistles of St Paul which foreshadowed much of Luther. Yet the reformism of Meaux, a compound of evangelism and mysticism, only acquired a Lutheran hue by associations. Briçonnet and Lefèvre always remained Catholics. Unfortunately, some of their ideas were open to misinterpretation. And their circle also included extremists who rejected the Mass, the Virgin, and clerical celibacy. The Sorbonne did not distinguish between moderate and extremist reformers – all were 'Lutheranizers'.

The King kept an open mind. His own confessor, Guillaume Petit, was one of the circle. His sister was by nature a friend to every reformer – Marguerite has been called 'la mère poule de la Réforme'. Her confessor too belonged to Meaux. The storm broke in 1523, when a friar was burnt for 'blasphemies'. The Sorbonne – led by Noël Bédier, a hunchback with a diabolical gift for inspiring terror – then arrested

Louis de Berquin. Berquin, a brilliant young professor and a friend of François, was an extremist. He had translated much of Luther besides writing a hilarious satire on traditional theologians. He was already being tortured when the King's archers arrived to demand his release.

Yet in temperament François was a natural Catholic. He took Communion seven times a year, was a great frequenter of shrines, and often went on pilgrimage. He touched frequently for the Evil – people came from all over Europe to be cured by him. In 1522 a Lutheran fanatic, one Pierre Piefort, stole the Host from the chapel at Saint-Germain and was caught; after his hand had been cut off, he was burnt alive. When the Host was brought back from Nanterre, where Piefort had left it, François accompanied the procession on foot, bareheaded and carrying a taper.

In the winter of 1520–1 the King suffered an odd series of personal mishaps at Romorantin, all on the Twelfth Day of Christmas. First, he was thrown to the frosty ground when his horse fell. Then, during the revels, having *par joyeuseté* covered his head with a basket and invited his friends to attack him, M. de Lorges set him on fire and he narrowly escaped being burnt to death. Finally, besieging the Comte de Saint-Pol's house with snowballs, François was hit on the head by a firebrand. He fell on the snow, unconscious. For two days doctors despaired of his life. It took him months to recover fully. He bore no rancour. 'Don't try to find out who threw the torch', he said. 'If I play the fool, I must take the consequences.' His mother was less forgiving. 'Innocent was the hand which struck him,' wrote Mme Louise, 'but by its carelessness it was in peril with every limb.' She was referring to the dismemberment which was the gruesome penalty for regicide. François's hair had to be cropped. Soon the French nobility were all wearing short hair.

In 1521 François took the initiative against Charles V. The Emperor had not returned southern Navarre to its rightful King, Henri II d'Albret, as he had promised. The Navarrese invasion began in the spring. Six thousand Gascon infantry and 300 of François's *gendarmerie* took part. The commander was André de Lesparre, a brother of Mme de Châteaubriant. He was assisted by the Chevalier Bayard and Richard de la Pole. Within a fortnight Henri d'Albret was reinstated in his capital of Pamplona. Among the Spanish casualties was the young commander, a certain Iñigo de Loyola – his broken thigh began a story which would culminate in the founding of the Jesuits. Lesparre, who had lost an eye, proved incapable of holding Navarre. Having sent most of his infantry home, he was taken by surprise when the Spanish launched a counter-attack. On 30 June 1521 he was routed at Esquiroz and fled back over the Pyrenees. In the north, with François's encouragement, Robert de la Marck – father of Fleurange – invaded Luxemburg. On the Emperor's orders the Count of Nassau attacked, driving Duke Robert from his Duchy of Bouillon. In July 1521 Charles V officially declared war. Nassau invaded Champagne in August. Mouzon fell. The French prepared to evacuate Mézières, but Bayard took command. The besiegers fired a barrage of bombs and mortar-fire, terrifying novelties, into the little town. Some French soldiers fled. The Chevalier commented, 'So much the better – such *canaille* are not fit to share our glory.' Nassau retreated before a relieving force. François wrote to Mme Louise, 'God has shown he is a good Frenchman.'

But the diplomatic situation grew worse every day. In August 1521 Henry VIII and Charles V signed another treaty; the Emperor was to invade France from Spain in the spring of 1523, while Henry was to attack from Calais – each would bring 40,000 men. Charles would marry Princess Mary. He also promised to make Wolsey Pope. None the less, when Leo X died in December 1521, the Emperor's old tutor was elected as Adrian VI. Even when the Dutch Pontiff – the last non-Italian to hold the office – died in autumn 1523, Charles V kept control of the Papacy. The new Pope was Clement VII, who as Cardinal Giulio de' Medici, had persuaded Leo X to desert France. Venice, François's last important ally, abandoned him in 1523.

If the French had been discontented in 1519, they now had real reason to be so. In February 1521 the English Ambassador, Sir William Fitzwilliam, wrote to Wolsey that 'both horse meat and man's meat are growing dear as they do in England'. In September he noted, 'As for money, the French King maketh all shift he can to borrow of every man still.' Sir William adds that he has never seen 'such poverty as is now'. By the summer of 1522 François was finding it almost impossible to collect taxes. Fitzwilliam believed that the peasants had nothing left to give – 'The poverty is so great many will die of hunger. To hear how rich and poor lament the war would grieve any man's heart.'

In the Milanese the Viceroy, Odet de Lautrec (another brother of Mme de Châteaubriant) failed to stop German reinforcements reaching the Imperial army in 1521. Throughout the autumn the latter's commander, Prospero Colonna – the general who had been captured before Marignano in 1515 – wore out Lautrec's troops with feigned attacks. Lautrec withdrew from Parma and Piacenza. At the end of November he abandoned Milan itself, but remained in northern Italy. In the spring of 1522 he advanced on Milan to try and turn Colonna out of an impregnable position by blockading him. Lautrec's Swiss pikemen would not wait. On 27 April 1522, at La Bicocca, they launched a frontal attack in their customary style. They were met by something new – organized volleys from massed arquebusiers. Three thousand Swiss fell, including twenty-two captains. Two days later the survivors marched home. Lautrec had to withdraw. Another Sforza, Francesco, was acclaimed Duke of Milan.

On Lautrec's return, François reproached him for losing the Duchy. According to du Bellay, Lautrec replied, 'Not he but the King lost it, that he had warned the King many times that were he not supplied with money, he would be unable to keep the *gendarmerie* who had had to serve without pay, and that the Swiss had made him fight against his better judgement which they would not have done had they been paid.' François answered that he had sent 400,000 crowns. Lautrec insisted he had never had them 'although he had had letters from His Majesty to say he was sending the said sum'. The Superintendent of Finances was summoned. Semblançay agreed that he had received François's order, 'but on having the sum ready to send,

Charles II, Duc de Bourbon and Constable of
France, by Jean Clouet.

Mme the Regent, the King's mother, had demanded the said sum from him, which
he had at once delivered to her'. François at once went to his mother's apartments,
'his face contorted'. He accused her 'of causing the loss of his fair Duchy, something
he could never have believed of her, by keeping the money which was to pay the
army'. Mme Louise sent for Semblançay, who said he had only spoken the truth.
Louise claimed, probably with justice, that though she had undoubtedly received
400,000 crowns, it was 'her savings from her revenues'.

By 1522 Charles V was demanding not only Burgundy but also Champagne,
Dauphiné, Provence, and Languedoc. At the same time Henry VIII was claiming the
provinces which had been conquered by Edward III and Henry V, together with the
Crown itself. France was threatened with extinction.

François was desperate for money. Despite his economies Louis XII had left a
deficit of 1,400,000 livres. This had been increased by such costly enterprises as the
expedition of 1515, the Imperial election, and the Field of the Cloth of Gold. By 1523
the deficit was nearly four million livres. François pawned his own plate, demanded
plate from every citizen in the realm, melted down the sacred vessels of the abbeys,
and sold the jewels of Rheims Cathedral. He even took the silver grill and the silver
statues of the Apostles from the shrine of St Martin at Tours. He extorted 30 per cent
of the clergy's benefices. He established *rentes* – a public loan of 200,000 livres which
he borrowed at $8\frac{1}{2}$ per cent from the Hôtel de Ville. Having sold all available offices,
he created a fourth Chamber in the Parlement of Paris, which brought in 1,200,000
livres. He also sold titles of nobility.

In 1523 the Trésor de l'Epargne – the Treasury for Economies – was established.
This attempted to increase efficiency and avoid corruption by combining the revenues
from Crown lands with 'extraordinary' revenues. The Epargne meant the end of
Semblançay. The previous year Louise had written in her journal, 'During the years
1515, 1516, 1517, 1518, 1519, 1520, 1521, 1522, without being able to prove it, my
son and I were continually robbed by the financiers.' In October 1523 Semblançay
was made to resign as Superintendent of Finances. In March 1524 a special commission
was set up to examine his accounts.

Taxes continued to rise. There were murmurings throughout France. In November
1523, three Councillors of the Paris Parlement went to the Bastille for saying, 'The
King has great revenues, yet he has not done a single thing of benefit for the Kingdom.'
One of their grumbles concerned Louise and the Duc de Bourbon. François had many
other reasons for being uneasy.

Charles II, Duc de Bourbon, was the last great feudal magnate in the style of the
old Dukes of Burgundy or Brittany. A Prince of the Blood, he was Duke of Bourbon,
of Auvergne, and of Châtelherault, Dauphin of Auvergne, Prince of Dombes, Count
of Clermont in the Beauvaisis, of Montpensier, of Forez, of La Marche, of Gien, and
of Clermont in the Auvergne, Viscount of Carlat and of Murat, Lord of Beaujolais, of
Combrailles, of Mercœur, of Annonay, of Roche-en-Reinier, and of Bourbon-Lancy.
From his great château of Chantelles in the Bourbonnais he ruled central France,

Armour c1535 said to have been given to François
by Archduke Ferdinand of the Tyrol. The King
wore an armour of this sort at Pavia. *Overleaf*
Pavia, 1525. A contemporary but stylized
representation by the school of Joachim Patinier.
François is surrendering to the Emperor's Viceroy.

almost as an independent sovereign. His court was hardly inferior to the King's –
he had his own archers of the guard under a captain, chamberlains, squires of the
body, gentlemen-in-waiting, twenty-four pages, singing men, and even his own
heralds, with a host of other officials and servants. In 1517, at the christening of a
short-lived son, to which he welcomed François, Bourbon was waited on by 500
gentlemen, each one dressed in velvet and wearing a triple gold chain. Despite his
vast wealth, he found it increasingly difficult to pay for this regal establishment.

A sketch by Clouet shows a fascinating face, thin and handsome with delicate,
overbred features. The large eyes have a sad, restless, expression. Slightly older
than François, his temperament was as reserved as the King's was warm and cheerful.
Louis XII had said of him, 'I wish he had a more open, a gayer, a less taciturn spirit –
stagnant water frightens me.' Neurotic, highly strung, the Duke was always fancying
himself slighted. Yet, despite his haughtiness, he inspired loyalty and affection.
Half Italian – his mother was a Gonzaga – he undoubtedly possessed considerable
charm.

Bourbon was a distinguished soldier. He had been an excellent Governor of Milan
until his replacement in 1517. Since then, although as Constable of France he ranked
as Commander-in-Chief, he had not been given even the smallest command. As the
Duke saw it, the upstart Bonnivet had usurped his place. Brantôme tells us the
Admiral 'was so loved and favoured by King François that, while he lived, he ruled
everything to do with war, just as Chancellor Duprat did with legal or financial
matters'. In the end, Bourbon believed that Bonnivet had deliberately turned
François against him.

The Duke had married Suzanne de Beaujeu, daughter and heiress of Charles VIII's
sister, Anne de Beaujeu, who as Regent had ruled France from 1483 to 1491. A large
part of his lands came from her inheritance. On 28 April 1521 Suzanne died. Though
she left a will bequeathing everything to him and although her mother, who was
still alive, also bequeathed everything to him, Bourbon faced ruin. There was a strong
case for the reversion of most of Suzanne's *apanages* to the Crown, as her children
had predeceased her. Other properties were also in dispute, the chief claimant being
Mme Louise. However, the case would have to be tried before the Parlement. It was
possible it might go in the Duke's favour. Nor could the Crown, even if it won the
case, reap any advantage until the death of Anne de Beaujeu.

Louise decided to marry Bourbon herself, though she was fourteen years older.
A scurrilous Burgundian chronicler, Robert Macquéreau, alleges that, at her request,
a mutual friend intimated to the Duke she was ready to become his Duchess. Bourbon
replied, 'Is it worthy of our friendship to bring me such an offer from such a woman?
You are counselling me, to whom the best woman in the entire kingdom of France
belonged, to marry the worst woman in the world. I will not do it, not even for all
Christendom.' When Mme Louise heard of the Duke's reply, she behaved as if out
of her mind, tearing her hair like a madwoman. She screamed, 'The matter will not
rest at that – by the creator of our souls, those words will cost him dear!' She told

The most convincing contemporary representation   ALL IS LOST SAVE HONOUR   125
of Pavia – a Flemish tapestry. Note the
arquebusiers who decided the battle.

François, 'My son, I will disown you and consider you a coward King unless you avenge me.' For, says the chronicler, she loved Bourbon 'with all her heart, however old she may have been'.

The case opened before the Parlement of Paris in the summer of 1522, although Anne de Beaujeu did not die until 14 November. A few days after her death, the King, ignoring the fact that the case was still being tried, granted Mme Louise the lands which she claimed. The Chancellor Duprat gave his private opinion that the Constable ought to be left with only a hedge squire's manor of 4,000 livres.

Men like Bourbon were doomed in the world of the Renaissance Prince. There is a tradition that, on the Field of the Cloth of Gold, Henry VIII told François that if he had a subject like the Duke he would not leave his head on his shoulders. Edward Stafford, Duke of Buckingham and Constable of England, was a feudal dinosaur very like Bourbon. He too possessed the greatest estates in the realm and royal blood, was haughty, and somewhat contemptuous of his King. In 1521, suddenly, and without warning, Henry VIII arrested him, accused him of treason, and beheaded him.

In March 1523 the English Ambassador, Sir Thomas Boleyn, described a recent incident at the Louvre. The Duke had been dining with Queen Claude, who liked him and hoped he would marry her sister, Renée of France. Suddenly François entered and, telling him not to get up, demanded, 'Seigneur, it is showed us that you be – or shall be – married. Is it true?' The Duke said it was not. The King insisted it was, that he would remember it, and that he knew about the Duke's dealings with the Emperor and would remember those too! Bourbon rose. 'Sire,' he answered, 'then you menace and threaten me – I have deserved no such cause.' Next day he left for Chantelles. François was perhaps referring to a secret betrothal to Charles V's sister. Yet he may have been trying to bully Bourbon into marrying his mother. In May 1523 Henry VIII told the Imperial Ambassador, 'There is great displeasure between King François and the Duke of Bourbon, perhaps because he will not marry Mme the Regent.' By now the Duke was frantic with outraged pride. Among his friends, he cried that he would return his Constable's sword.

In the summer of 1523 François was preparing for another descent into Italy. Once again, a great army assembled at Lyons. By now Genoa had been lost, and the French had abandoned their last footholds in northern Italy. Events at home made it impossible for François to lead the expedition.

The last words of Anne de Beaujeu to her son-in-law, on her deathbed, were, 'I beg and command you to make an alliance with the Emperor.' Even before Suzanne died, Charles V had offered his sister, Eleanor, to the Duke. Now Bourbon acted like some great feudatory of the previous century, allying with the Emperor, just as the Dukes of Burgundy had allied with the Kings of England. Charles's secret envoy, Adrien de Croy, Sieur de Roeux, came to him at Montbrison. There, an hour before midnight on 11 July 1523, Bourbon signed a secret treaty which, in the words of du Bellay, delivered up 'France's entrails'. Charles was to have Burgundy, Henry VIII Paris and the provinces of the north-west, while the Duke would take Provence for his own kingdom, together with Poitou, Champagne, and the domains he already possessed. In addition he was to have Eleanor of Austria for his bride. When François left Lyons for Milan in August 1523, the Emperor would strike from the south-east, Henry VIII from the west, while the Duke, joined by 10,000 Germans from Franche-Comté, would seize the King and imprison him at Chantelles. Whatever he may have agreed to in the treaty, Bourbon meant to seize Paris and proclaim himself King of France.

Two Norman gentlemen whom he tried to recruit had scruples. They consulted the Bishop of Lisieux who immediately informed Louis de Bréze, Seneschal of Normandy. By chance, François was on progress near the Duke's capital of Moulins. Strengthening his escort with some Germans under Richard de la Pole, the King went to Moulins, to find Bourbon in bed, apparently ill. François either refused to believe in the Duke's treason or else tried to save him. He assured Bourbon that though he had heard of a plot he could not believe it was true, and that should the lawsuit go against the Duke he would return his estates. He begged Bourbon to accompany him on his campaign in Italy. François then left to join the army.

The Duke procrastinated. At the beginning of September, François, his patience exhausted, arrested Bourbon's two most loyal followers, the Sieur de Saint-Vallier and the Bishop of Autun. He sent 4,000 men to Chantelles. By the time they arrived the Duke had fled, clad in black velvet and carrying 30,000 crowns in his saddlebags, escorted by 240 gentlemen. Next day he said goodbye to them all, save for the Sieur de Pompérant. The latter was a sinister Auvergnat murderer whose life he had once saved. Soon heralds were proclaiming Bourbon a traitor in every town in France. Hoping to reach Spain, the fugitives rode south, the Duke disguised as a servant. Eventually they turned east. They came to the Rhône at midnight. Pompérant went forward to reconnoitre the bridge at Vienne while Bourbon hid behind a house. They decided to cross the river by the ferry. Some troops on the boat greeted Pompérant cheerfully, much to the Duke's terror. They were nearly recognized at an inn where they were told that a royal official had been looking for them only an hour before. At last, having been hunted for three weeks and after a detour up into the mountains, they reached Imperial Franche Comté and safety.

'No-one ever saw any man so overcome by rage' as François when he learnt of Bourbon's flight. He had to stay behind to mop up the expected rising. Bonnivet was given command of the Italian expedition and marched off to blockade Milan. But there was no rebellion. Admittedly, many must have pitied the Duke. Brantôme says that Bourbon had to act as he did, otherwise 'he would have been imprisoned and dishonoured for ever'. There was considerable sympathy for him in Paris. Yet less than 100 gentlemen followed the Duke into exile. His strongholds surrendered without firing a shot.

Henry VIII now attacked. He saw himself within reach of the French crown. King François would have to give way to him 'as King Richard did for his father'. Letters from France said that the French commons, cruelly taxed, were crying 'Long live the

King of England.' In August 1523 12,000 English troops under the Duke of Suffolk landed at Calais. At the end of September, after briefly investing Boulogne, Suffolk marched on Paris. Within a month he was less than forty miles away. But he expected to be joined by Burgundian allies and rebellious French lords. Instead came news of Bourbon's flight. A terrible winter set in. Frostbitten, then drenched by rain, Henry's army, its spirit broken, retreated to Flanders to await evacuation.

By now the Imperial forces in northern Italy had been reinforced by 10,000 *landsknechts* under Bourbon. On 30 April 1524 they attacked Bonnivet in his entrenchments at Sesia. The Admiral was wounded and the French army badly mauled. The French retreated over the Alps carrying Bonnivet in a litter.

Bayard, fighting in the rearguard, was shot by a Spanish *arquebusier*. According to du Bellay, Bourbon found him dying beneath a tree and, somewhat stiffly, expressed his regrets. The Chevalier replied, 'I do not need pity, who am dying like a gentleman – but you need it, who are serving against your King, your country and your oath.' Bayard's squire has a different story, simply that the Spanish came to the tree where Bayard lay and complimented him on his gallantry. Even the Emperor's envoy wrote to his master that the Chevalier had made a fine end, concluding, 'The loss is no small one for the French.'

The Emperor entrusted 20,000 men to the former Constable of France, who assured him that Provence would rise against François. Bourbon marched out from Besançon in the summer of 1524, crossing the Alps without opposition and capturing Antibes, Fréjus, Toulon, and many other towns. In August he besieged Marseilles. His guns bombarded the walls but the Marseillais refused to surrender. The King sent 1,500 men to reinforce them, with a fleet loaded with flour, wine, and livestock. In a letter, he told the defenders that 'he would remember their services for evermore', and that he was coming to their rescue. When the Duke heard that François had reached Avignon with 40,000 men, he sent his guns away by sea and retreated in confusion down the wild coast road along the Riviera.

There had been private griefs for François during 1524. First, the death of Charlotte of France, only eight years old. By now, Queen Claude was worn out by child-bearing. Madeleine, a future Queen of Scots, had been born in 1520, a third son, Charles, in 1522, and another daughter, Marguerite, in 1523. Ambassadors' dispatches spoke constantly of the Queen's illnesses. About noon on 26 July Queen Claude, 'the universally beloved', died some days after saying good-bye to the King when he left for Italy. All France mourned 'the very noble and very good lady' as the Bourgeois de Paris calls her. Another chronicler speaks of 'the very pearl of ladies and clear mirror of goodness, without stain', claiming that when people prayed at the Queen's tomb she worked miracles. Fleurange considered her 'one of the truest princesses that ever walked the earth and the most beloved by everyone great and small', and thought 'if she is not in paradise, then very few people will go there'. And, says the Young Adventurer, 'She had borne the King many beautiful children, the most beautiful I ever saw; among rich or poor there were never lovelier children than they, nor sweeter

Four of François's children, by Jean Clouet. *Left to right*: Charlotte (1516–24); Madeleine (1520–37), later Queen of Scots; Charles (1522–45), Monsieur d'Angoulême; Marguerite (1523–74), later Duchess of Savoy. *Opposite* Clement VII, Pope 1523–34, by Sebastiano del Piombo.

natured.' François had been told that she would die, but not until the autumn. He had to leave her to deal with the invasion. In tears, he told Marguerite, 'Could I buy her life with mine, I would do it with all my heart. I never thought that the bonds of marriage, ordained by God, could be so hard to break.' Claude's will bequeathed her Duchy of Brittany to *'son seul très aimé mary'* – her own most beloved husband.

Instead of pursuing the Duke, François went over the Alps. He ignored three letters from his mother who begged him not to fight in Italy. When he appeared before Milan on 24 October, Bourbon and his exhausted troops were still toiling along the Riviera. The Imperial Viceroy, Lannoy, withdrew to Lodi, where Bourbon eventually joined him. After briefly investing Milan, which he dared not enter because of plague, the King laid siege to Pavia on 28 October. His troops were over-confident. A small band of Spaniards tried to defend a tower which guarded a bridge over the Ticino – when they surrendered Montmorency hanged them 'for daring to resist the King's army in a pigeon-loft'. A messenger came to François from Clement VII to say that he wished to change sides. A secret treaty was signed on 12 December. Clement intimated that he might persuade Florence and even Venice to join their new alliance. The King's judgement was unbalanced by this coup. In the depths of winter he sent 15,000 men under the Scots Duke of Albany to conquer Naples. It was to prove a fool's errand.

The first assault on Pavia was beaten back. A scheme to divert the River Ticino failed. 5,000 *landsknechts* defended the great fortress, commanded by Antonio de Leyva, who, according to Blaise de Monluc, would have been the best general in Europe had he not been tortured by gout. Throughout the winter the besiegers crouched in muddy entrenchments, drenched by rain and decimated by sickness. François and his lords lodged in local abbeys and castles. At Rome a humorist offered a prize to anyone who could discover an Imperial army lost in the Alps. But Lannoy somehow managed to obtain fresh troops. Bourbon, relentless in his thirst for revenge, went to Germany and hired 6,000 *landsknechts* and 500 Flemish horse, with money lent to him

by the Emperor. Lannoy, Bourbon, and Pescara marched on Pavia at the end of January 1525. They had 17,000 infantry and perhaps 1,000 cavalry.

François now moved his field headquarters to the Park of Mirabello, a nearby hunting-lodge, placing himself between Pavia and the Imperialist army. He was in a strong position, his front guarded by the little River Vernavola, a tributary of the Ticino. The enemy dug in on the opposite bank. Both sides brought up artillery, to fire at each other across only fifty yards of mud. For three weeks the confrontation anticipated the trench warfare of 1914–18. On 3 February François wrote to his mother, 'According to the view I have always held, I think the last thing our enemies will do is fight, because, to be frank, our strength is too much for them . . . Pavia will be lost to them unless they find some means of reinforcing it, as they have now tried everything in attempting to hold it to the last gasp, which I think is not far away, because for more than a month those inside have not drunk wine or eaten meat or cheese.' Leyva had demolished houses for firewood, and had melted down church vessels, and even the gold chain he wore round his neck, to pay his troops. But Lannoy, as François suspected, did not feel strong enough to relieve him.

Then, on 20 February, 6,000 of François's Swiss insisted on returning home. At the same time 2,000 Germans deserted. His army had dwindled to less than 20,000 men – 1,300 *gendarmerie*, 4,500 Germans, 9,000 French and Italian foot, and 5,000 Swiss. Marshal de la Palice and Marshal de la Trémouille, with most French generals, advised François to retreat. However, Bonnivet, speaking after la Palice, told the veteran that he and his friends were too old and had lost their nerve. The Admiral argued that the French always won when led by a King. 'We Frenchmen', he boasted, 'never refuse battle, are not used to waging war by little stratagems, but instead show forth our banners proudly, especially when we have for general a brave King who can make even cowards fight.' He ended, 'Sire, give battle!'

Leyva now warned Lannoy he could no longer hold Pavia. The Imperialists outside were themselves short of food. Bourbon begged them to attack and the Neapolitan Pescara, a most cautious general, agreed they had to fight. Yet, if the Swiss had not deserted François, it is unlikely that Lannoy would have risked a battle.

About midnight on 23–4 February, under cover of an artillery barrage, the Imperialist army moved north, along the east bank of the Vernavola until the river was fordable, outflanking the French. It was a black, stormy night, and the Imperialists wore white shirts over their armour to recognize each other in the dark. Crossing the brook, they found themselves in front of the unguarded wall of the Park. Pioneers wielding battering-rams, picks, and shovels, made three breaches, without attracting attention. François had not had sufficient troops to throw out a cavalry screen which would have guarded him against such a manœuvre. The enemy were now able to attack the French flank. Before dawn, an advance party under the Marques del Vasto burst into the château of Mirabello – but François was spending the night with his troops.

When dawn broke on Friday, 24 February 1524, the Feast of St Matthew, the King

Below Plan of the Battle of Pavia, 24 February 1525. *Overleaf* A contemporary German picture of Pavia. Only two *arquebusiers* are shown although it was they who defeated the French.

saw the enemy army advancing from the north. It was a clear, chilly morning. The Imperialists had forced him to reverse his front and his troops were in total disarray. François had to move quickly. He left most of the French foot to hold the Vernavola. He himself took his *gendarmerie* to what was now the centre, positioning the Swiss on his left and the Germans, under Richard de la Pole, on his right. But it was impossible for him to make full use of his strength. Alençon, who was guarding the western approaches to Pavia far out on the left, was thrown into confusion by a well-timed attack from Leyva – it prevented a large part of the French army from taking part in the King's turning movement.

It was about eight o'clock. François knew he must attack at once. If he waited, the

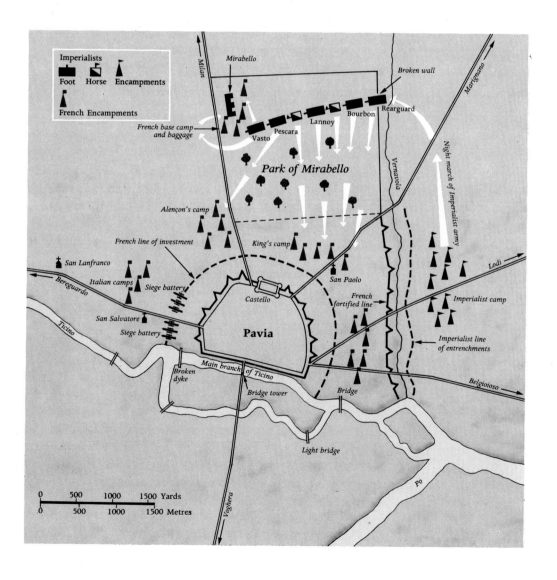

Cannon of the sort used at Pavia, from a
contemporary woodcut by Erhardt Schoen.

enemy would simply overrun his scattered army. Galiot had managed to open fire with
a forward battery, tearing an Imperialist company to pieces. But the King had to charge
across his line of fire – Galiot's guns fell silent. François's charge dispersed some Flemish cavalry whose commander was cut down. Exultantly, the King turned to Lescun
and said, 'Now I really can call myself Duke of Milan!' The Imperialists began to lose
heart. The French instead of being caught off their guard were attacking in good order.
Lannoy said grimly, 'There is no hope but in God', and made the Sign of the Cross.

However, the French infantry were too slow in following up the King's charge. The
Imperialists held them. On the right, de la Pole and his Germans fought bravely
against the Imperialist *landsknechts*. But, outnumbered, they were overwhelmed when
the enemy charged them in flank – the White Rose died with most of his officers.
On the left, Pescara had had time to recall del Vasto's advance party. The King's Swiss
pikemen went in half-heartedly, flinching at rolling volleys from the enemy *arquebusiers*. Suddenly they broke: François rode back to try and rally them, without success.

The battle was decided by the arquebus. Admittedly, it was primitive and unreliable.
Its trigger was the bottom of an S-shaped hook, the top of which held a lighted fuse or
'match'. When applied to the touch-pan, the match fired the gun. A shower of rain or
a poor-quality match could make an arquebus useless, and it took several minutes to
load. Nevertheless, though inaccurate, the best arquebuses sometimes had a killing
range of as much as 400 yards. Protected by pikemen or good cover, *arquebusiers*
firing in volleys could destroy any troops sent against them.

Left Loading an arquebus, a woodcut by Sebald Beham. *Middle* An *arquebusier* with a spring-driven matchlock, by Niklas Stoer. *Right* The firemaster of a mercenary regiment, by Erhardt Schoen.

Again and again, François and his men-at-arms charged. But their long lances were hard to use amid the Park's trees and bushes. Hiding behind tree-trunks, *arquebusiers* shot point-blank at them. More Frenchmen fell at every charge, bewildered by these completely new tactics. Bussy d'Amboise brought his infantry up from the Vernavola, but they were soon broken by the enemy *landsknechts*. Many drowned trying to swim the Ticino. Alençon – 'a man of shallow understanding' – who had been left without orders, never joined the King. When he realized that the day was lost, he retreated, destroying the bridges behind him.

In the pale winter sunshine, amid the rattle of the arquebuses, François and his court fought on alone. There they died, his captains and his chamberlains, the friends of his boyhood and the heroes of Marignano. Two Marshals of France were among the slain, la Palice and la Trémouille, who had both ridden with Charles VIII – la Trémouille was nearly seventy. Bonnivet deliberately sought death. 'I cannot survive such disaster, such destruction, for anything in the world', he cried. 'I must die!' He opened his visor, exposing his throat. Bourbon found his corpse after the battle. 'Wretch!' said the Duke. 'You were the cause of France's ruin – and of mine!' Many other great lords died for the Spaniards preferred killing to taking prisoners. It was the Flodden Field of France.

At the end, François, a splendid figure in a silver surcoat and with long plumes which swept down over his shoulders, was fighting by himself. Swinging a great gold-hilted sword, he killed several Spanish officers. His horse was shot beneath him,

The sword which François surrendered at Pavia. It
remained abroad until it was brought back
to France in 1808 on Napoleon's orders.

but he continued to fight on foot. He was wounded above the eyebrow, in the arm,
and in the right hand. At last he was struck to the ground. Spanish *arquebusiers*
tore off his surcoat and his armour. Not knowing who he was, they were about to kill
him. Then M. de Pompérant, his face covered with blood, rushed up and asked the
King to surrender to Bourbon. François refused to surrender to a traitor. Eventually,
Lannoy and his bodyguard forced their way through a greedy mob. The Viceroy
dismounted, kissed the King's hand, and, on his knees, received François's sword.
(It stayed abroad until Napoleon had it brought back to France.) The Spaniards were
shouting, '*Vittoria! Vittoria! España! España!*' It was not yet ten o'clock. In less than
two hours 8,000 Frenchmen and their mercenaries had fallen, as opposed to only 700
Imperialists. Among those captured were Fleurange, Galiot, Montmorency, and Henri
d'Albret.

François did not wish to be taken to Pavia. The courteous Viceroy took him to a
monastery where his wounds were bandaged. Here the King had the humiliation of
meeting Bourbon, whom he ignored. He was then brought to the fortress of Pizzighettone. He at once wrote to the Regent:

> Madame. To let you know the extent of my misfortune, nothing remains to me but my
> honour and my life which are safe. And so that news of me may be of some small comfort
> to you, I have begged to be allowed to write this letter, which favour has been given to
> me freely. I beg you not to lose heart but to employ your usual good sense, for I have
> confidence that in the end my God will not desert me. I commend unto you my little
> children, who are also yours, and beg you to hasten the bearer of this on his road to and
> from Spain – he is on his way to the Emperor to enquire how he wishes me to be treated.
> And I recommend myself humbly to your kindness.
>
> Your very humble and obedient son, François.

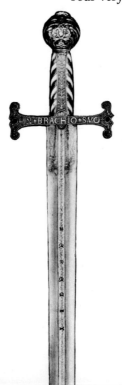

Now
I am King
Again

Mme Louise answered her son's letter on 8 March 1525:

> My Lord, I cannot begin this letter better than by thanking Our Saviour that it has pleased Him to guard your honour, life and health, of which last, by your own handwriting, it pleases you to reassure me – which in our tribulation has been such comfort that I cannot write enough – and also that you are in the hands of so good a man [Lannoy] and one by whom you are so well treated. Assuring you, My Lord, having learnt the above matters and how you are content to bear bravely everything God pleases to send you, as Montpezat [the messenger] tells me, that I too for my part can endure whatever your fortune and your desire may ordain, for the succour of your little children and the good of your realm. So that I will never give you further cause for sorrow. Begging the Creator, My Lord, to have you in His holy protection as I heartily pray Him.
>
> Your very humble, good mother and subject, Loyse.

Marguerite adds her signature 'Your very humble sister, Marguerite.'

François had also written to Charles: 'I have no comfort in my plight other than in my esteem for your kindness. I pray you decide in your own heart whatever you may be pleased to do with me, certain that the good pleasure of such a prince as you can only be joined with honour and magnanimity.' If the Emperor would have pity, continued this tactful letter, then he would have 'a friend in place of a desperate man'. Charles did not reply. When he received the news of Pavia, he showed no emotion, apart from retiring to his room to pray.

Henry VIII heard the news with less restraint. Jumping out of bed, he told the messenger that he came 'like St Gabriel announcing the coming of Christ' and called for wine. He inquired especially after the White Rose. Learning that his Yorkist rival was dead, Henry thanked God and called for more wine. But, by withdrawing from the struggle in 1524, he had deprived England of any share in the victory.

France was in safe hands – those of Mme la Régente, who was well advised by the Chancellor Duprat. Du Bellay recalls how 'as a woman of fine quality, she considered carefully how to make best use of what was left, and to this end summoned to her side those princes and lords who had stayed in France'. Despite years of cruel taxation, the French remained loyal to François. Louise also raised a small army to guard the frontiers. She evacuated Albany and 11,000 men from Naples. At her own expense, she ransomed many of those captured at Pavia. Some who were without means had already been released by Bourbon. 'Of which number', wrote Monluc, 'I was one, for I had no great treasure; he gave us indeed a troop of horse and a company of foot for our safe conduct but the Devil a penny of money or a bit of bread, in so much that not one of us had anything but turnips and cabbage stalks, which we broiled upon the coals to eat, till we came to Embrun.' One survivor, Alençon, found no welcome on his return. Reviled by all, he died within two months, accusing himself of cowardice.

Abroad, the Regent negotiated with the Pope, with Venice, with England, even with Turkey. Pavia had upset the balance of power – every European ruler now feared Charles V. To him too Louise wrote, flattering and persuasive letters.

An Imperial envoy waited on François at Pizzighettone. He demanded that Burgundy be returned to Charles as its rightful Duke, that Dauphiné be surrendered to him as an Imperial fief, and the county of Toulouse as an Aragonese fief. Bourbon must have his lands back, together with Provence which would be made into a kingdom. Henry VIII was to have whatever lands belonged to him by right. François refused the terms and, somewhat optimistically, asked for the hand of the Emperor's sister in marriage.

Lannoy was frightened that the King might escape. Henri d'Albret had already done so. In May François left Genoa by sea, ostensibly bound for Naples, but in June he landed at Barcelona. A French scheme to intercept him came to nothing. The King's progress to Madrid was almost a triumph. Dressed with his usual splendour and riding a magnificent horse he was received with acclaim. The Spaniards were deeply impressed. At Valencia, the ladies – who particularly admired his legs – visited him every day, bringing sumptuous gifts and dancing with tambourines. At Guadalajara he was entertained with tournaments and bullfights, with combats between lions, tigers, and leopards.

A rude shock awaited him at Madrid. Charles had ordered him to be imprisoned in a tower of the Alcázar. Saint-Simon, who visited the tower 200 years later, describes the King's prison in his memoirs: 'This room was not big, and had only one door through which one entered. It was made a little larger by an embrasure on the right as one came in, facing the window. The latter was wide enough to give some daylight, it was glazed and could be opened, but it had a double iron grill, strong and stiff which was welded into the wall. . . . There was enough room for chairs, coffers, a few tables and a bed.' From the window there was a drop of more than 100 feet and the tower was guarded day and night by two companies of troops. The King's exercise was limited to an occasional mule ride under strong escort.

Later, he wrote, *'Le corps vaincu, le cœur reste vainqueur'* – 'The body conquered, the heart remains the victor.' But, not surprisingly, François to whom hard physical exercise was an essential part of life, fell ill. The Spanish cuisine may have been a contributory factor. In the opinion of two doctors, his fever had all the signs of death – he was unable to speak, see, hear, or recognize anyone. Then Marguerite arrived, wearing white mourning for Alençon. Mass was said in his room and brother and sister took Communion together. Miraculously, his fever broke. He had been ill for three weeks. The Emperor, who had been told that he was dead, came hastily to Madrid – François would be of no use in the grave.

Left Antoine, Cardinal Duprat (1464–1535), from a drawing by Jean Clouet. *Right* Mme la Régente, François's mother, from a presumed portrait-bust by a contemporary French sculptor.

Again, the King refused the terms. He sent Marguerite to Paris with a declaration that 'Our very dear and very beloved eldest son, François, Dauphin of Vienne' should be proclaimed King 'under the regency and authority of our very dear and most beloved mother the Duchess of Angoulême.' François retained the right to take back the Crown should God grant him deliverance. The Parlement refused to register the abdication, as he was unable to exercise his free will. The news of his illness shocked France. The Bourgeois de Paris records: 'In the said year 1525, at the beginning of the month of October, there came the news to Paris that the King of France, being a prisoner of the Emperor in Spain, in a town called Madrid which is about ten leagues from Toledo and in the Kingdom of Castile, was dead and people received it as truth. At which the people of Paris and of all the Kingdom of France were greatly troubled and worried. . . .' Erasmus, the recognized leader of Europe's intellectuals, wrote to the Emperor to plead for François's release.

France was not easy for Louise to govern. The greatest thorns in her flesh were the Parlement of Paris and the Sorbonne. In April 1525 the lawyers, encouraged by the University, sent their 'Remonstrances' to the Regent. These demanded, among other matters, that the Concordat of 1516 be cancelled and the Gallican Church be restored to its former independence; that the Judiciary be made independent, without any obligation to submit cases to the Grand Conseil; and that there should be a reform of the Kingdom's finances. The lawyers also attempted to try Chancellor Duprat, who was blamed for the Concordat and for all the vexatious taxation of recent years. They were particularly incensed by his recent spiritual elevation – when Duprat's wife died,

Anne de Pisseleu, Duchesse d'Etampes, c1540 by
Corneille de Lyon – François's great mistress at the
height of her power. *Overleaf* A Parisian music
party c1540 (representing the parable of the
Prodigal Son) with Notre-Dame in the background.

Mme Louise had had him ordained and had then made this rather disreputable old politician Archbishop of Sens and a Titular Abbot. In addition, the Parlement began a ferocious persecution of heretics, and the victims were whipped and branded and even burned alive. Lefèvre, who was certainly not a heretic, fled to Strasbourg. To maintain order, Mme Louise needed the Church's support – she did not dare to oppose the burnings. François was so horrified by the news of this persecution that he wrote from Madrid, beseeching the Parlement to cease such actions.

The King had recovered his health, but remained despairing. One comfort was a little dog which Marguerite had left him and which jumped into his bed every morning. It was not very much. An attempt to escape, disguised as a Negro servant, failed. Finally, the King decided that if abdication under duress was invalid, so was a treaty. In December 1525 he informed the Emperor that he would agree to all demands. The Treaty of Madrid was signed in January 1526. By it François promised to give up Burgundy, Flanders, and Artois, to abandon his claims to Milan and Naples, to rehabilitate Bourbon, and to send his two elder sons as hostages. In return the Emperor would give him his sister Eleanor for his bride. Mass was said in his chamber and François swore on the Gospel that he would keep the treaty. Then he rode into Madrid with Charles, in the same litter. Here he solemnly kissed Eleanor on the mouth, to seal their betrothal.

On 15 March 1526 King François crossed the River Bidassoa, the frontier into France, to land at Hendaye. The boat bearing the eight-year-old Dauphin and the seven-year-old Duc d'Orléans into captivity passed him in mid-stream. François told them to take care of themselves and to eat well, and that he would soon send for them. Tears rolled down his cheeks as he made the Sign of the Cross over his sons. He wept again when he set foot on French soil. He was greeted by the great lords of his Kingdom, by 200 gentlemen of the household, by 400 archers of the Guard in white velvet trimmed with gold, and by 100 Swiss Guards in velvet tunics and red caps. Then, crying 'Now I am King again!' he galloped to Bayonne where he gave thanks in the Cathedral. His mother and Marguerite were there to give thanks with him.

At Dax he held the first Council of his renewed reign. Montmorency was made Master of the Household and Galiot de Genouillac Master of the Horse, in the places of René of Savoy and Galeazzo de San Severino who had both been killed at Pavia. Chabot de Brion was made Admiral in place of Bonnivet. Fleurange became a Marshal of France. However, after his captivity the King was less interested in affairs of State than in *divertissements*, hunting, dancing, and going on progress to places with happy memories. He acquired the most beloved of all his mistresses. Anne d'Heilly was one of the thirty children of the Sieur de Pisseleu – a name meaning 'worse than wolf' – from Picardy. Only eighteen years old, an elegant blonde, she was sensitive with a taste for the arts. Louise and Marguerite were fond of her – in fact they had deliberately introduced her to François. Claude was dead, he had had no women in Spain and he was ready to wait a long time for Eleanor of Austria.

Françoise de Châteaubriant was at home in Normandy when she heard of the King's return. She hastened to the court where she abused Mlle d'Heilly as 'a fuzzy chit'.

François thereupon wrote to Mme de Châteaubriant that he no longer loved her and that she must leave court and retire to her husband's estates. Apparently, enraged by her abuse of Anne, he also told his former mistress that she was 'a rabid beast'. According to Brantôme, Anne asked the King to take back all the gold ornaments which he had given to Mme de Châteaubriant, because they were engraved with vows of undying love. A messenger was sent to Normandy: Françoise had the jewels melted down into ingots and then returned them. The King commented, 'Give them all back to her – I wanted them not for their value but for the inscriptions. I do not want the gold now she has destroyed them. She has shown more courage and generosity than I would have expected from a woman.'

François began to build again. Work at Chambord recommenced in 1526. In 1527 the King demolished the great keep of the Louvre, to make its apartments less gloomy. François now abandoned the Loire Valley. Paris became his centre. In 1528 a new château was begun near Paris, in the Bois de Boulogne. The Parisians christened it 'Madrid-en-Boulogne'. Fontainebleau, also within easy reach of Paris, engaged François's affections the most. Here, in what he called 'our delightful wilderness', he decided to build a new Blois. Fontainebleau, beside a beautiful lake and deep in the forest, was an ancient royal residence. The château had thick medieval walls built round an oval courtyard, and a great square keep. In 1527 François began to improve it, without any intention of a radical rebuilding.

There was much which needed attention, despite Mme Louise's careful stewardship. The Parlement must be checked. In July 1527 François held a *lit-de-justice*, the full session of the Parlement, at the Palais-Royal. Seven steps, covered in blue velvet sewn with gold lilies, led up to the King's throne. On his right were the lay peers and the great lords, on his left the spiritual peers, the bishops, and the lawyers in their red robes. Duprat stood at the bottom of the throne, with three Presidents of the Parlement. One of the latter, Guillart, began with a careful address in which, while claiming that the Parlement had been perfectly respectful to Mme Louise during the royal captivity, he attacked the Concordat and the sale of offices. Guillart admitted that the King was above the law, but none the less told him that he could only do what was reasonable and just. François's edict was then read out. 'The King forbids you to meddle in any matter of State or in anything else save law', it declaimed. The Parlement must not interfere in clerical affairs. Any limiting ordinances enacted during the Regency were revoked. 'The said Lord declares that you have no jurisdiction or power over the Chancellor of France' – the lawyers had to erase all criticism of Duprat from their journal. The King knew just what was at stake. Brantôme tells us how he consciously modelled himself on Louis XI, before whose reign the Kings of France 'had only been half-Kings', because the States General and the Parlements 'controlled and censured their actions, wishes and edicts'. France had taken another step towards the fatal absolutism of Versailles.

Three weeks later, Bourbon was tried in his absence before the Parlement of Paris and the Grand Conseil of the realm. He was found guilty of *lèse-majesté*, rebellion, and

The King presiding over the Parlement.

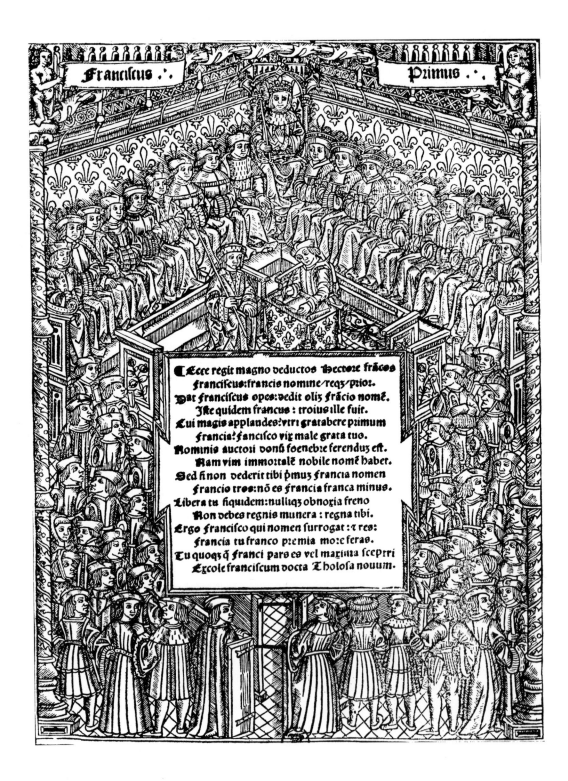

felony. All his lands and possessions were declared forfeit. His arms were effaced – he was even deprived of the name of Bourbon. The door of his house in Paris was painted yellow, in token of his degradation.

Next, François dealt with the financiers. Semblançay was executed at Montfaucon on 12 August 1527. On the scaffold this old, white-bearded man – he was over seventy – behaved with such dignity that Clément Marot wrote some lines in admiration:

> *Lorsque Maillart, juge d'enfer, menoit*
> *A Montfaulcon Semblançay l'âme rendre . . .*

He says the Superintendent's bearing was so possessed that one would have thought it was the judge who was going to hang, not Semblançay. François has been accused of callousness, but he was outraged at what he conceived to be betrayal by a trusted friend, whom he had even called 'mon père'. It is unjust to say that François destroyed Semblançay because he owed him over a million livres – most of the Superintendent's money had come from the royal coffers. He had undoubtedly feathered his own nest and his execution was meant to frighten other financiers who were exploiting the King.

Meanwhile, Parlement and the Sorbonne continued to persecute heretics. The Meaux circle had been harried out of existence – Briçonnet himself was summoned before the Parlement in 1525. In March 1526, the works of Berquin – 'most learned of noblemen' – were condemned. Later in the year he was arrested. Once again François saved him from the flames, ordering the Parlement to free him. Courtiers were inclined to experiment with the new ways – Clément Marot found himself imprisoned for eating lard in the Lent of 1526. However, even dislike of a stultifying orthodoxy was shaken by the Reformers' more senseless excesses. In May 1528 a statue of Our Lady was found near the Porte Saint-Antoine, hideously mutilated with its head cut off. The King offered 1,000 crowns for the criminal's discovery, replacing the statue with one of silver. In 1529 Louis de Berquin was arrested for the third time. On 16 April he went to the stake. François was not in Paris to save him. Had Berquin lived, Luther, not Calvin, might have been the model for French Protestantism.

The King also busied himself with foreign affairs. At Angoulême, in June 1526, he inaugurated the League of Cognac, with Venice, Milan, Genoa, Florence, and the Papacy. Its declared purpose was to liberate Italy from the Emperor. François openly repudiated the Treaty of Madrid, as having been signed under duress. He compared his treatment with that of King Jean II who had been captured at Poitiers in 1356; far from imprisoning him, Edward III had lodged him in his own palace, dined with him every day, and invited him to all the English court's amusements. The Emperor had treated François as a criminal, to drive him to despair. But 'how many times did I not warn him that it was not in my power to dismember the Kingdom?'

Charles V was so furious that he ordered the Dauphin's gentlemen to be sent to the galleys. Henceforth François's two sons were served by Spaniards. They were reduced to straits reminiscent of the English Princes in the Tower. In 1529 M. Bodin, a gentleman-usher of Mme Louise, visited them in their prison. It was 'very dark, without any

The Dauphin François (1518–36) and *right* Henri de
France (1519–59), Duc d'Orléans – the future
Henri II. From drawings by Jean Clouet *c*1524.

carpet or decoration save a straw mattress, in the which chamber my Lords were
seated on small stone stools beneath a window, barred inside and out with great iron
bars, and with walls eight or ten feet thick, the said window so high that scarcely
could my said Lords have air or the pleasure of daylight'. So shabby were their clothes
that Bodin could not keep back his tears. They had been captives for three years – the
Dauphin François was now eleven, Henri d'Orléans ten. When Bodin addressed them

in French they could not understand him. The Dauphin explained in Spanish that
they had forgotten French because there was no one with whom they could speak it.
They went into another room, even barer, where a little dog jumped up to greet
them. '*Voilà tout le plaisir des princes*', said an observer.

Meanwhile, Bourbon had been left in Italy without orders. No doubt he was beginning to fear that he might be handed over to François by some future treaty. The
Duke had become half war-lord, half outlaw, adored by the *landsknechts,* who bel-
lowed his praises. A sketch by Titian shows the change from Clouet's haughty dreamer
(p. 118) – he now appears as a wild man of the woods, with hollow eyes, bristling
hair, and bony features. By March 1527 the Imperial army, unpaid for months,
was in a state of murderous mutiny. Bourbon hailed the mutineers as his brothers
and promised to make them rich – by sacking Rome. Many were German Lutherans

who welcomed this plan with delight. They reached the Eternal City in May. The
Duke stormed it easily, his followers shouting 'Kill, kill, blood, blood, Bourbon,
Bourbon!' The terrified Pope took refuge in the Castle of Sant'Angelo from a sack,
unparalleled since the days of the Goths. It continued for weeks. Cardinals were
tortured, nuns raped, altars plundered, relics thrown into cesspools, and horses
stabled in St Peter's.

Bourbon was dead. He had been mortally wounded by an arquebus bullet when
attempting to storm Sant'Angelo – Benvenuto Cellini claims he was the marksman.
No doubt the Duke, never small-minded, expected to recoup his fortunes by holding
the Pope to ransom. It was less than four years since he had left Chantelles. The
landsknechts buried him in St Peter's but later his corpse was exhumed, to be exhibited
at Gaeta as a curiosity until the eighteenth century.

The English had by now abandoned Charles V. Henry VIII's aim, as yet undeclared,
was to obtain a divorce from Charles's niece, Catherine of Aragon, so that he could
marry Anne Boleyn. In the autumn Cardinal Wolsey crossed the Channel to discuss
policy with François. He spent a fortnight at Amiens with the King and 'My Lady
Regent'. Mr George Cavendish, his gentleman-usher and biographer, was much
impressed by François's suit of purple satin slashed to show a silver lining. He also

admired the tall Scots archers, 'much comelier persons' than the French guards. When Wolsey and Duprat – the latter now a Cardinal himself – fell out, Mme Louise 'handled the matter so discreetly and wittily' that they soon resumed their discussions. Cavendish marvelled at the 'dangerous hunting of the perilous wild swine' – the King 'was in his doublet and hose, without any other garments, all of sheep's colour cloth', and 'had on a leash a fair pair of great white greyhounds'. Finally, a Perpetual Peace was signed between England and France. François wept during the ceremony – his overriding purpose was to bring his sons back from Spain.

In December 1527 the King summoned to Paris an Assembly of Notables – three cardinals, three archbishops, and seventeen bishops, the great nobles, the entire Parlement of Paris, delegates from provincial Parlements, and the capital's leading citizens. He would not call the States General, who might question his absolutism. François explained to the Assembly that he had not sufficient money to make peace with the Emperor and ransom his children. He recalled his wars in Italy, Bourbon's plot, the Imperialist invasions, his defeat at Pavia and cruel imprisonment, and the unjust treaty. Should he break the treaty? Or should he go back to Spain? 'I offer to take the penalty upon myself', said the King, 'being ready to live all my life a prisoner, to spend my days in captivity for the salvation of my people.' Greatly moved, the Assembly urged François to break the treaty, and agreed that he should impose new taxes.

In January 1528 Guyenne Herald delivered François's defiance to the Emperor at Burgos. In March, at Paris, a cartel challenging Charles to trial by battle was read to the Imperial Ambassador in the presence of the King. In September Burgundy Herald brought the Emperor's acceptance to François. Charles's cartel told François, 'You lie in your throat', and proposed they should meet at a place between Hendaye and Fuentarrabia, to fight to the death. But what might have been the most dramatic spectacle in European history never took place.

François had continued to intervene in Italy, though not in person. In November 1527 Lautrec advanced on Naples. For many months he invested the delectable city. Famine had brought it to the verge of surrender when, in July 1528, the Genoese fleet which was blockading it deserted the French. Then plague set in, killing two-thirds of the besiegers, including Lautrec himself. What was left of them surrendered. Next year François made a final effort. But, on 21 June 1529, at Landriano in Lombardy the last French army was destroyed by Leyva – its commander, the Comte de Saint-Pol, was taken prisoner.

Mme Louise now approached the Emperor's aunt, Marguerite of Austria, who governed the Low Countries for him. In July 1529 the Archduchess visited Paris, where she was received by Louise with much splendour. Together the two great ladies heard Mass at Notre-Dame, praying to the Virgin to bless their enterprise.

The Ladies' Peace, named after Louise and Marguerite, was signed at Cambrai on 3 August 1529. Charles gave up his claim to Burgundy, but in return he received the county of Charolais and French recognition of his sovereignty in Flanders and Artois.

François abandoned all claims in Italy. He had to pay two million *écus-au-soleil* (gold crowns) in ransom for his sons, including a lump sum of 1,200,000 crowns – four and a half tons of gold. In addition, he was to reimburse Henry VIII for any sums lent to the Emperor. To raise such vast amounts, François had to resort to the most drastic taxation. Every landowner had to pay a fourth part of his annual income, besides every other levy and tax, the clergy had to subscribe four-tenths of their revenues, and enormous sums were demanded from all the towns.

The treaty represented the zenith of Charles V's power. Yet François would have his sons back. So overjoyed was he that, after the signing, heralds threw fistfuls of gold and silver coins among the crowd in the streets of Cambrai – its citizens lit bonfires in token of their delight at the peace.

Blaise de Monluc was a professional soldier who welcomed war. Yet, looking back on the conflict between Charles V and François I, he could write:
'God almighty raised up these two great princes sworn enemies to one another and emulous of one another's greatness, an emulation that has cost the lives of 200,000 persons and brought a million families to utter ruin.' The Peace of Cambrai was only a breathing-space in these wars. Even so, François knew he had failed as a war-lord – the experience of Pavia had been too bitter. He had brought suffering on himself, on his people, on his own children. But, through his patronage, the arts might still give him 'immortal glory'.

Above Fresco by Primaticcio in the bedroom of Mme d'Etampes at Fontainebleau. *Below Danaë*, from a set of tapestries woven at Fontainebleau *c*1545 which reproduce the frescoes in the Galerie François I.

The School of Fontainebleau

At the time of the Ladies' Peace, François was thirty-five years old – in the prime of life. A terracotta bust of him, once at the château of Sansac, has a strange, almost faun-like face with a secret smile and mocking eyes – it is saved from any coarseness by high, fastidious eyebrows and an unmistakable delicacy of expression. The King enjoyed reasonably good health, keeping himself fit by hard exercise. The Peace denied his energies their accustomed outlet in campaigning. Also, the 1530s saw great changes in the circle closest to him. No doubt these unsettled him, contributing to the ferment of what was to be his most creative period.

He gave his court new settings. The little château of Madrid in the Bois de Boulogne has already been mentioned. In those days the Bois abounded in game. Four storeys high, the basic plan of Madrid consisted of two great square blocks joined by a narrower block which contained one enormous State room flanked by galleries. The façade was made up of narrow, rectangular towers linked by external galleries whose arcades had round Venetian arches. Its roof – three high-pitched canopies with tall chimneys – had an unmistakably French appearance. Indeed, the architects may well have been Frenchmen. However, the château was decorated by a Florentine, Girolamo della Robbia, who worked on Madrid until 1566, enriching it with his strange, ceramic decoration. He employed violently coloured terracotta for his statues, medallions, and reliefs, even for the fireplaces – on which, as usual, the salamander appeared. He was particularly fond of caryatids which were much in evidence. A contemporary, Philibert de l'Orme, called Madrid-en-Boulogne 'a château of faience'. It was demolished in the eighteenth century.

Like so many of François's châteaux, Villers-Cotterêts was originally an old manor-house deep in a forest, in this case the great Forest of Compiègne. Among those who directed the work, which began in 1532, were Guillaume and Jacques le Breton (who may have been brothers of Gilles le Breton, the master-mason at Fontainebleau). The basic plan of Villers-Cotterêts consisted of two courtyards opposite each other, one large and one small. The central block, which joined the two courtyards, was the dominant feature, a two-storeyed building under a great, high-pitched roof with tall, narrow windows. Above the gateway was a loggia, like that at Blois but much more Italian in feeling. The château was far plainer than Madrid, built with noticeable simplicity in brick and stone, though the cornice bore the usual crowned F's and salamanders. Inside the central block two staircases which entered the chapel were splendidly carved and vaulted, one with scenes from ancient mythology, the

The Galerie François I at Fontainebleau by
Rosso c1534–7. Its décor was revolutionary
when compared with a medieval interior.

THE SCHOOL OF FONTAINEBLEAU   155

other with rosettes and salamanders. The chapel – since known as the Salle des Etats,
also in this block and one of the few parts of the château to survive – was decorated
with a great carved frieze of garlands of fruit and royal badges. Villers-Cotterêts was
both French and Italian, with an unmistakably hybrid flavour.

In Paris, the King inhabited a number of palaces, none of his own creation. He
soon came to dislike the Hôtel des Tournelles. This was a rabbit-warren of old buildings
near the Bastille – twenty of its rooms had to be refurnished when Queen Eleanor
arrived in Paris. New State apartments and kitchens were added to the Louvre,
where the court generally stayed after 1534. For important occasions, François set
up his throne in the great Gothic hall of the Palais-Royal, which was the home of the
Parlement – almost the French Westminster. With its painted statues of the Kings of
France, and lit by myriads of candles hanging from the roof in the shape of a cross,
the hall was considered to be 'the finest room in Paris'. Sometimes the King gave
banquets in the courtyard of the Bastille, which was illuminated by a thousand pine
torches, its grim walls hung with tapestry and garlanded with ivy. He also made use
of apartments in the Bishop's Palace, behind Notre-Dame.

If François I had a home anywhere, it was Fontainebleau. He called it 'chez moi'.
Brantôme speaks of it with awe: 'What a building is Fontainebleau, where, out of
a wilderness, there has been made the finest house in Christendom . . . so rich and fair
a building, and so big and spacious that one might house a small world in it, and so
many lovely gardens and groves and beautiful fountains, and everything pleasing
and delightful.' The King's improvements to the château began in 1527 and continued
for the rest of his life. They were organized haphazardly – there was never any over-all
planning – but grey sandstone and pale pink brick, enhanced by yellow plaster,
were used throughout. The first embellishment was the gateway into the old Cour
Ovale (see pp. 218–19), centred on the ancient keep of Louis IX. This was the Porte
Dorée – the Golden Gate – constructed by the master-mason Gilles le Breton in 1528.
Three storeys high, with pedimented windows and open *loggie*, it followed Italian
models, though its tall roofs and chimneys are completely French. An immense,
rectangular courtyard was built next to the Cour Ovale. Named the White Horse
Courtyard it consisted of a series of pavilions, one of which contained the great Galerie
d'Ulysse. The new courtyard was joined to the Cour Ovale by the famous Galerie
François I. Fontainebleau always remained a haphazard collection of mediocre buildings – it was never as impressive as Blois or Chambord. Its glory was its interior.

Mannerism is the name given to the art of the later Renaissance – the period between
the High Renaissance and the Baroque. The term comes from the word *maniera* or
'style'. The movement began in about 1520. A group of young artists working in
Rome – among them Giulio Romano, Parmigiano, and Rosso – sought to refine their
work in a new way. They abandoned harmony for complexity and elaboration,
naturalism for idealization, cultivating artificiality and elegance, bizarre conceits and
capricious fantasies. There was also a curiously reserved note, a desire to please the
individual rather than impress the world at large.

by Gilles le Breton. *Left* Putti in the bedchamber
of Mme d'Etampes, by Primatticio. *Right Mars
disarmed by Cupid, with Venus disrobed by the
Graces* – Rosso's allegory of Eleanor persuading
François to make peace with Charles V.

In 1530 François, delighted with the drawing (below) by Rosso, invited him to work
at Fontainebleau. He arrived next year. Giovanni Battista di Jacopo, surnamed Il
Rosso and called 'Maître Roux' by the French, had the manners of a great nobleman and
the culture of a great humanist, but was an introspective, seemingly tormented, soul.
His sadness may have been the result of horrible experiences during the sack of
Rome. Even Cellini, hardly lavish with praise for anyone other than himself, acknowledged Rosso to have been 'a man of great genius'. Rosso spent the rest of his life at
the château, with the title 'Director of stuccoes and paintings'. From 1534 until 1537
he worked on the Galerie François I. Beneath a carved and gilded ceiling and above
a wainscot of intricately carved walnut, with gold F's and crowned lilies, he created
an extraordinary décor. There are twelve frescoes, mysterious allegories of Kingship,
constituting a *roman-à-clef* whose meaning has now been lost – possibly they tell
the story of François's life in terms of Homeric symbolism. They have a strange,
almost surrealist, quality. The figures are elongated and angular, the colours startling,
even clashing. The over-all tone is one of enigma and exaggeration. Yet there is great
beauty.

In addition, Rosso used stucco as sculpture. Each picture, crowned by a golden
salamander, has its stucco cartouche. Each is flanked by stucco reliefs made up of
caryatids, sphinxes, and putti, of masks and medallions, of gaily coloured swags
and garlands of fruit. Michael Levey has said of this 'fusion of all the arts', that 'what
began as scarcely more than a corridor has become a grotto-like tunnel, overgrown
with white unnatural stalactites, all paying tribute to the bizarre inventive powers
of art to transform the ordinary into the unexpectedly extraordinary'.

It may be that Rosso was not the sole inventor of this revolutionary combination. In 1532 he was joined by another exponent of *maniera*, a pupil of Giulio Romano, the young Francesco Primaticcio, who had considerable experience of both fresco and stucco. 'Le Primatice' also possessed graceful manners and soon became a favourite of King François. He, not Rosso, decorated the King's bedchamber, the Queen's bedchamber, the bedchamber of Mme d'Etampes (converted into a staircase by Louis XV, though the frescoes remain), and the Galerie d'Ulysse. The last contained sixty frescoes, depicting the adventures of Ulysses, which while designed by Primaticcio, a subtle and delightful draughtsman, were in fact painted by Niccolò dell' Abbate who did not arrive in France until after François's death. Like Rosso, Primaticcio fused the present with the mythological past. However, his art is gentler, less intellectual. It conveys a sense of suave, luminous fantasy anticipating the world of Poussin

Ulysses and Penelope by Primaticcio.
Although this painting is usually ascribed
to *c*1563, some have dated it to the later
years of François's reign.

or Watteau. Indeed, in the next century, the young Poussin considered the Galerie
d'Ulysse to be 'the place most proper for forming a painter and nourishing his genius'.

The frescoes of both Rosso and Primaticcio concentrate the viewer's eye on the
human body. One wonders if the impossibly slender and elongated nudes, with
their tiny heads and elaborate coiffures, represent François's own ideal of feminine
beauty. Kenneth Clark, discussing 'the exquisite ladies of Fontainebleau', says that
'in spite of their remoteness from ordinary experience they are calculated to arouse
desire; indeed their very strangeness of proportion seems to invite erotic fantasies
for which the substantial bodies of Titian offer less opportunity'.

Rosso and Primaticcio were assisted by a host of other Italian painters and decorators;
Bartolommeo di Miniato, Luca Penni, Domenico del Barbiere, Niccolo da Modena,
Giovanni-Battista Bagnacavallo, Francesco Caccianemici, the sculptor Lorenzo

An enamel plaque of the Crucifixion by Léonard
Limosin from a design by Niccolò dell' Abbate. It
was commissioned for the Sainte-Chapelle by
Henri II shortly after François's death.

Nardini, and many more. Frenchmen worked with them, including Geoffroy Dumoustier, Pierre le Roy, Charles Carmoy, Claude Badouin, and Pierre Bontemps. There were
also Flemings, such as Léonard Thiry. The château housed artists great and small,
painters, sculptors, workers in mosaic, woodcarvers, and printmakers.

François was so fond of his enchanted palace that, towards the end of his life, he
had tapestries woven which reproduced the frescoes and the stucco-work. He could
take them on progress and, when they were hung, imagine that he was at Fontainebleau. Yet the art of Fontainebleau is not to everyone's taste. It is a court art, which
seeks to glorify the King and to entertain a spoilt, aristocratic audience. Its over-refine-
ment, its perversity, are for jaded palates. But it also has an aristocratic art's elegance
and distinction, and is full of the spring-like exuberance of the Renaissance. The rich
rewards received by Rosso and Primaticcio are significant. François loved the strange
and beautiful world which they had created. The King's face, with its enigmatic
smile, was that of a man who enjoyed private pleasures, secret laughter, things to
be shared with only a very few.

François filled the château with his most prized possessions. Père Dan, who
visited Fontainebleau a century later, speaks of it as 'a treasure house of marvels'.
Here the King hung his Leonardos, his Raphaels, his del Sartos. He continued to
add to that awe-inspiring collection. He acquired the *Visitation* by Sebastiano del
Piombo, and *Portrait of a Man Armed* by Savoldo. In addition, he obtained works by
Sogliani, Ridolfo, Ghirlandaio and Pontormo and also a Perugino. Nor did François
confine himself to Italian Masters. In 1528 he invited a Dutchman, Jan Schoreel of
Utrecht, to work for him. Schoreel declined, but shortly afterwards the Fleming Joos
van Cleve, a far greater artist, arrived to paint two fine portraits of François and Queen
Eleanor.

A minor art which François did not disdain was that of the enameller. For centuries
the enamels of Limoges had been the most prized in Christendom. In 1530 the King
appointed the young Léonard Limosin to be one of his *valets-de-chambre* – later he
made him Director of the royal factory at Limoges. In a long working life Limosin,
who was the greatest *émailleur* of the sixteenth century, produced nearly 2,000
translucent enamels – cups, vases, ewers, plates, and plaques. Normally he employed
a background of the brilliant blue for which Limoges is so famous, but sometimes
he worked in the exquisite *grisaille d'or* – subtle shades of grey picked out in gold.
His decoration was clearly influenced by what he must have seen at Fontainebleau.
Limosin's subjects range from mythology to portraiture (*see* p. 190). A magnificent
plaque in the Louvre, a Crucifixion, has roundel miniatures of the King and Queen
Eleanor; François kneels at a prie-dieu, clad in purple and ermine – his face is aged
and heavy, with a distinctly lugubrious expression. Designed by Niccolò dell'
Abbate, the plaque was made for the Sainte-Chapelle shortly after the King's death.

The galleries of Fontainebleau were flanked by rows of statues. In 1529 the King
at last obtained a work by Michelangelo, a *Hercules*, which has since disappeared,
though Tribolo's *Goddess of Nature*, commissioned by François in 1528, has survived.
There may also have been a bronze horse by Giovanni Francesco Rustici, a Florentine

INRI

NVTRISCO
ET
EXTINGOR

Hercules, Ruben's drawing of the only statue by
Michelangelo which François succeeded in
acquiring.

sculptor who worked in France. The King was particularly proud of a Roman *Venus*, which had been discovered near Naples in 1530 – one of Marot's epigrams commemorates the excitement aroused by this acquisition.

The King collected antique weapons, as well as antique statuary, but, despite splendid trophies, his courtiers must have been more impressed by his tapestries. Many were bought in the Low Countries, though later François was to set up a factory at Fontainebleau. One hears of an arras woven of gold and of silk, of pictures of Leda, of Actaeon, of the Acts of the Apostles (from cartoons by Raphael), of a Story of St Paul, of a History of Scipio Africanus (from cartoons by Giulio Romano), of a Story of Joshua, of a Creation of the World, of a Story of Romulus and Remus. Such needlework glittered, not merely with silk but with gold and silver thread which gleamed in the

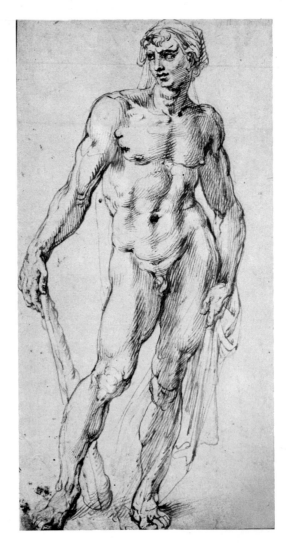

Mars and Venus in the bath – the baths at
Fontainebleau were probably of this sort. From a
design by Primaticcio etched by Fantuzzi c1543.　　THE SCHOOL OF FONTAINEBLEAU　　163

candlelight. These tapestries were supplemented by hangings of red or green Cordovan in leather, gilded, bronzed, or silvered, and embossed with arabesques.

In the top storey of the Pavillon Saint-Louis, François kept two rooms, or cabinets, of precious objects. One, the Cabinet of Rings, contained his jewels, with his cameos and intaglios. The other, the Cabinet of Curiosities, was filled with antique vases and statuettes, with coins and medals, and with strange prints and drawings. There was also what appears to have been a stuffed crocodile with seven heads – it was popularly believed to be the mythical Hydra.

Unlike the stucco-work, the furniture of Fontainebleau tended to be massive and functional – buffets, dressers, tables, cabinets, and coffers. However, the arabesques and medallions of its decoration reflected Mannerist influence. So little survives that one must resort to conjecture. Walnut replaced oak. Surfaces were often inlaid, with ivory, tortoiseshell, metal, marble, and rare woods – François possessed a bed inlaid with mother-of-pearl. Some furniture was painted in bright colours and gilded – Primaticcio is known to have decorated several *armoires* (wardrobes). Coffers were sometimes covered with gilded leather or with velvet studded with brass and silver. Often tables were spread with Turkey carpets or Persian rugs. Much of the furniture must have come from Italy; no doubt it included folding 'Dante' chairs, marble tables, and the gorgeous *cassone* or wedding-chests. None the less, a distinctive French style was evolving.

It was even a comfortable palace. In trying to recapture the atmosphere of a Renaissance château, one has to remember the almost total lack of sanitation. Refinements like earth closets did not exist. The King and a few magnates possessed *chaises percées* – upholstered in velvet, furnished with metal pans, and covered by a tent-like canopy. The greatest lords were accustomed to relieving themselves in any convenient corner,

usually the fireplace, though in the royal châteaux a room was reserved for this purpose. Such was the smell that floors were strewn with rosemary, juniper, and other sweet-scented herbs and sprinkled with rose water and orange-flower water while courtiers carried pomanders. All the more extraordinary, therefore, was François's installation of bathrooms on the floor beneath the Galerie François I. The largest bath measured 14 feet by 10 and was $3\frac{1}{2}$ feet deep; hot and cold water came from great brass coppers. The Chambres des Bains included six retiring-rooms decorated by Primaticcio. The King seems to have made frequent use of the baths as he kept his favourite pictures in these rooms.

A mere list of treasures does not convey how much enjoyment each one gave to its owner and his friends. Rosso's designs for a set of sixteen masks for a pageant at Fontainebleau make a more personal impression. Clément Marot's nostalgic little poem, *Adieux aux Dames de la Cour* recalls the gaiety of Fontainebleau:

> *Adieu vos plaisans passetemps,*
> *Adieu le bal, adieu la danse,*
> *Adieu mesure, adieu cadence,*
> *Tabourins, hautboys, violons . . .*

Fontainebleau was not simply an attempt to create a décor, but an ideal world. François wanted his mistress, his sister, his children, his friends, and his courtiers to share it. Everyone had a part to play.

For this reason, any attempt to re-create the Fontainebleau of François I must take clothes into account. While great lords in Spain – almost until the present day – obeyed Castiglione and wore black, in France, before the Revolution, it was accepted that the great must wear great clothes. The bird-of-paradise apparel of François's courtiers surprised even their Renaissance contemporaries. All the chroniclers of sixteenth-century France devote considerable space to clothes – it was a principal means of conveying atmosphere. A passage from Rabelais, written about 1532, which describes the dress worn at his fictitious Abbey of Thélème, depicts the clothes of François's court as he had seen them himself:

> The men were apparelled after their fashion. Their stockings were of fine worsted or of cloth-serge, white, black, scarlet, or some other ingrained colour. Their breeches were of velvet, of the same colour with their stockings, or very near, embroidered and cut according to their fancy. Their doublet was of cloth of gold, of cloth of silver, of velvet, satin, damask and taffetas, of the same colours, cut, embroidered and suitably trimmed up in perfection. The points were of silk of the same colours, the tags of gold well enamelled. Their coats and jerkins were of cloth of gold, cloth of silver, gold tissue or velvet, embroidered as they thought fit. Their gowns were every whit as costly as those of the ladies. Their girdles were of silk, of the colour of their doublets. Everyone had a gallant sword by his side, the hilt and handle whereof were gilt, and the scabbard of velvet, of the colour of his breeches, with a band of gold, and pure goldsmith's work. The dagger of the same. Their caps or bonnets were of black velvet, adorned with jewels and buttons of gold. Upon that

they wore a white plume most prettily and minion-like parted by so many rows of gold spangles, at the end whereof hung dangling in a more sparkling resplendency fair rubies, emeralds, and diamonds, but there was such a sympathy betwixt the gallants and the ladies, that every day they were apparelled in the same livery.

Rabelais devotes far more space to the ladies. He rhapsodizes over their scarlet stockings, their garters, their shoes of red, violet, or crimson velvet, their taffetas petticoats of white, red, tawny, or grey, their gowns of cloth of gold, their upper coats of satin, damask, or velvet – 'either orange, tawny, green, ash-coloured, blue, yellow, bright red, crimson, or white' or 'of cloth of gold, cloth of silver, or some other choice stuff, enriched with purple'. He is particularly impressed by the way in which they dress according to the season:

In the summer, some days, instead of gowns, they wore light handsome mantles, made either of the stuff of the aforesaid attire, or like Moresco rugs, of violet velvet frizzled, with a raised work of gold upon silver purl, or with a knotted cord-work, of gold embroidery, everywhere garnished with little Indian pearls. . . . In the winter time they had their taffaty gowns of all colours, as above named and those lined with the rich furrings of hind-wolves, or speckled linxes, black spotted weasels, marten skins of Calabria, sables, and other costly furs of an inestimable value. Their beads, rings, bracelets, collars, carcanets, and neck-chains were all of precious stones, such as carbuncles, rubies, baleus, diamonds, sapphires, emeralds, turquoises, garnets, agates, beryls, and excellent margarites. Their head-dressing also varied with the season of the year, according to which they decked themselves. In winter it was of the French fashion; in the spring, of the Spanish; in summer, of the fashion of Tuscany, except only upon the holy days and Sundays, at which times they were accoutred in the French mode.[1]

Such clothes might constitute the better part of a man's entire fortune. The sixteenth century tended to judge people's wealth by what they spent – the *bella figura* was everything. It was said that some courtiers came to the Field of the Cloth of Gold wearing their manors on their backs.

When one looks at the background of the courtiers of François I one can understand why they were so staggered by Fontainebleau. The majority must have been noblemen who came from the countryside. The châteaux of all save the greatest were big farms, despite their towers and battlements – their courtyards piled with manure, filled with wandering geese and chickens. The manors of the lesser had thatched roofs and out-side staircases. Floors were carpeted with rushes and windows were frequently glazed with horn or oiled paper. The sole illumination was that of rushlights. Everyone dreaded the winter. Not only was the decoration of Fontainebleau a matter of wonder, but so were its parquet and mosaic floors and its dazzling illumination.

Scholars mingled with the courtiers at Fontainebleau. They must have been particularly in evidence after 1529, the year of the most cerebral of François I's creations. This was his foundation of the Collège des Lecteurs Royaux – the future Collège de France. It has been said that the opening of its doors marks the real breaking-

[1] *The Inestimable Life of the Great Gargantua* (1534)

point with the Middle Ages. The hidebound University of Paris did not cater for
humanists – it did not even offer a Greek course. Colleges of Greek, Hebrew, and
Latin had been founded at Rome, at Zürich, at Strasbourg, at Louvain, and at Alcalà
de Henares. The King had visited the last in 1525 and had been most favourably
impressed. In one of his prefaces Guillaume Budé exhorts François to encourage
humanist studies by setting up a college of this sort. The 'Royal Readers' included
the Hebraist François Vatable and the Hellenist Jacques Toussaint. Latinists were
largely excluded owing to fierce rivalry with the Sorbonne. In 1530 there were two
Greek and two Hebrew courses, as well as a mathematics course. In the same year
the King nominated the great mathematician Oronce Finé to a lectureship. Later, the
brilliant though half-mad Guillaume Postel was appointed to a Chair of Oriental
Languages. Later still, a certain Guido Guidi was given a Chair of Medicine. The
courses were held in the Lecture Hall of the Collège de Cambray. The King and his
sister sometimes attended them in person. The Sorbonne fulminated, with little
effect. François intended to erect a magnificent building for his beloved college, with
accommodation for 600 students. His Treasury could not afford it. It remained to
Henri IV to give the 'trilangue et noble académie' its first real home.

Another lasting creation was François's library, which later provided the basis
for the Bibliothèque Nationale. He transferred it from Blois to Fontainebleau where,
after 1530, it was housed in a gallery on the floor just under the roof and above
the Galerie François I. It had thirteen windows overlooking the Fountain Court,
between each of which were presses and cupboards containing the books; on the
opposite side of the gallery were desks and work-tables. No less a personage than
the famous Guillaume Budé was 'Grand Master of the King's Library'. Special funds
were allotted to pay men to keep the books in a good state and preserve them from
dust, damp, and worms. François allowed any genuine scholar to use his library.
Foreign princes who visited France preferred, so it was said, to see the wonderful
library, rather than the bravest heroes or the richest jewels in the Kingdom.

It contained nearly 3,000 books. Many were inherited from the family collections
of the houses of Angoulême and Orleans, while others had been purchased, like the
Flemish manuscripts of Louis de Bruges bought by Louis XII. Some had a more
dubious provenance, such as the volumes looted from the Sforza Library at Milan
or those which had once belonged to Bourbon. François sent agents into Italy, like
Hiérosme Fondule, who returned in 1529 with sixty manuscripts. In 1536 he commissioned Guillaume Postel to look for manuscripts at Constantinople and in Egypt
and Syria. He also ordered his Ambassadors at Rome and Venice to join in the search.
Fondule was sent again and again into Italy. If he could not purchase a manuscript,
a copy had to be made.

François did not restrict himself to manuscripts. In 1536 he ordered that no book
should be printed in any language without sending a copy to M. Mellin de Saint-Gelais,
the Librarian at Blois. He patronized printers like Simon de Colines, Geoffroi Tory,
Michel Vascosan and, above all, Robert Estienne. Colines was one of the pioneers

Left Title-page of Oronce Finé's translation and exposition of Euclid, printed by Simon de Colines, Paris 1544. *Right* The works of the Church Father Gregory Nazianzen bound for François, bearing his personal achievement of arms.

who gave France good Roman type in place of the crabbed black-letter. Tory produced some of the most beautiful illustrated books of the entire Renaissance. Estienne was both a printer and a famous scholar who enjoyed an intimacy with the King amounting to personal friendship. There is a story that on one occasion the King sat waiting in Estienne's workshop rather than disturb him while correcting proofs. In 1527 Estienne published a pamphlet entitled *Lettres de François I*er *au Pape* which, with its careful exposition of Government policy, has some claim to be considered the first White Paper. Besides being the father of French lexicography, Estienne printed many of the new works, including translations of the Bible. He was frequently in trouble. François protected him from the fury of the Sorbonne, giving him the title of Imprimeur du Roy. François took particular interest in Greek typography and commissioned Claude Garamond to design and cast an elegant type which became known as *les grecs du roi*. The monopoly was given to Estienne – in 1538 the latter was ordered to present a copy of each book printed by him in Greek to the royal library. The King even issued a list of regulations for printers. Every printer must henceforward adopt an easily identifiable mark.

Many of the books published during François's reign were translations. Some were from the Italian, which the King spoke fluently. Among these was Castiglione's *Book of the Courtier* rendered into French by the humanist Jacques Colin and published in 1537. There were also some from the Spanish, such as *Amadis of Gaul*, which was translated by Herberay des Essarts at François's command. Those from the Latin

François listens as Antoine Macault reads from
his translation of Diodorus the Sicilian. In
the foreground are his three sons, on his left
Cardinal Duprat, on his right probably Cardinal
Jean de Lorraine. From a miniature c1530.

and Greek were most numerous. It was the King who ordered Jacques Amyot to produce a French rendering of Plutarch's *Lives*. (Sir Thomas North's English interpretation of Amyot's version was to be the Plutarch used by Shakespeare.) A delightful miniature of about 1530 shows François, surrounded by his three sons and playing with a marmoset, listening to Antoine Macault read one of his translations.

In 1532 the King commissioned Clément Marot to prepare a new edition of the works of François Villon, the haunting poet from the Paris underworld of the 1460s. Already his language had become so old fashioned as to be incomprehensible. That a writer so medieval and so uncourtly should appeal to François is a vivid testimony to the breadth of his tastes.

The King's favourite poet was certainly Marot. The charming, feckless courtier had left Marguerite's service in 1526 to enter that of François. Always in trouble – in some ways his career was a courtly version of poor Villon's – he even wrote a poem to the King from gaol asking to be set free. This was in 1527 when he had been arrested for helping a prisoner escape from the watch. Amused, the King ordered the release of his 'dear and well-beloved *valet-de-chambre*, Clément Marot'. Another poem beseeches François to give him money after he had been robbed – the prayer was answered. Clément was something of a poet laureate. He wrote on the return of the King's sons from captivity, on an illness of the King, on the death of the King's mother. He was famous for his teasing, elegant wit. He wrote of his many creditors, of his equally numerous mistresses, in praise of wine and dancing and of all the follies of court life. Yet Marot's ruin was to be none of these failings but his deep religious vein. Probably he was never a Lutheran but an evangelical Catholic after the fashion of Meaux. He began his translation of the Psalter in 1533, with the King's encouragement. Only fifty Psalms had been rendered into French when he ended in 1541. Nevertheless, the ladies of the court were soon singing them so enthusiastically that it has been said that the court of François I became Lutheran without knowing it. It was unfortunate for Marot that Reformers sang them with equal enthusiasm.

Marot's first book, a collection of verse entitled *Adolescence Clémentine*, was published in 1532, at the insistence of Marguerite of Navarre. Though soon to be overshadowed, Marot was the most important French poet of his day. He was the first to make use of classical imagery – he introduced the epigram and consciously modelled himself on Ovid and Catullus. An admirer of Petrarch, he brought the sonnet into France. Yet in some ways he remains the last French poet of the Middle Ages. His verse, with its mixture of *naïveté* and sophistication, helps us to understand how people actually felt at François's court. His *aubades,* love lyrics, drinking-songs, carols, *ballades*, have a spring-like freshness.

Clément Marot had his imitators. The most important was his fellow courtier, Mellin de Saint-Gelais. Brantôme considered 'M. de Sainct-Gelays' to be 'a fine poet of his time, who retained nothing of the barbarous old-fashioned poetry'. Born in Angoulême, Saint-Gelais was a brilliant scholar who had studied at Padua and Bologna, a theologian and a musician as well as a poet. His verse, if not without charm, is

An arch of the Grotte des Pins at Fontainebleau,
the arbour of imprisoned giants created for
François by Primaticcio c1543.

somewhat rustic, though like Marot he was a pioneer of the sonnet. The King respected
him for his erudition rather than his poems.

Contemporaries believed that François had brought about an intellectual revolution.
In Gargantua's letter to Pantagruel – written in 1533 – Rabelais claims: 'Now it is,
that the minds of men are qualified with all manner of discipline and the old sciences
revived, which for many ages were extinct. Now it is, that the learned languages
are to their pristine purity restored – Greek, without which a man may be ashamed
to account himself a scholar, Hebrew, Arabic, Chaldaean, and Latin . . . there was
never such conveniency for studying as we see at this day.' Rabelais continues, 'I
see robbers, hangmen, freebooters, tapsters, ostlers and such like, the very rubbish
of the people, more learned now than the doctors and preachers were in my time.'

However, François's most inspired work of patronage was undoubtedly his
employment of Rosso and Primaticcio. To appreciate their genius their creation at
Fontainebleau has to be taken as a whole. It is hard to exaggerate its novelty. What
happened at Fontainebleau must have appeared to the eyes of the older generation
rather as though King George V had redecorated Sandringham in the style of the
Bauhaus. The glittering ensemble of fresco and plaster amazed contemporaries. To
realize why, one has only to visit the Hôtel de Cluny with its Arthurian arras and
Gothic fireplaces.

The fame of Fontainebleau spread throughout Europe. A few years after François's
death, Vasari spoke of it as a new Rome. Reports of its magnificence made Henry VIII
dissatisfied with his own rustic splendours. In 1538 he began to build a rival, in Surrey,
the palace of Nonsuch near Epsom. The exterior of Nonsuch may have been suggested
by Chambord, but its interior was inspired by Fontainebleau. At least one artist from
Fontainebleau, Nicolas Bellin, was employed at Nonsuch where he constructed
stucco chimney-pieces. He had worked with Primaticcio but fled to England after
being charged with embezzlement. But King Henry had neither the talent nor the
money to compete seriously with François as a patron.

Little survives from the Fontainebleau of François I. The remaining frescoes have
recently been restored. Otherwise there are only a few pictures and some prints
and drawings. But there is still enough to show that François's patronage of Rosso
and Primaticcio decided the course of French art for the rest of the century. Perhaps,
as Kenneth Clark says, 'northern mannerism is no more than a bewitching byway
in the history of European art'. Even so, it has its glories. Nothing can detract from
François's achievement in bringing Mannerism to France from Italy, long before it
reached any other country. Without him there would never have been a school of
Fontainebleau.

Inuenit [...] prieiofam
margaritam [...] quam [...]
ceptit [...] [...]

Henri d'Albret c1527. The inscription reads, 'I
have found the pearl [*margarita*] and placed it in
my heart.' Henri had just married Marguerite.

173

The Great
Monarchy
of France

The death of Mme Louise took place on 22 September 1531, at Grez-sur-Loing near
Fontainebleau. She was only fifty-five but had for long been ailing. In her last moments
she called for her son. François was unable to reach her deathbed in time. The King's
grief was both deep and demonstrative. He dissolved into tears on hearing the news
and fainted when he saw her corpse. His mother's coffin was wrapped in cloth of
gold, sixteen prelates officiated at her Requiem in Notre-Dame, and she was buried
at Saint-Denis with the honours of a Queen of France. François was too overcome
to be present. He composed an epitaph:

> *Ci gist le corps, dont l'âme est faicte glorieuse*
> *Dans les bras de Celuy qui le tient precieuse . . .*

The King laments that Mme Louise has been cut off in 'la fleur de son âge' and credits
her with the courage of a man. He had reason to be grateful to her. Some 1,500,000
gold crowns – many millions in modern money – was found in her coffers.

The Trinity had been dissolved. For François also saw less of his sister. Marguerite
in her thirties was gracious and elegant rather than beautiful. A sketch of her by
Clouet in white mourning for Alençon in about 1527 (*see* p. 225) is the best likeness we have of this fascinating creature. She has a pretty mouth, delicate eyebrows,
and very fine eyes, but her nose is much too big. Even so, she is obviously a very
attractive woman. She had taken a new husband in 1527, Henri II d'Albret, King of
Navarre, who was nine years younger. He was King only of that tiny part of his realm
which lay north of the Pyrenees. A late portrait shows a hard, clean-shaven face with
cold eyes. In his youth he wore a yellow beard. A charming miniature, painted in
the year of his marriage, depicts King Henri standing in a beautiful garden and holding
a marguerite, the flower which was his wife's badge; a Latin inscription proclaims,
'I have found a pearl [*margarita*] and taken it to my heart.' Yet, although Marguerite
bore him a daughter – Jeanne d'Albret, mother of Henri IV – the marriage proved
loveless. Henri's only love was his lost Kingdom. The Queen of Navarre turned more
and more to her scholars. She could not spend as much time at her brother's court as
hitherto. This was because her husband, who possessed huge tracts of south-western
France, kept his own court at Pau or at Nérac in Armagnac. Nevertheless, the bond
between brother and sister remained as strong as ever.

François's friends and advisers were changing too. Bonnivet's place had been taken
by the Grand Master, Anne de Montmorency, another companion from the early days
at Amboise. Captured at Pavia, he had been confined with the King at Madrid. In 1529

Montmorency was thirty-six, coarse-featured, harsh, and intolerant. He was the most professional of François's war-lords. Rather surprisingly, he advocated a policy of peace with Charles V. Like his master, to whom he was genuinely devoted, Montmorency patronized the arts. His château of Chantilly, according to Rabelais, rivalled Chambord. He employed Rosso to decorate his other palace, Ecouen (it is said that the designs in its windows would have made even Rabelais blush). He possessed a work by Michelangelo, he commissioned paintings and illuminated manuscripts and he was the friend of Marot.

Montmorency's chief rival was the new Admiral, Philippe Chabot, Seigneur de Brion. Although much older – he had been born in 1480 – Chabot too was a friend from Amboise, who had been captured at Pavia. This round-faced, snub-nosed, bushy bearded Poitevin was greedy, devious, and a little unstable. He advocated an aggressive policy towards the Emperor. Chabot was also a patron, with a splendid château at Pagny in Burgundy.

The person who might have been expected to have most influence on King François had least. This was his new Flemish wife, Eleanor of Austria. The sister of the Emperor, born in 1498, she had briefly been the third wife of the aged King Manoel of Portugal before his death in 1521. She arrived in France in June 1530 and was married in July at a little convent near Villeneuve-de-Marsin. Next year on 5 March she was crowned Queen of France at Saint-Denis – the diamonds, emeralds, and rubies with which she was encrusted were worth more than a million gold crowns. Tall, with a long, sallow face and the jutting lower lip of the Habsburgs, Eleanor was none the less not ill looking. However, many years later, one of her ladies in waiting, Mme de Chalandray – 'la belle Torcy' – told Brantôme that although the Queen seemed pretty enough, 'when undressed she was seen to have the trunk of a giantess, so long and big was her body, yet going lower, she seemed a dwarf, so short were her thighs and legs'. And while only in her early thirties, Eleanor was already middle aged, placid and colourless. Montmorency, probably because she encouraged his policy of peace, displayed an extravagant devotion. The rest of the court took little notice of her.

François was preoccupied with Anne d'Heilly. The shocked English Ambassador reported, in cipher, that when the Queen made her ceremonial entry into Paris in March 1531, the King and Mlle d'Heilly sat in a window together watching, talking for two hours 'in the sight of all the people'. The King's poem *Alone by a window one morning* seems to have been written for Anne. It was probably for Anne too that he composed a pathetic ballad of his expedition to Italy, defeat at Pavia, and cruel imprisonment. Anne d'Heilly remained François's acknowledged mistress and constant companion till the day he died, even though he was occasionally unfaithful. There were other women in his life. Among them was Marie de Canaples. There was also the mother of his son, Nicolas d'Estouteville (who never knew the identity of his father but to whom the King left 200,000 crowns). Perhaps Anne herself was unfaithful – Clément Marot has, most implausibly, been suggested as one of her lovers. Brantôme says that of all François's mistresses 'there was not a single one who was not far more

Left Eleanor of Austria, François's second Queen, from a portrait *c*1530. *Right* Jean de Brosse, Duc d'Étampes (*c*1505–65), husband of François's favourite mistress, from a drawing *c*1535–40 by Jean Clouet.

THE GREAT MONARCHY OF FRANCE   175

fickle than any of his hounds stag-hunting'. At Chambord the King scratched a couplet with a diamond on a window-pane in his bedchamber:

Souvent femme varie
Bien fol est qui sy fie

(Woman is often fickle. Mad is he who trusts her.) Nevertheless, François stayed in love with Anne.

She was made a lady-in-waiting to Queen Eleanor and governess to the King's daughters, the Princesses Louise and Charlotte. François regularized her position by finding a complacent husband, willing to be cuckolded in return for advancement. This was Jean de Brosse whom she married in 1533. The Sieur de Brosse was eager to win the King's favour as his family estates had been confiscated after his father's involvement in Bourbon's plot. Next year he was made Governor of Brittany and Duc d'Etampes. Mme d'Etampes owed her influence over François as much to her intellect as to her beauty – she was known at court as 'la plus belle des savantes et la plus savante des belles'. The King enjoyed showing her his treasures. Anne's semi-regal status is symbolized by her magnificent bedroom at Fontainebleau. She was also given splendid châteaux of her own at Etampes and Limours, besides an hôtel at Paris in the rue de l'Hirondelle.

It would be wrong to assume that François I was disinterested in matters of State. Certainly he liked to get any business over as quickly as possible, preferring to leave the details to others. He spent the better part of his time hunting but in this he was no

different from the great Henri IV. François understood how to employ Ministers. There was no need for him to attend meetings of the Grand Conseil, a purely judicial body, or those of his Privy Council. Nor had he to preside over the Conseil des Affaires which dealt with really important matters – its half-dozen members, chosen from among his intimate friends, knew exactly what he wanted. In the end, François took all the decisions – including the introduction of breaking on the wheel as a punishment for highwaymen. He also made use of secretaries who often had responsibilities comparable with those of a modern Junior Minister.

François was obviously determined to make his authority absolute. There were many theories as to the nature of French kingship. In 1515 Claude de Seyssel, a former Minister of Louis XII, wrote a treatise entitled *La Grant Monarchie de France*. A conservative, Seyssel, while stressing the supremacy of the Crown, argued that the King must respect the realm's established laws and customs. In practice François frequently ignored established laws and customs, as in his enforcement of the Concordat and cowing of the Parlements. In 1538 Charles de Grassaille published his *Regalium Franciae* – he claimed the sovereignty of a Roman Emperor for the King. François's own views probably reflected those of Grassaille.

The King's model was Louis XI. Like the Spider, François went endlessly on progress. Even in the depths of winter, one might see King François riding through the snow on his mule, wrapped in a great cloak lined with marten and sable; next to him, in the golden cavalcade, rode his soldiers and servants in their royal livery of black, white, and tawny. Personal contact between the King and his subjects was essential – government was based on a vast, interlinked chain of local contracts with the monarchy. To some extent at least, absolutism had to be tempered by consultation.

Thus, from the end of 1531 until the beginning of 1534 the King was seldom at Paris or even at Fontainebleau. He spent the early part of 1532 in Picardy and Normandy, the summer in Brittany. September was passed in the Val de Loire, before François went up to Artois in October. After this he was in Paris where he stayed until Lent 1533. He spent the spring of that year in Champagne, Berry, and the Lyonnais, June at Lyons, July in the Auvergne, August in Languedoc, and September in Provence, before going on to Marseilles. François did not leave Marseilles till November 1533, but then rode through Dauphiné and Burgundy, to keep Christmas with Philippe Chabot at the latter's château of Pagny. The King only returned to Paris in February 1534, after nearly a year's absence. Wherever he had been, he had reinforced the Crown's prestige, dispensing justice on the spot to high and to low.

The fate of Brittany is an example of François's determination to strengthen the monarchy. Many Breton barons still spoke Celtic, and the entire peninsula looked back with nostalgia to the reign of Duke François II who had died in 1488 and whose beautiful tomb was to be seen at Rennes. The King seems to have liked the Bretons even if he detested their wine – he told a story of an unfortunate dog who had been made ill through eating Breton grapes. None the less, he was determined to destroy any aspirations to independence, to forestall any revival of what might have been a

French Scotland. On 14 August 1532 the Dauphin, who was now fourteen (the age of royal majority), was invested as Duke François III in Rennes Cathedral. Wearing blue velvet and the Ducal coronet and seated on a throne, he was presented with a Sword of State by the Bishop of Rennes. Henceforward, the Duchy was part of France. Another Celtic country had finally been conquered by a larger, alien neighbour.

François looked further abroad for the expansion of his realm. His inquiring mind was naturally intrigued by the new lands beyond the seas. He was particularly attracted by the possibility of finding gold. It is said that when he heard of Pope Alexander VI's apportioning the New World between the Kings of Spain and Portugal, François cried out, 'The sun shines for me too — what clause is there in Adam's will which cuts me off from a share?' In 1523 the King commissioned Giovanni da Verazzano, a Florentine, to make more discoveries. Although Verazzano and his ships from Dieppe sailed along the coast of North America, reaching Hudson's Bay, his voyage had no tangible results. Later François instructed Admiral Chabot to send expeditions 'to seek a passage from Europe to China and to occupy new and fertile lands'. Two such expeditions were made in 1534 and 1535 by the Breton Jacques Cartier. On his first voyage Cartier reached Newfoundland, where he erected a thirty-foot-high wooden cross with the inscription *Vive le Roy de France*. He brought back two natives who told glowing tales of a land abounding in gold and precious stones. On the second voyage Cartier took three instead of two ships – these were the *Grande Hermine*, the *Petite Hermine*, and the *Ermillion*, all named in honour of Brittany, with a combined tonnage of 240 tons and a complement of 112 men. This time he discovered Canada, penetrating as far as Montréal and making friendly contact with the 'Indians'. He took twelve of them home to France – François had a long talk with their leader who had acquired some knowledge of French. (Rabelais was so intrigued that he went to Saint-Malo to meet Cartier – some of the details of Pantagruel's 'prodigious long voyage' in search of the Oracle of the Holy Bottle originate from their subsequent discussions.)

By 1532 Henry VIII was nearing the climax of his struggle with the Papacy. Clement VII would not give him a divorce from Catherine of Aragon, partly for fear of angering her nephew the Emperor. French pressure might counteract this fear. Henry had pleasant memories of the Field of the Cloth of Gold, and wished to impress Anne Boleyn. Also, he seems to have been genuinely fascinated by François. Deciding to renew the acquaintance, he told a French envoy that there must be no 'precious apparel of gold, no embroidery, nor any other sort of nonsense'. The two Kings should bring no more than their households and 600 men-at-arms each. Henry made it plain that Queen Eleanor, as niece to Catherine of Aragon, would not be welcome: he disliked Spanish clothes so much 'that he seems to see some devil in them' writes the French Ambassador, Jean du Bellay. Henry wanted Marguerite of Navarre; she declined gracefully, on the grounds that no other Queen would be present. Perhaps Marguerite had no wish to meet Anne Boleyn, now 'the lady Marquess of Pembroke', whom Henry insisted on bringing. Henry set sail from Dover on board the *Swallow* at five o'clock in the morning of 11 October 1532, landing at Calais five hours later. It had been a perfect crossing. François arrived at Boulogne on 19 October, to take up quarters in the abbey of Notre-Dame. The two Kings met on English territory at Saint-Inglevert – known to the English as Sandyngfield – at about 10 a.m. on Monday, 21 October. They were no longer the young men who had met near Ardres twelve years ago. Henry was forty-one, heavier and fuller faced every day. He wore a suit of russet velvet, braided with gold and embroidered with trefoils of pearls. The French King, still only thirty-eight and better preserved, was in slashed crimson, with cloth of gold appearing through the slashes. It was a lovely autumn morning. Bareheaded, both galloped through the fields to each other. They embraced five or six times, still on horseback, and then rode on hand in hand together for a mile towards Boulogne. Dismounting, in a field near a place called Paradise, they drank to one another, then remounted and rode on through the rolling countryside. Before they reached Boulogne, they were met by the three Princes of France – the Dauphin François aged fourteen, Henri d'Orléans aged thirteen, and Charles d'Angoulême aged ten. All were dressed in black velvet trimmed with silver. It is hard not to feel sorry for Henry who had been unable to beget in wedlock a single son capable of life. He kissed each one on the mouth. The two elder boys told him how grateful they were to him for having helped to free their father from captivity. Listening, François told them never to forget the Englishman's kindness. Henry took a particular fancy to little Charles d'Angoulême, whom he embraced again and again. With notable stamina, he also kissed, individually, every great lord of France, including the Cardinals. Finally, King Henry entered Boulogne to be greeted by a 1,000-gun salute which could be heard twenty miles away.

Both monarchs lodged in the abbey of Notre-Dame. Of Henry's suite of four rooms, one was hung with cloth of gold and silver branches and needlework panels depicting scenes from Ovid's *Metamorphoses*. They dined in the abbey refectory which had been converted into a hall. It was hung with tapestries portraying Charity – a woman suckling an old man – on the one hand, and scenes from the life of Scipio Africanus on the other, including an image in fine gold wire of the sun going down and various marvellous beasts. There was also a buffet laden with gold and silver plate, and great cups set with precious stones.

The entertainment continued for four days. The Kings attended Mass together every morning, while in the afternoons François's sons – who may now have changed from black into the suits of white, grey, and yellow velvet which their father had ordered for them – played tennis. Henry placed bets on their games, losing over £150 in a single day. Neither King jousted; each was getting older. Nor was there any dancing – Anne Boleyn had stayed behind at Calais. The Tudor lavished gifts on his hosts. To the Children of France he gave 300,000 gold crowns, the exact sum he was owed by their father, while he presented François with splendid horses and falcons – the latter were little English hobbies. François gave Henry his own bed, of crimson velvet embroidered with pearls, six horses, and a suit of white velvet similar to one he wore himself. The English King was hardly shabby – on one occasion he appeared in a doublet sewn with rubies and diamonds though he was outshone by François in a coat covered entirely by diamonds. The weather was perfect and the two sovereigns and their nobles passed the time in discussions of the utmost amiability. On Friday, Henry's last day at Boulogne, a Chapter of the Order of Saint-Michel was held, in which the Dukes of Norfolk and Suffolk were made Chevaliers.

On the same day François left Boulogne with Henry, to spend four days as the English King's guest at Calais. Before they reached it, they were greeted by the Tudor's bastard son, Henry Fitzroy, Duke of Richmond, 'a goodly young prince and full of favour and beauty'. To the sound of deafening cannonades the French King rode into the last bastion of the Hundred Years War. The streets were lined on one side with English soldiers in blue and red, on the other by 'the serving men of England' in coats of tawny and caps of scarlet with white feathers. He was conducted to the Staple Inn, the great hall of the Calais merchants. That evening, François sent a large diamond to Anne Boleyn.

On Sunday, 26 October, Henry VIII excelled himself as host. There was bear- and bull-baiting in the courtyard of the Staple until nightfall. At supper, everyone was impressed by the multitude of wild fowl and abundance of venison, both red deer and fallow, and the extraordinary variety of fish. King Henry in a robe of violet cloth of gold, wore a collar of fourteen rubies – the smallest as big as an egg – and fourteen diamonds 'not so large'; between were two rows of pearls, hanging from which was the great ruby (really a garnet) of the Black Prince. After supper Anne Boleyn and seven ladies danced, masked in 'apparel of strange fashion' which was made of cloth of gold and crimson satin woven with silver thread and fastened with gold laces. Anne danced with François, until Henry took off her mask. An ungallant Venetian observer noted that, 'Madame Anne is not one of the handsomest women in the world; she is of middling stature, swarthy complexion, long neck, wide mouth, bosom not much raised, and in fact has nothing but the English King's great appetite and her eyes, which are black and beautiful'. However, François continued dancing with 'the goggle-eyed whore', as Londoners called her. Then he took Anne to a window-seat, where they sat talking for a full hour.

On Monday, Henry held a Chapter of the Garter, in which Anne de Montmorency and Philippe Chabot were made Knights. During the ceremony François wore the blue mantle of the Garter. The two Kings also made the enjoyable gesture of pledging themselves to fight the Turk. Less majestically, there were wrestling matches between English and French – the latter, 'all priests and big men and strong', received some nasty falls. On Tuesday, 29 October, it was time to say goodbye. Henry rode with François for seven miles until they reached French soil. After a farewell drink in the fields – it was still fine weather – 'with princely countenance, loving behaviour and hearty words, each embraced the other' and so departed.

All observers agree that the two Kings could not have shown more friendliness to each other. According to Henry, François promised to forward his divorce. It seems that he encouraged the Tudor to marry Anne Boleyn. Soon Cardinal de Tournon was at Rome, protesting the perfect friendship between the Kings and demanding a Council of the Church. However, he also proposed that the Pope should meet François at Nice or Avignon. Nor, after Henry VIII had married Anne and been excommunicated by Clement VII, did François give him what might be termed moral support, even if in September 1533 he became godfather to the future Elizabeth I.

François had never ceased to dream of Italy. A marriage was negotiated between Henri d'Orléans and Catherine de' Medici, who was the daughter of a former Duke of Florence and the Pope's niece. The King went to Marseilles for the ceremony in October 1533, making a pilgrimage *en route* to the tomb of the poet Petrarch recently discovered at Avignon. At dawn on 11 October, almost exactly a year after François's meeting with Henry VIII, eighteen galleys hung with purple silk and scarlet satin swept into Marseilles. On board one was the Blessed Sacrament, on board another was Clement VII, seated beneath an awning of red, green, and yellow damask. François arrived the next day, to kiss the Pope's toe. The wedding took place on 28 October.

Henri was fourteen years old, a cold, reserved boy. Already he was in love with Mme de Brézé, wife of the Seneschal of Normandy. Diane de Poitiers, as she is better known, was one of the ladies who had met the young Duke at the frontier on his return from Spain – the passion which he then conceived for her would last for the rest of his life, although she was almost twenty years older. The bride was also fourteen, black

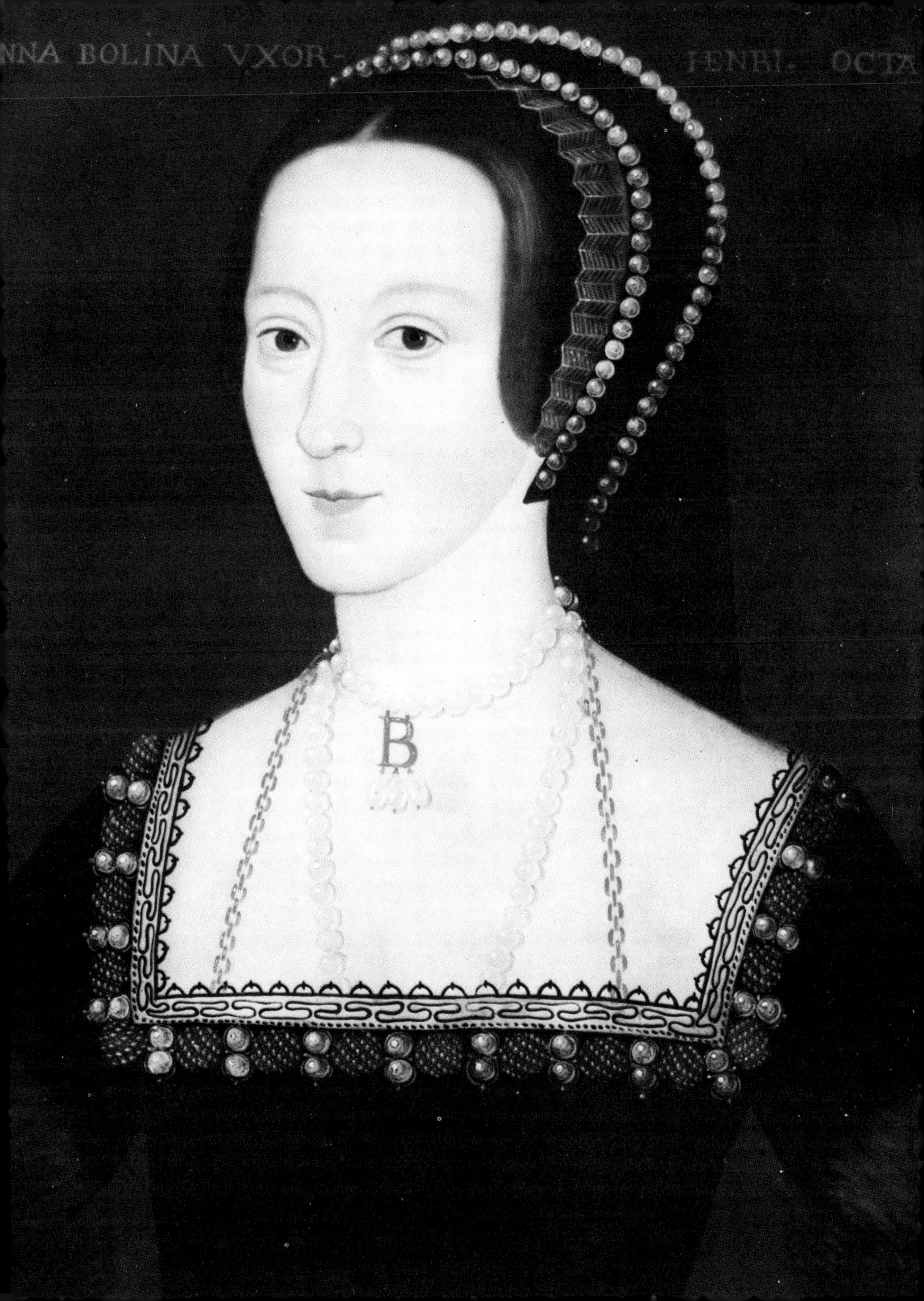
NNA BOLINA VXOR-
IENRI. OCTA
B

haired with a pale, fat face and bulging eyes. An orphan – who had barely escaped being sent to a brothel by the anti-Medici faction in Florence – her life had hitherto been spent in convents. So overcome was this 'shopkeeper's daughter', as the French court called her, that she kissed her father-in-law's feet. On her wedding-day, Catherine wore a Ducal coronet and a dress of violet velvet trimmed with ermine. The King himself was in white satin. Pope Clement performed the ceremony, rejoicing at this exaltation of his family. The Pontiff, who knew François's tastes, had had a marvellous casket specially made by Valerio Belli, which he presented to the King; it consisted of crystal panels set in silver-gilt and carved with scenes from the life of Christ. Another gift was beyond price – a unicorn's horn, three feet long, which had the useful property of sweating if placed near poison.

There is a painting of the wedding by Vasari, in the Palazzo Vecchio in Florence. Clement is joining the hands of the young couple. Looking on are King François, Queen Eleanor, and Cardinal Ippolito de' Medici, together with many lords, ladies, and prelates. Also in the picture are François's tame lion – given to him by Barbarossa – and his dwarf Gradasse.

The ostensible aim of the marriage was to obtain Milan for Henri and Catherine on the death of Duke Francesco Sforza who was childless. The Pope, doubtful of the young husband's virility, would not leave until he was sure it had been consummated. As a result, King and Pontiff had to spend several weeks together at Marseilles. However, the alliance lost its value when Clement VII, 'most unhappy of Popes', died the next year. His successor was Cardinal Alessandro Farnese, who took the name Paul III. Although friendly to François and an enemy of the Emperor, the new Pope had little time for the Medici. Catherine was now an encumbrance instead of an asset. But the ugly little Duchess possessed remarkable powers of survival. With her tastes for Greek, mathematics, astrology, and hunting she soon contrived to ingratiate herself with her father-in-law.

The Sorbonne, not without reason, was relentless in its attempts to root out heresy. The gentle reformism of Meaux had been largely superseded by a radical Protestantism. Burnings, floggings, and mutilations continued throughout France. Probably even some who were not heretics suffered, although the persecution was to some extent held in check by the King. François did not dabble in the sacred sciences like Henry VIII, but he was by nature sympathetic to new ideas. While condemning Lutheranism as 'pernicious', he admitted to Cardinal Aleander that Luther had said certain things which seemed sound enough. Undoubtedly, François found the intolerance of the Sorbonne most distasteful. In addition, he was angry with it for condemning Henry's divorce. He was also anxious not to antagonize the German princes.

In 1531 the Sorbonne made an embarrassing blunder. A book of devotional verse, the *Mirror of the Sinful Soul* – later translated by Princess Elizabeth for Henry VIII – was placed on the list of forbidden works. Unfortunately its author proved to be Marguerite of Navarre, who complained to her brother. Alarmed, the Sorbonne explained that the book had only been condemned because it had not received authorization from the Faculty of Theology; it publicly withdrew its censure, declaring that the book contained nothing but good. This incident lost the Sorbonne its privilege of authorizing works of theology.

The Reformers were even more encouraged in 1533 when Gérard Roussel, who had been accused by the Sorbonne of preaching heresy before Queen Marguerite, was exonerated by Cardinal Duprat. Instead, Noël Bédier, the ferocious leader of the conservatives, was first banished and then in the following year imprisoned. In 1534 François had a meeting with Philip of Hesse, leader of the Protestant princes of the Reich. In the same year he dispatched a mission to Germany under Guillaume du Bellay, brother of the Bishop of Paris. Its task was to establish friendly relations with the Reformers, with such men as Bucer and Melancthon. For a time it seemed that the latter might visit Paris, until the Sorbonne condemned him. Like Melancthon, like the Emperor, and like the Popes at this period, François hoped for a *rapprochement*.

The University continued to anger the King. Its younger members performed a farce which mocked Marguerite of Navarre and her sympathies. Montmorency, always a champion of orthodoxy, rebuked her to her face. 'You are only the King's servant,' she replied, 'I am his sister!' When someone complained of Marguerite to François, he shouted, 'Do not even mention her! She loves me too much – she will only believe what I believe.' It seems more than likely that the King himself was an evangelical Catholic. 'My Kingdom', said he, 'is free of the fashionable heresies, and I leave the cure to those whom it concerns.'

Yet everywhere images were being smashed and churches profaned. Such excesses were typical not of Lutherans but of Anabaptists. At this time the latter were horrifying Europe by their excesses at Munster – Anabaptism meant social as well as religious revolution. On the night of 17 March 1534 placards were posted in every public square and thoroughfare in Paris, Rouen, Orleans, Tours, and Blois, and on the door of François's bedchamber at Amboise. They were entitled *True articles upon the great, horrid and unbearable abuses of the Papal Mass, devised contrary to the Holy Supper of Our Lord, the one mediator and only saviour, Jesus Christ*. It was the first real attack on the Mass in France. Their author was a certain Antoine Mercourt, who had prudently retired to Switzerland.

The effect was the reverse of what he intended. Paris and the great cities were filled with mobs howling for 'Lutheran' blood. François at last recognized the emergence of a French Protestantism. He gave the Sorbonne and the Parlements a free hand. Two hundred suspects were arrested, twenty-four of whom were sent to the stake. These included people of all classes – a rich merchant, a weaver, a stonemason, a paralysed cobbler, a schoolmistress, and the singing man who had posted the placard at Amboise. Many of the others were stripped and beaten with rods. Even to possess a Lutheran book was suspect. On 25 January 1525 the Parlement proscribed seventy-three more, including several printers and writers.

Among the latter was poor Clément Marot. He had already fled. It was unfortunate that his translation of Psalm VI had only recently been published. Nor had his jokes

Woodcuts by Geoffroi Tory showing
opposite an edict against heretics, *below
left* condemnation, *right* torture.

THE GREAT MONARCHY OF FRANCE   185

about the guzzling 'Friar Lubin' endeared him to the clergy. At first he had thought of
going to the King and proving his innocence but his nerve failed him. Arrested at
Bordeaux, he managed to escape. He then found a temporary refuge with Marguerite
of Navarre at Nérac where the young Jean Cauvin – or Calvin – had also sheltered. In
the spring of 1535, pursued 'by men on foot and by men on horses', Clément rode across
the Alps to a safer refuge at Ferrara. Here the Duchess was Queen Claude's sister, Renée
de France, who was a devoted adherent of the new religion. Marot had to stay in Italy
for over a year, writing doleful verses which protested his innocence and accused the
Sorbonne of calumny. Although he must have enjoyed meeting Italian humanists, he
was miserable away from the French court:

> Dieu gard la cour les dames, où abonde
> Toute la fleur et l'élite du monde

On 13 January 1535 King François issued a Draconian edict. 'Under pain of the gallows', it forbade *any* book to be printed. On 21 January he took part in a long, winding
procession of atonement to Notre-Dame. The bourgeois of Paris marched in parishes,
two by two, each holding a wax candle. Queen Eleanor rode in their midst, on a white
hackney. After her came Swiss Guards, heralds, the royal musicians, and then the
clergy bearing the holiest relics. The Blessed Sacrament was carried by the Bishop of
Paris, Jean du Bellay, under a canopy of crimson velvet sewn with gold lilies whose

four poles were held by the three Princes and the Duc de Vendôme. François walked immediately behind, in a black velvet gown, bareheaded, clasping a guttering taper. He was followed by his entire household, by the civic dignitaries, and by 400 archers of the Guard. The crowd shouted 'Sire, do justice!' That same day six heretics were burnt. Pontifical Mass was sung in the Cathedral and the King returned to dinner.

After dinner, seated on his Chair of State, and surrounded by his sons, François addressed the clergy, the University, and the bourgeois of Paris. 'It is fitting that I should use another fashion and speech, another face and countenance', he told them, 'for I do not speak to you as King and master but as subject and servant to those who with me are subjects and servants of the same King, the King of Kings and Master of masters, which is almighty God.' As to those things which concerned the Holy Catholic Faith, he had never abandoned them. France was the only Power which had not nourished monsters. Yet there were 'wicked and unfortunate persons who wished to spoil her good name, sowing damnable and execrable opinions'. 'This good town of Paris, since the time when studies were transferred to it from Athens, has always been resplendent in reputation for good and pious letters', continued François. He begged his listeners to return to 'the way of the Holy Catholic Faith', exhorting them to denounce any whom they knew to be inclined to heresy, to do so 'without regard for alliance, lineage or friendship'. His hearers were weeping. The King, seeing it, said, 'I rejoice in the piety, good zeal and affection which I read in your faces', and went on, 'Our fathers have shown us how to live according to the doctrine of God and of Holy Mother Church, in which I hope to live and die . . . I would see these errors chased out of my kingdom and no one excused, in such sort that if one of my arms were infected by this corruption I would cut it off. And were my children stained by it, I myself would burn them.' He ended by beseeching the University to guard its pupils from heresy and the citizens to do the like by the simple people. 'Who is accused justly shall be punished, though I promise no less punishment for false accusers.'

Two days before, on 19 January, François had approved two more savage edicts. The first forbade any appeal by heretics who had been condemned. The second ordered that those found sheltering heretics should be punished as though they themselves were heretics. Burnings – and recantations – continued until the summer.

By then, the authorities were ceasing to find heretics. There had never been very many, even including the moderates, and those who had not been caught had fled abroad. A somewhat shamefaced reaction set in. François was temperamentally averse to extremism. His sister and his mistress, who both favoured the Lutherans, must have been deeply shocked. In any case, Churchmen like du Bellay (now a Cardinal) advocated moderation. Even Clement VII and the new Pope, Paul III, were against repression; Rome still hoped to come to terms with the Reform.

On 16 July the King issued an edict from Coucy. France, it stated, had been cured of heresies and new sects, as much by 'divine goodness and clemency as by the diligence with which, under God's providence, we have submitted to exemplary punishment all sectaries and followers of error'. Henceforward, persons accused or suspected of heresy were not to be arrested or molested in any way. Those in prison were to be set free, those who had fled abroad might return in safety. But all must live as 'good catholic Christians ought to' and must formally abjure their errors within the next six months.

Clément Marot did not return at once. He hoped to escape the abjuration – probably from pride rather than from any deeply held conviction. He had had to leave Ferrara. Duke Ercole II, a strict Catholic, had suddenly ordered all Lutherans to leave his court, setting the local Inquisition on them. Clément fled to Venice. In France Marguerite of Navarre and her new secretary, Bonaventure des Periers, pleaded for him, but the authorities were adamant he must recant. Finally, Clément crossed the Alps, in October 1536, riding through snowy mountain passes. His baggage contained the Italian sonnet. When he came to Lyons the King had left, so he presented himself to Cardinal de Tournon. On 14 December, before the Cathedral of St John, Clément Marot, barefooted, naked save for a white shirt and holding a lighted taper, came solemnly to abjure his errors – the Cardinal gave him a slap between the shoulder-blades in token of punishment. Clément's *amour propre* was soothed by the warm welcome he received from the poets and scholars of Lyons. He did not return to the court until March 1537. Much had changed during his absence.

The Chancellor Duprat had died in July 1535, consumed by worms and gangrene. His funeral was the first occasion on which he visited his archiepiscopal cathedral of Sens. With his frog face and bull neck, his avarice and his gluttony, he had been much laughed at. He was notorious for recommending donkey flesh as a succulent dish for the poor, infamous for his merciless taxation. Yet, if hardly a Richelieu, Duprat had been a very great servant of the Crown – his shrewd advice had considerably furthered the growth of royal absolutism. The new Chancellor was Antoine du Bourg, a President of the Parlement of Paris and an old friend of the King's, who had been taken prisoner at Pavia. But he was never to command the same influence as Duprat.

François retained sufficient energy for an aggressive policy abroad. He was far from exhausted by his progresses and his patronage. Montmorency had been ousted in 1535 by a cabal including Philippe Chabot, Antoine du Bourg, and Cardinal du Bellay. In place of Montmorency's policy of peace, they urged war. Charles V was too powerful. He had just conquered Tunis from the Muslims and made it a fief of Spain, an achievement which gave him intolerable prestige. By now France felt herself in the grip of the Habsburg vice. Nor had the King forgotten his Italian dreams. The last Sforza Duke of Milan, Francesco, died in November 1535, without heirs. Charles V refused to let either a Valois or a Medici inherit his throne.

For some time François had been negotiating with the Protestant princes of anti-Imperialist Germany. The Schmalkaldic League, which had sprung up in 1531 under the Elector Philip of Hesse, with Luther's blessing, was a political organization of Protestant lords and cities. With its own chancellery, troops, and financial structure, the League negotiated with foreign powers almost as a new State. It constituted a

deadly threat to the Emperor. The French envoy, Guillaume du Bellay, swiftly
established excellent relations with the League.

Even more astonishing were the approaches by the Eldest Son of the Church to
Sultan Suleiman II, 'the Magnificent', of Turkey. This mighty war-lord had wrested
Belgrade and Rhodes from the Christians in 1521 and 1522, and had conquered Hungary in 1526. More recently, he had threatened Vienna itself, which was only ninety
miles from the new Turkish border. His ships swept the Mediterranean, raiding
the Spanish and Italian seaboards and dragging their inhabitants off to slavery. In
1534 Khair ed-Din Barbarossa, the pirate ruler of Algiers, had attempted to kidnap
Duchess Giulia Gonzaga, the most beautiful woman in Italy, as a present for Suleiman's
harem. Yet only the year before François had received Barbarossa's envoys with every
honour. It was said that the King had sent his ring to Suleiman on the evening of
Pavia. He had sent another secret envoy during his imprisonment, while later an
entire embassy was dispatched to Constantinople. François is credited with the
cynical explanation: 'When wolves fall on my flock, it is necessary to call upon dogs
for help.' In February 1535, the King sent one of his secretaries, Jean de la Forêt,
to Suleiman in Constantinople. La Forêt brought with him a complete plan of campaign.
Barbarossa, Admiral of the Turkish Navy, was to attack Corsica and Genoa and
would be aided by the French Navy. François, who asked the Sultan to lend him a
million gold crowns, would attack in Italy at the same time. Suleiman must attack
the Emperor, but not in Hungary as this might antagonize the Schmalkaldic League.

An offensive and defensive alliance was concluded in February 1536, together
with a commercial agreement; the subjects of the Sultan and of 'the Padishah of
France' were to be free to trade in each other's countries – Frenchmen in the Sultan's
domains would only be answerable to the French Ambassador at Constantinople and
the French Consuls in Alexandria and Damascus. This treaty is known as The Capitula-
tions. François had altered the entire balance of power in the Mediterranean.

He had also taken steps to prepare his country militarily. In July 1534 he had
issued an edict which created a national infantry by ordering the raising of 'provincial
legions'. Each of these numbered 6,000 men – mixed *arquebusiers* and pikemen –
under the command of a colonel. Originally, the King had intended to raise seven
of these corps, but lack of money restricted him to four – those of Picardy, Champagne,
Normandy, and Languedoc. It was a revolutionary innovation: Swiss or German
mercenaries had been considered the only worthwhile infantry for a French army.

François's uncle, Charles II of Savoy, had been Duke since 1504. He was the half-
brother of Mme Louise. The King had a good claim in law on certain of his uncle's
lands, while the Duke had sheltered Bourbon and had publicly rejoiced at the news
of Pavia. To attack him was to attack the Emperor. François decided on invasion.
He assembled an army of 40,000 men, including 12,000 of the new legionaries, and
by the end of March 1536 had occupied all the Ducal territories – Savoy, Nice,
Piedmont, and Turin. Chabot, apparently confused by contradictory orders from
François, failed to take the golden opportunity of regaining Milan.

The Constable of Montmorency *c*1550, from an enamel by Léonard Limosin. He lived on until 1567 when he was killed in battle by the Huguenots at the age of seventy-five.

Charles V reacted violently to the rape of Savoy. The news reached him when he was returning from Tunis, on his way to a triumphal entry into Rome. On Easter Monday 1536, in the presence of Pope Paul III, the Emperor publicly challenged the King of France to personal combat.

Pavia had taught François caution. Instead of advancing into Italy he waited for Charles to invade France. Provence was laid waste, farms and villages being razed to the ground, vineyards, orchards, and olive groves cut down, mills and granaries demolished, wine poured down drains, livestock slaughtered or driven into the towns. Every possible source of food or shelter was destroyed. Thousands of peasants died of starvation. Anne de Montmorency was put in over-all command. The King had lost confidence in Chabot who was replaced as commander in Provence by the Marquis of Saluzzo. Unfortunately, the latter promptly deserted to the Emperor – an astrologer had told him that Heaven had doomed François to destruction.

The Imperialist strategy was to attack on two fronts, in Picardy and in Provence. In July 1536 Charles V, accompanied by Antonio de Leyva, the hero of Pavia, personally led 50,000 men over the Alps. Their objective was Marseilles. Montmorency and the bulk of the French army stayed near Avignon in a fortified camp on the banks of the Durance – only if the Emperor tried to cross the Rhône would they attack. In August Charles entered Aix, which was undefended, and had himself crowned King of Arles. Advancing on Marseilles, he found the great port strongly defended, as were Arles and Tarascon – François had filled them with troops and artillery. The Emperor was in a desert. His food-supplies began to run low. Even water was hard to find as the wells had been poisoned. Dysentery broke out among his troops. Peasants ambushed his convoys and murdered stragglers. On 13 September Charles V raised the siege of Marseilles, to start a long, agonizing retreat. Twenty thousand died from hunger and disease, among them the great Antonio de Leyva. An eyewitness, Martin du Bellay, says that 'all the roads were strewn with dead and dying men, with lances, pikes, arquebuses and other weapons, with horses abandoned because they could not keep up. You could see men and horses piled in heaps, one on top of the other, the dying mixed with the dead.'

In the north the Count of Nassau had invaded Picardy in July. He intended to march on Paris, but was held up at Péronne. Here M. de Dammartin took charge of the little town, making its citizens fight like heroes, even after he himself was killed. Nassau raised the siege when he heard the news from Provence and withdrew over the frontier.

Yet François had suffered a terrible blow. On 10 August 1536 the Dauphin François died at Tournon. He was eighteen. Father and son had delighted in each other's company, despite the Dauphin's sober, solitary tastes. 'Sombre and bizarre', he dressed in black like a Spaniard and preferred books to soldiering. None the less, he already had a mistress – Mme d'Estranges. The circumstances of his death were suspicious. Playing tennis with his young Italian secretary, Count Montecuccoli, the Dauphin had become very hot and had asked for a cup of iced water, which the Count brought him. After drinking, he at once fell ill and died within a very few days. The unfortunate Montecuccoli was known to be interested in toxicology – a book on arsenic was found in his lodgings. He was accused of being an Imperial agent and under torture confessed to having poisoned the Dauphin. Montecuccoli was sentenced to be torn in pieces by horses at Lyons, in the Place de Grenette – the mob played football with his head. In fact the Dauphin almost certainly died from some form of tuberculosis.

At first the Cardinal of Lorraine dared not break the news to the King. He merely said that the Dauphin was very ill. François guessed the truth. Groaning, in tears, he stared out of a window. Then he turned and faced his nervous courtiers. Taking off his hat, the King raised his eyes to heaven. 'Oh God', he prayed, 'you have afflicted me by humiliating my kingdom and my army and now you have taken away my son. What else remains save to destroy me utterly? When it shall please you to do so, at least warn me that it is your will so that I do not rebel. . . .' Marguerite came to comfort her brother.

François had little in common with his new heir. Henri d'Orléans, now Dauphin and Duke of Brittany, was a tall, dark youth, cold and inhibited. He seldom spoke – many courtiers said they had never seen him laugh. He had a violent streak, loving war and the tourney – on one occasion he raped a beautiful Piedmontese girl. His pastimes were wrestling, long jumping, and peculiarly savage horseplay. The only person for whom he felt any affection was his mistress, Diane de Poitiers. There was little love between Henri and his father. The King much preferred Charles d'Angoulême, who now became Duc d'Orléans.

One afternoon in the autumn of 1536, François was resting in his chamber, still grieving. There was a knock on his door. Then Henri's voice said, 'Sire, it is the King of Scotland come to see Your Grace and to comfort you.' Jumping up, François opened the door and embraced this very welcome visitor. James V was twenty-four, well built and handsome, with red hair and a red beard 'like fine shining gold'. Brilliant, impetuous, charming, fond of women and building, in many ways James resembled François. He liked to wander among his subjects, disguised as a poor traveller – the Scots called him the *gaberlunzie* (beggar-man) King. He hated the English who, when he was one year old, had killed his father at Flodden Field. His uncle, Henry VIII, persisted in bullying him to marry Mary Tudor but James was determined to find a French bride. He arrived in France in September 1536, after a long, dangerous voyage, before which he had been three times beaten back to Scotland by contrary winds. A marriage had already been arranged with Marie de Vendôme whom King François had adopted as his daughter. However, James found her so 'hunchbacked and misshapen' that he broke off the engagement. It is said that she later died of chagrin.

King James then met François's eldest surviving daughter, Madeleine de France. She was riding in a 'chariot' because she was too sickly to ride a horse. 'From the time she saw the King of Scotland, she became so enamoured with him and loved him so well that she would have no man alive to be her husband but he alone.' Unfortunately,

Madeleine de France, Queen of Scots (1520–37),
from a portrait by Corneille de Lyon.

Madeleine, who was just sixteen, was consumptive. Doctors warned that she could
never bear children and that if she left France 'she would not have long days'.
Madeleine insisted on marrying James. In November François reluctantly consented –
he would have preferred him to marry his younger daughter, Marguerite, who had
better health. He promised a dowry of 100,000 gold crowns. In return, James ratified
'the old band betwixt Scotland and France'. He wrote home, summoning his great
lords to his wedding.

On the last day of 1536 James V rode into Paris, wearing a coat of crimson velvet
slashed with gold. He was received with honours normally accorded only to a King
of France, then escorted to his lodging in the Hôtel de Cluny. Next day, 1 January
1537, at ten o'clock in the morning, the marriage took place on a great dais in front
of Notre-Dame. The dais was surmounted by a canopy of fine cloth of gold supported
by four pillars of 'antique work'. Madeleine was frail but lovely, tall and slender,
with small, delicate features and with light brown hair which hung down to her
shoulders. A picture, once in the Luxembourg, showed her in a dress of white and
gold damask with a jewelled collar. Her bridesmaids were also in white, but with
green sleeves, while the bridegroom wore white satin hose and a cloak of dark blue
velvet edged with sable. Those present included the Kings and Queens of France and
Navarre and François's two sons. It was the first time François had given a daughter
away in marriage. Heralds threw gold and silver coins into the crowd, shouting,
'Largesse de par Madame Madeleine, fille du Roy!' The ceremony was performed by
the Cardinal de Bourbon. Among the guests from Scotland were six bishops, six
earls, and twenty barons.

The wedding-breakfast was in the Bishop's Palace, behind Notre-Dame. The
Scots were particularly impressed by the public entertainments which had been
devised by 'cunning carvers and profound necromancers' – birds flew through the
air spouting flames and ships fought each other on rivers running through the
streets of Paris. Supper was held in the Great Hall of the Palais-Royal, hung with rich
tapestries. The Parlement attended in their red robes. The King and Queen of Scots
sat on one side of a marble table, the King and Queen of France on the other. There
were two towering buffets at each end, laden with every sort of gold and silver
plate. High above, on specially constructed platforms, were orchestras who played
during the supper and during the masked ball which followed. While the meal was
in progress King James set cups before the more important French lords, announcing
that these were filled with the fruits of his realm – the fruits turned out to be coins
of Scots gold. Later, a peculiarly Scottish note was struck by François having to
pay all his new son-in-law's expenses.

A fortnight of tourneys and jousting followed, in the courtyard of the Louvre.
The young couple stayed in Paris until the spring. James tried to wander disguised
through the streets of Paris, as he did in Edinburgh, but was always recognized –
urchins pointed out the King of Scots to passers-by. Before he left François presented
him with two ships, one called *The Salamander*, with twenty of his best horses and

with twenty suits of gilded armour. He also invited Madeleine with her lords and ladies to inspect his wardrobes and take any bales of cloth of gold, velvet or satin which they might fancy. In addition he gave his daughter rings and jewels so that she took to Scotland 'ane infinite substance'. James and his bride left France in May. Among those who sailed with them was a thirteen-year-old page, the poet Ronsard. After a stormy voyage of five days, they reached the port of Leith. When they landed, Madeleine knelt down and kissed the earth and 'thanked God that her husband and she was come safe through the seas'.

The war with the Emperor had begun again. In Picardy Montmorency fought the Imperialists to a standstill and a truce was signed at Bomy in July 1537. However, this only applied to the northern front. In Italy, François formally annexed Turin to France. But the French troops in Piedmont were driven back. Then, on 8 October, Montmorency and the Dauphin forced the seemingly impregnable pass of Susa. Within three weeks Montmorency, waging merciless war and hanging prisoners, had reconquered most of Piedmont. François and Charles V recognized stalemate. On 16 November a truce was signed at Monzon in Aragon.

Meanwhile, François had suffered another tragedy. Queen Madeleine had been

greeted with joy by the Scots. However, according to Brantôme who had spoken with Ronsard, she found Scotland a very different country from what people had told her. None the less, she concealed her disillusionment, only saying over and over again, 'Alas, I wanted to be Queen!' Soon after her arrival she fell into what was obviously a galloping consumption. James wanted to take her to Balmerino Abbey, where the climate was thought to be milder. He spent all his time in her sick-room. She wrote to her father that she was cured. But Madeleine died at Holyrood on 7 July 1537 – she was not yet seventeen. Ronsard says that 'she died without pain in her husband's arms'. James tried to kill himself with his own sword. The Scots mourned passionately for their beautiful midsummer Queen of only forty days. 'Triumph and merriness was all turned into dirges and soul masses, which was very lamentable to behold.' James wrote to her father the same day of 'the death of your daughter, my dearest companion'. He says that he cannot write at length. François was lying ill at Fontainebleau when the news came, so ill that the Cardinal of Lorraine would not admit the messenger. It was some time before his courtiers dared tell the King. Yet despite their grief, both James and François were determined to hold to 'the auld alliance'. Within the year, a new French Queen arrived in Scotland, Marie de Guise.

On 10 February 1538, François created Anne de Montmorency Constable of France. Montmorency had been tireless in the fight against the Emperor. Etienne Dolet admiringly compared him to an enraged wild boar. Brantôme gives a sample of his conversation. 'Go on, hang that man there, run this one through with a pike or shoot him, at once, in front of me!' Montmorency would order, or 'Cut those scoundrels in pieces for daring to hold a steeple against the King', or 'Burn that village, set fire to everything for a quarter of a league about.' He punished the slightest insubordination with torture or death. The ceremony took place in the château of Moulins, once the home of the Constable de Bourbon. No doubt this was by deliberate design on François's part. It was a suitably martial occasion, with troops marching to the music of drums and fifes. Montmorency, in a tunic of crimson velvet, was girded with the royal sword in its gold scabbard. The King declared that he was worthy of 'perpetual praise, commendation and reward'. Then heralds cried 'Vive Montmorency, Constable of France!' Finally, there was a High Mass in thanksgiving.

The Emperor Charles was bewildered by his failure to crush the French. He was also worried about the Turks. Sultan Suleiman was gathering an enormous army – Hungary and Venice were in danger. The monstrous alliance with the infidels even made François himself uneasy. He knew that he was outraging Christendom. He must have been shaken by two open letters from 'Aretino'. Pietro of Arezzo, poet, playwright, and pornographer, was the one outstanding publicist of Renaissance Europe, a precursor of cosmopolitan journalism. His gossiping correspondence with European courts commanded an enormous audience. In 1532 Ariosto called him *'flagello dei Principi'* – 'scourge of princes'. The name stuck. To incur Aretino's enmity was, in modern terms, the equivalent of having the entire Press of Europe against one. Both the Emperor and the King of France vied for his goodwill. In 1533

François had sent him a massive gold chain with little pendants enamelled red, 'as if poisoned', which bore the inscription 'His tongue uttereth great lies.' Though delighted by this enigmatic gift, Aretino feared that François's alliance with the Turks might bring disaster on Venice, his home. He also enjoyed a handsome pension from the Emperor. He wrote that he doubted whether he could call François a 'most Christian' King. He continued, 'Now I regret bitterly, that I can call you neither King of France nor François. For how can a man be called either King or free, which last quality is implicit in both France and François, if he goes and begs aid from barbarians, foes of his race, and turns against his creed? My lord, for so I still address you, you have thrust the sword of the Ottoman into the heart of Christendom!' Aretino was only voicing the general indignation.

Pope Paul III was particularly distressed. The war between France and the Emperor was hindering his great design – the summoning of a Council to reform the Roman Church. In June 1538 an abortive peace conference took place at Nice, attended by the Pope, by François, and by Charles. The last was in an evil temper because the Duke of Savoy had refused to lend him the citadel for a residence. Nice, then called Nizza, was the Duke's sole remaining possession, so his caution may be understood. The Emperor stayed on board his galley in the harbour, while François remained at a near-by château. They did not meet. However both talked with the sixty-five-year-old Paul III, a formidable and awe-inspiring figure with a presence and a beard like those of an Old Testament patriarch. He would not let François kiss his toe but embraced him. Negotiations, presided over by the Pope, dragged on in a desultory fashion. The problem was that François still hoped for Milan. The conference ended after three weeks, having achieved nothing.

Henry VIII was alarmed. The thing he dreaded most was a Franco-Imperialist coalition. Luckily he was a widower again: both Anne Boleyn and Jane Seymour were dead. He sent hastily to France for a new bride who would cement his friendship with François. Five great ladies were suggested. Portraits were submitted. 'By God,' said Henry, 'I trust no one but myself – the thing touches me too near. I wish to see them and know them some time before deciding.' He asked for all five to be sent to Calais for his personal inspection. The French Ambassador suggested that he sleep with each in turn, keeping the one who performed best, as 'the Knights of the Round Table treated the ladies of this land in time past'. Henry laughed but blushed. François later commented that 'it was not the custom in France for demoiselles from such families to be shown off like hackneys for sale'. If the English King asked for one in particular, he might perhaps receive a favourable answer. The beauty contest never took place.

On 14 July Charles and François finally met at Aigues-Mortes the great medieval port in the Camargue. Their meeting may well have been arranged by Queen Eleanor – she longed to reconcile her husband with her brother. King and Emperor embraced, to the general astonishment and delight. François could not resist saying, 'My brother, I am your prisoner once again!' Yet next day the display of friendship was even more affecting. Queen Eleanor beamed and the King appeared to have tears in his eyes when Charles embraced his sons. After dinner, he presented the Emperor with a diamond ring, whereupon Charles took off his collar of the Golden Fleece and hung it round François's neck. The meeting lasted only two days, but seemed completely successful.

A ten-year truce, if not a peace, was speedily negotiated. King and Emperor united against the enemies of Christendom. They agreed to wage war on the Turks, on the Lutheran heretics, and on Henry VIII. François kept Savoy and two-thirds of Piedmont. These were territories which protected the borders of France. It was the greatest triumph of his middle years. Nothing was said about Milan.

An Autumn Landscape

François was always happiest at Fontainebleau. His 'delicious wilderness', as he himself called it, has been conjured up by Michelet: 'An autumn landscape, both strange and wild, gentle and meditative. Here were rocks warmed by the sun where one might take refuge from illness, wild shadows tinted purple by October hues to make one dream before winter came, only two paces from the young Seine flowing between golden vineyards. It was a delightful retreat in which to rest and savour what remained of life, the last drops from the *vendange*.' Here François loved to hunt

Left A copy of the *Ariadne*, from a bronze model cast by Primaticcio in 1543. *Right* The *Boy drawing out a thorn*, a bronze cast of the statue by Sansovino. It was given to François in 1540.

and picnic with those lords and ladies with whom he was most at ease. In these later years he preferred hawking to hunting, as a less demanding, more cerebral pastime. Not only did the King fly his mighty gerfalcons and peregrines but also a grey shrike. If he did not feel like violent exercise, he could walk in the long Italian gardens and terraces, with their fountains, pavilions, and arbours, their avenues of lime trees. Primaticcio built him a strange resting-place of carved stones, the Grotte des Pins whose pillars are shaped like imprisoned giants.

In 1538 François was painted by Titian in his studio at Venice. As the King was not there to sit for him, he used a medallion as a model (*see* p. 217). He was also advised by the Cardinal of Lorraine, who was living in Venice at that time. An earlier, bareheaded, attempt, which still survives, was rejected. The outcome was the most splendid of all the portraits of François and is now in the Louvre. The King is shown in profile with a feathered hat. Under a cloak he wears a doublet of wonderful crimson and the Saint-Michel hangs round his neck. His hair, still dark, straggles in spikes over his forehead, his smile is as mocking and enigmatic as ever, his neck is almost

François I, from a portrait c1540 by François
Clouet.

bull-like. The over-all expression is one of enormous vitality and confidence.

Yet however much the portrait may be like the King in his prime, it is not François during his later years. In the autumn of 1539 'the King, being at Compiègne, fell ill with an abscess which was below his stomach and from which he was in great danger of dying'. Henceforward, the abscess, probably tubercular, broke out once a year, though each time François seemed to make a complete recovery. It has been suggested, plausibly, that after this illness François became less high-spirited than hitherto, more suspicious and harder to please.

In the seventeenth century a legend grew up that the abscess had been venereal, that the husband of 'La belle Ferronière' one of François's mistresses, had deliberately gone to a brothel and infected himself to be revenged on the King. In the nineteenth century Michelet claimed that François had really died eight years before his actual death, becoming a shadow of the man he had once been, because of 'a horrible malady from which his doctors could only save him by destroying him'.

François had certainly contracted some sort of venereal infection, but many years before, in 1512, as his mother had recorded. There is little substance in the allegation of tertiary syphilis in 1539. How little may be seen from the description of the King by Marino Cavalli who met him in 1546:

> His appearance is completely regal, so much so, that without ever having seen his face or his portrait, merely seeing him one would say 'It is the King.' All his movements are so noble and majestic that no other prince can rival him. His nature is robust despite the excessive fatigues he has always had to endure and which he still has to endure in all his progresses and journeys. There are few men who could bear such hardship. He purges himself of any evil humours which he may have contracted by a method which nature provides once a year – which is why he may well live for a long time. He eats and drinks heartily, he sleeps even better and, what is more, he likes to spend his days in pastime and pleasure.

After commenting on the King's exquisite clothes, Cavalli says that this 'delicate and fastidious way of life will undoubtedly help his health'.

François was not always regal. Once, during Mass, a gentleman engaged in picking the pocket of the Cardinal of Lorraine turned and saw the King watching him. With curiously bold presence of mind, he placed his finger on his lips, whereupon François made a similar gesture in response. Afterwards, when the Cardinal shouted he had been robbed, the King broke into fits of laughter, announcing, 'I was the accomplice.'

The two best likenesses of François I during these autumn years show a different man to that drawn by Jean Clouet or Titian. One is a small equestrian portrait, now in the Uffizi, which was painted by François Clouet, Jean's son, in about 1540. The King is tired and a little flabby but scarcely Michelet's syphilitic ruin. A half-length bust, possibly by Jean Cousin, is the strangest and yet in some ways the most convincing of all likenesses of François I. The face is almost a caricature, like some laughing mask from antiquity. None the less, it conveys perfectly the King's characteristic blend of mockery and enigma (see p. 13).

In 1543 Primaticcio was sent to Rome to commission models of the greatest surviving works of antiquity. Among these were the *Emperor Commodus as Hercules, Marcus Aurelius*, the *Venus of Cnidus*, the *Laocoön*, the *Capitoline Horse*, reliefs from the Column of Trajan, and *Cleopatra* and *Apollo*. When he returned, he had them cast to ornament the corridors of Fontainebleau. Later, François also acquired a model of Michelangelo's *Pietà*.

Rosso had died in 1542, probably by his own hand. But together he and Primaticcio had transformed French art. New means were found to make their works known to a wider audience. From about 1542 until 1548 a school of printmakers worked at Fontainebleau including etchers and engravers. Among them were Fantuzzi, Jean Mignon, Pierre Milan, and Domenico del Barbiere. They reproduced works by Rosso, Primaticcio, Luca Penni, Giulio Romano, and Parmigiano. Etchers such as Geoffroy Dumoustier and Juste de Juste produced designs, which although their own, reflected the taste of Fontainebleau. Another means of disseminating the new art was tapestry, and the King took a personal interest in setting up special workshops.

An aesthetic revolution was already apparent. Jean Cousin the Elder, who settled in Paris towards 1540, was one of the first French painters of the nude. A vigorous *Charité* by him, of about 1543, shows a woman with the strong thighs and tiny head

Left and right The Triumphs of Scipio, a drawing of his procession and an etching by Fantuzzi of his banquet, from Romano's tapestry designs. *Middle* Mannerism at its most absurd: 'François in war is a furious Mars, in peace a Minerva and a Diana at the hunt' (c1545).

so typical of the Fontainebleau school. It may have been Cousin who made the strange bronze bust of François which has been described. Cousin was also a designer of tapestry and of stained glass and worked on the decorations for the entry of Charles V into Paris in 1540. In the same year, the youthful Antoine Caron came to Fontainebleau to work under Primaticcio – later Caron became the most famous of the native French Mannerists and was Court Painter to Charles IX, Henri III, and Henri IV. In 1541 François Clouet succeeded his father as 'Painter to the King'. Like 'Janet' he too was a decorator who painted furniture as well as portraits.

Another delightful artist who worked in France during these years was Corneille de Lyon. Like the Clouets he was of Flemish origin. He produced a large number of small panel-portraits, on wood, in a naturalist style. Some are particularly convincing, especially his likeness of Marot (*see* pp. 189, 141). Corneille, whose studio seems to have been at Lyons, created a vogue for these little pictures, which, apparently, were usually hung in small *cabinets*. He played a role rather like that of a Court Photographer, just as Jean Clouet had done with his drawings in the 1520s. Other painters tried to produce similar portraits but were less successful. Those by Corneille are characterized by apple-green or peacock blue backgrounds. Although not a Mannerist, in 1541 he was rewarded with the title 'Painter to the Dauphin'.

Venus, Cupid, Time and Folly, an allegory c1546 by
Agnolo Bronzino, commissioned by Duke Cosimo I
of Tuscany as a gift for François.

François's collection of Masters continued to grow. His acquisitions included Titian's portrait of himself and a *Magdalen* by Titian. In 1545 Duke Cosimo de' Medici of Florence sent the King Bronzino's *Venus, Cupid, Time and Folly*, which the Duke had specially commissioned. It is perhaps the greatest of all Mannerist paintings. Vasari considered it to be of 'singolare belleza' – 'outstanding beauty'. In addition François may have also acquired Flemish works of art, though no evidence survives. He had undoubtedly purchased some Flemish paintings in 1529, mainly of religious subjects but there is no clue to the artists' identity.

François was still building. He repaired his château of Le Pavillon, at Folembray near Laon, which Charles V's troops had sacked and burnt in 1538. This hunting-lodge is one of the least known of the King's palaces – from du Cerceau's sketch it also seems to have been one of the least interesting, save for a magnificent tennis-court. However, Brantôme considered it 'a lovely, pleasant mansion'. In Paris François had been building a new Hôtel de Ville since 1533. It was designed by Domenico da Cortona but an important part in its construction was played by a French master-mason, Pierre Chambiges. Later the King employed Chambiges to build three more châteaux – Saint-Germain-en-Laye, La Muette, and Challuau.

According to du Cerceau, François was his own architect at Saint-Germain. Here an entirely new palace was added to the Gothic keep and the chapel of St Louis. As it was built on the foundations of the old castle, its shape was that of an irregular pentagon. The lower storeys were of creamy white stone, the upper of pale pink and straw-coloured brick. The windows were under arches deeply recessed between buttresses and there were slender round towers at each of the five angles. Within, the five-sided courtyard also had round towers at its angles – balustrades were ornamented with the salamander. The State rooms were on the first floor, reached by a great staircase. Instead of a steep-pitched roof, the top storey was vaulted and crowned by a flat terrace walk – to enable the court to watch the King hunting in the forest far below. Work on Saint-Germain began in 1532, but by 1540 so little progress had been made that François commissioned Maître Pierre Petit to 'pursue, worry and hustle' the masons. (The château was over-restored under Napoleon III and only survives in a greatly altered form.)

If François was his own architect at Saint-Germain, he must also have been responsible for La Muette and Challuau which greatly resembled it. La Muette was begun in 1541. A smaller version of Saint-Germain, also in brick and stone, it was built for Mme d'Etampes, only six miles from Fontainebleau. (It must not be confused with a château of the same name at Passy.) Challuau too was built for her, near Fontainebleau. Likewise in brick and stone, it consisted of a central block with four square pavilions at the corners and was only three storeys high. These two little châteaux, La Muette and Challuau, have disappeared without trace.

One must not forget that François possessed other palaces besides those which he had built. They included Amboise, Cognac, Romorantin, Plessis-lès-Tours, Angoulême, Montargis, Creil, Vincennes, and Coucy. Some, like the last two, were

Benvenuto Cellini's salt-cellar, c1540–3. When
François saw it 'he burst into an exclamation of
surprise and could never admire it enough'.

AN AUTUMN LANDSCAPE   209

frowning medieval fortresses rather than palaces. In addition, the King had Chenonceau
and Azay-le-Rideau, both confiscated from guilty financiers, and likewise the great
châteaux which had once belonged to Bourbon. There were also hôtels, or *maisons-du-
roy*, in Beaune and in Marseilles. François visited most more than once, some frequently.
He kept them in good repair and in many cases improved or embellished them – a
new wing was added to Amboise in the 1540s.

The King's example was followed all over France. The great lords built splendid
châteaux, the lesser graceful *manoirs*. The small folk had their churches. The same
architectural ferment produced what is still the finest church in Paris after Notre-
Dame – Saint-Eustache. Begun in 1532, essentially a Gothic structure with Renaissance
decoration, it is a dazzling monument to the impact of Italy upon France.

In 1537 Sebastiano Serlio sent a copy of the first section of his illustrated treatise
on architecture to François – it was intended for the use of architects and their
patrons. He asked to be taken into the King's service but nothing came of this request.
However, after he had dedicated the next section to François in 1540, he was invited
to France. He was given the title 'Architect to the King' and put in over-all charge
of the work at Fontainebleau. François seems to have employed him more as an
adviser than anything else – it is likely that he assisted the King with the building
of Saint-Germain. Although Serlio built châteaux for other patrons, his significance
lies in the fact that he helped to make Frenchmen aware of the really important
architectural achievements of the High Renaissance in Italy.

In 1540 the most colourful of François's Italian protégés arrived at Fontainebleau.
This was Benvenuto Cellini, the Florentine goldsmith and sculptor. Pope Paul III
had imprisoned him, largely on account of certain disrespectful comments on Pontifical
taste. He was released after Blaise de Monluc had repeatedly assured the Pope that
François needed Cellini's services and Cardinal Ippolito d'Este had persuaded him
that the King of France was 'much more complaisant' than he imagined.

Benvenuto tells how, at their first meeting, François spoke to him in Italian, 'in
a free and easy manner'. The King assigned him 700 crowns a year – 'the same salary
that he allowed Leonardo da Vinci the painter'. At his own request he was given
the *castello* of the Petit Nesle.

The Tour de Nesle was an ancient bastion of the city walls, on the Left Bank, in a
seedy neighbourhood infested with footpads. This round tower, ninety feet high,
was a place of sinister legend. It was said that a Queen had once lived there who
enticed lovers inside and then had them thrown from the battlements in sacks.
(A version of the tale was known to François Villon, who referred to it in his famous
Ballade des dames du temps jadis.) Today the Institut (the home of the Académie
Française) stands on the site.

Cellini took up residence in the Petit Nesle, which swiftly became notorious. He
evicted the previous occupants and filled it with whores who served as his models
and whom he beat. François visited the artist in this unsavoury studio, bringing a
party which included Mme d'Etampes, the Cardinal of Lorraine, the King and Queen

The château of Saint-Germain-en-Laye, from an
engraving by Jacques Androuet du Cerceau.

of Navarre, the Dauphin, and Mme Catherine. 'In a word', boasts Benvenuto, 'all
the nobility of the court of France came to my shop.' They arrived when he had just
given a tremendous kick to a French assistant, for clumsiness – the boy fell over the
King. Fortunately, François laughed. Not only did he pay the artist compliments,
but he treated him as an equal.

One day in 1542, one of the King's First Secretaries – M. Antoine le Maçon – came
to the Petit Nesle. The Secretary, 'a very polite, well-bred man who spoke Italian
incomparably well', gave Cellini some documents. 'His Majesty', he said, 'makes you
a present of these to encourage you to serve him with even greater zeal. They are
your letters of naturalization.' M. le Maçon added that the King had done this of
his own accord, a mark of distinction which had never been shown to any other
foreigner. Puzzled, the artist asked what were 'letters of naturalization'? The
Secretary burst out laughing. He explained that they were a great honour, greater
than that of being made a Venetian patrician. François himself laughed when he
heard of Benvenuto's bewilderment. 'I will see he understands why I sent him letters
of naturalization', said the King. 'Go and make out his patent as Lord of the Tour de
Nesle where he lives, as it's my property – he ought to understand that more easily
than he did the letters of naturalization!'

When Cellini showed François his models for the palace gate at Fontainebleau

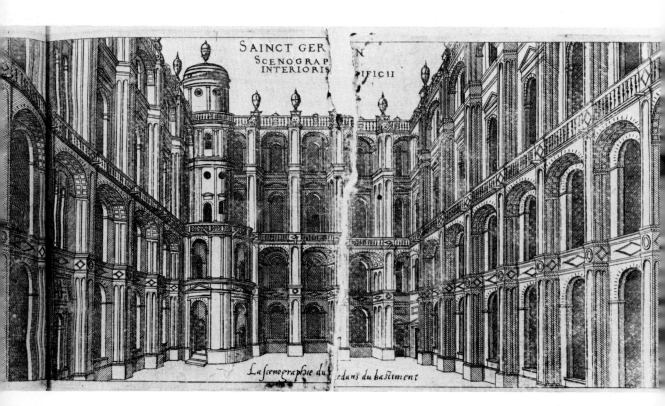

SAINCT GER   N

SCENOGRAP
INTERIORIS   IFICII

La scenographie du edans du bastiment

The Tour de Nesle, Benvenuto Cellini's studio, from a seventeenth-century engraving by Jacques Callot.

AN AUTUMN LANDSCAPE 211

and for a bronze fountain with figures of the Virtues, the King exclaimed, 'At last I have found a man after my own heart!' He clapped Benvenuto on the back saying, 'Mon ami, I do not know which is happier – the prince who meets a man after his own heart or the artist who finds a prince generous enough to give him all he needs to create his sublime dreams.' Cellini answered that, if he were the artist, the happiness was entirely on his side. Laughing, François said, 'Let us say they are equally happy.'

Unfortunately, Benvenuto somehow made an enemy of Mme d'Etampes. He ascribes this to neglecting to show her the works he had shown the King. He angered her still more by evicting one of her servants from a cellar under the Petit Nesle. (The eviction was perhaps understandable as the man was using the cellar as a gunpowder factory!) The Duchess made Primaticcio ask François for the commissions given to Cellini. Very unwillingly, the King agreed to let Primaticcio try his hand. Cellini visited his rival, threatening to kill him 'like a mad dog'. Primaticcio wisely went off to Rome to look for antiquities. Later, according to Cellini, Mme d'Etampes complained 'I rule the whole kingdom yet this little man defies me.'

In 1543 Cellini presented François with the most famous of all his works, the wonderful golden salt-cellar which is now at Vienna. Oval in shape, exquisitely cast and chiselled, it is flanked by two figures, the legs of one placed between those of the other. The left-hand figure is a beautiful naked woman, representing the Earth –

The *Nymph of Fontainebleau* – a bronze panel cast by Cellini for the palace gate. *Right* His drawing of *Juno*, a design for the twelve life-sized silver candelabra commissioned by François. (Only the *Jupiter* was completed.)

the right-hand figure is a naked man, holding a trident and representing the Sea. When the King saw the salt-cellar, he 'burst into an exclamation of surprise and could never admire it enough'. Benvenuto also cast a bronze panel for the Fontainebleau gate. It depicted the Nymph of Fontainebleau – the model was his mistress, Caterina. In addition, he prepared a design for the fountain, with a colossal figure of Mars.

In particular, Cellini hoped to impress François with a silver Jupiter six feet high. It was to be the first of twelve life-size gods and goddesses which were to serve as candlesticks at Fontainebleau. (Cellini's drawing for a Juno still survives – it is in the Louvre.) By 1544 the Jupiter was finished. It had a plinth of gilt-bronze on which were bas-reliefs of Leda and the Swan and of the Rape of Ganymede. The artist brought his statue to the Galerie François I for inspection. In the evening the King and Mme d'Etampes came to see it. Immediately, François cried out, 'This is one of the finest works of art that has ever been seen! I, who love such things and understand them, could never have imagined anything a hundredth part as beautiful!' However, the Duchess made disparaging comparisons between the *Jupiter* and the bronze casts of antique figures which stood in the gallery. The King disagreed. 'This statue is superior to them in every way,' he said. 'Benvenuto deserves the highest esteem since his works, instead of merely equalling those of the ancients, have greatly surpassed them.' Undeterred, Mme d'Etampes observed that by daylight it would not look so fine, that the veil draped round it must conceal some blemishes. At this, Benvenuto angrily tore away the veil, revealing Jupiter's prominent private parts.

Indeed, Cellini was impossible. Boastful, ridiculously touchy, he quarrelled with

Junone

era stera esfiecie di
grāde piu del uiuo
franceseho · in
auenono a essere
stimi il cia...

almost every other Italian artist whom François employed. He brawled no less noisily with Frenchmen and was constantly involved in street fights. His mistress, Caterina, accused him of sodomizing her – the penalty for this was burning alive. She was routed by Benvenuto's histrionics. In court he abused the judge and demanded that 'the shameless whore' herself should be burnt, shrieking, 'The fire! The fire!' He was acquitted but the affair can have done him no good.

In 1544, some time after the incident of the *Jupiter* and Mme d'Etampes, François came to the studio and gave Cellini a stern warning. 'It is important, Benvenuto, for you to realize that, however great your talent may be, you can only show your skill and prove your genius through the opportunities we give you. You must be a little more obedient, a little less proud and opinionated.' The King complained that the artist had done just what he pleased instead of what had been commissioned. 'If you are determined to go on like this', François threatened, 'I will show you how I can be when I want to have things done my way. I repeat that I insist on your carrying out exactly what I order – should you persist in doing just what you please, you will suffer!' All present trembled save, by his own account, Cellini. Later, in a conversation with M. de Saint-Pol, the King joked that he would let him hang Cellini if he found an artist who could take his place.

Despite his brave words, Benvenuto was obviously very frightened. He knew that François suspected he might try to run away. He therefore went to the King, bringing two beautifully wrought silver vases and asked for permission to visit Italy. He reminded François that such a favour had been granted to Primaticcio. The King was suspicious – several times he gave Cellini 'one of his terrible looks'. He told him, 'Benvenuto, you are a fool – take those vases back to Paris at once as I want them gilded.' Shortly after, however, through the intervention of the faithful Cardinal d'Este, Cellini was allowed to leave. In 1545 he returned hastily to Italy while François was ill, though the King's Treasurers had to gallop after him to prevent him from stealing three more silver vases. He never dared to set foot in France again.

There was at least one Frenchman as colourful as Cellini – Rabelais, 'master of all happy men'. Although the good doctor was never one of the King's protégés, like Budé or Marot, François undoubtedly enjoyed the adventures of those kindly giants, Gargantua and Pantagruel. He certainly read the first and third books and very probably the second too. He protected their creator, the 'hundred-headed monster' whom both Catholics and Protestants wanted to burn. Rabelais came into contact with the court as Physician to Cardinal du Bellay. He is known to have been present at the meeting between François I and Charles V in 1538. The King at some time made him a Master of Requests, a legal office of vague honour rather than duties or emolument. Rabelais himself says that the King had had read to him *The Inestimable Life of the Great Gargantua* – it is not known if the reading was by the author in person. Despite the outraged hostility which he provoked, this bibulous ex-friar, ex-monk, ex-canon, wandering physician, occasional lecturer, and parish priest, spoke for his age. Lytton Strachey wrote of his mighty work:

The whole vast spirit of the Renaissance is gathered within its pages: the tremendous vitality, the enormous erudition, the dazzling optimism, the courage, the inventiveness, the humanity, of that extraordinary age. . . . Rabelais's book is a history of giants, and it is itself gigantic; it is as broad as Gargantua himself. It seems to belong to the morning of the world – a time of mirth, and a time of expectation; when the earth was teeming with a miraculous richness, and the gods walked among men.[1]

Bottle! whose mysterious deep
Does ten thousand secrets keep,
With attentive ear I wait;
Ease my mind and speak my fate.

Soul of joy, like Bacchus, we
More than India gain by thee.
Truths unborn thy juice reveals,
Which futurity conceals.
Antidote to frauds and lies,
Wine, that mounts us to the skies,
May thy father Noah's brood
Like him drown, but in thy flood.
Speak, so may the liquid mine
Of rubies or of diamonds, shine.

Bottle! whose mysterious deep
Does ten thousand secrets keep,
With attentive ear I wait;
Ease my mind, and speak my fate.

In 1546 a proof-copy of *The Third Book of the Heroic Doings and Sayings of the Noble Pantagruel* was read to the King who laughed uproariously, crying that the author was the merriest devil in the realm – and the new volume received the royal imprimatur despite the Sorbonne's imminent condemnation. Laughter was what really mattered to Rabelais. Quintessentially French and hilariously funny, the advocate of 'The Divine Bottle' had a zest for life which is still infectious. His Utopian Abbey of Thélème, with its motto *'fais ce que voudras'* – 'do what you want' – and his orgy of swirling, experimental, prose continue to fascinate and bewilder twentieth-century minds. It says a good deal for the King's discernment that he saw that Dr Rabelais was neither heretic nor atheist. Anyone who loves Panurge and Friar Jean must have at least a little in common with François I.

[1] *Landmarks in French Literature* (1912, 1969)

François c1538 by Titian. Although based only on
the medallion by Cellini, it is a remarkable
likeness. *Overleaf* The Cour Ovale at
Fontainebleau.

François's last work of patronage was, if only indirectly, his mightiest. For he began
the new Louvre. In August 1546 the King commissioned Pierre Lescot to erect a
two-storey building with a projecting central pavilion and flanking galleries on the
site of the old keep. Lescot was an interesting choice. He was not a mere master-mason,
like Pierre Chambiges or Nicholas Le Breton, but came from a family of successful
lawyers and had studied mathematics and painting. Although he does not seem to
have visited Italy before the 1550s, he already had an excellent understanding of
the principles of classical architecture, with a clear grasp of 'the orders'. The style
which he developed was the first French architecture which was truly classical.
When François died, only a few months after approving the plans, Henri II confirmed
Lescot's appointment 'to carry on the work in accordance with the design and
specifications made for the late King'. Shortly after, however, the original plan was
replaced by one for a square château with four corner pavilions, whose area was
later quadrupled – the present Cour Carrée. Most of the work which had been done
in the previous reign had to be demolished. Today a staircase near the west entrance
is probably all that remains of François I's new Louvre.

Emperor Charles V c1548 by Titian. Charles is thirty-eight, the same age as François in the Titian portrait.

221

Everything Goes Ill

Despite all his achievements as a patron, the later years of François I's reign were far from happy. He was plagued by overreaching or inadequate Ministers, by a quarrelling court, and by an unsympathetic heir. His Kingdom was increasingly infected with heresy, was almost bankrupt, and suffered a bloody and humiliating invasion.

At the end of 1539 the people of Ghent rebelled against Charles V. To reach the Low Countries as quickly as possible, he asked François to let him pass through France with an escort of only fifty men. The King readily agreed. The Emperor was met at Bayonne by the Dauphin, M. d'Orléans, and the Constable. François joined him on 10 December at Loches, from whence they rode to Amboise. Night had fallen when they arrived. They entered the château together, riding up the spiral ramp inside one of the great towers, whose walls were hung with tapestry. The ramp was lined by such a multitude of torches that it seemed like midday. Then a page dropped a torch and the tapestry went up in flames. The Emperor was almost stifled by the smoke and nearly trampled to death in the panic. François wanted to hang the page, but Charles dissuaded him.

Next day the King and the Emperor proceeded to Blois, thence to Chambord, where the avenue was strewn with flowers. When they entered Orleans, Charles was given a triumphant reception by the entire city. At Fontainebleau he was greeted in the forest by woodland gods and goddesses who danced a rustic dance to the music of hautboys. Within the palace, says the chronicler, 'rooms, chambers and galleries were so richly hung with tapestries and decorated with such costly and beautiful pictures and statues that no mortal man could describe them or give a true account, for it seemed more like paradise, the work of gods rather than human hands . . . '

On 1 January 1540 the Emperor Charles V entered Paris. He rode on a black horse beneath a golden canopy emblazoned with the arms of his kingdoms and principalities. At his right hand rode the Dauphin, at his left M. d'Orléans. He was greeted by a salute of 300 guns, fired at the Bastille and on the city walls, and welcomed by the leading citizens of Paris – lawyers, merchants, clerics, and academics. His suit of plain black cloth was in sober contrast to their rainbow apparel. For a fortnight François entertained him in his capital, with banquets, masked balls, jousting, combats on foot and on horseback, and hunting-parties. Charles slept in the Louvre in a chamber hung with green velvet, on a bed covered in crimson velvet embroidered with pearls

By 1540 François I and Henry VIII were on friendly terms: among other gifts, François gave the English King this magnificent clock salt (restored to its original condition in 1972).

and precious stones. He was presented with a life-size silver statue of Hercules whose lion skin was of gold.

The Emperor can hardly have enjoyed every moment. Despite keeping to a diet of iced wine, oysters, and as much fish as possible, he was often ill. He passed entire nights in prayer, in rooms draped with black and lit by corpse candles. The stiff pride of his Spanish courtiers was bruised by the contrast between the splendour of the French and their own sombre attire.

François obviously took pleasure in his guest's uneasiness. A seventeenth-century historian tells how on one occasion the King, pointing towards Mme d'Etampes, said – no doubt with his malicious grin – 'Brother, that lovely lady advises me to bind you by a treaty of Paris, to undo that of Madrid!' Charles smiled faintly, answering, 'If advice is good, one should take it.' Next day when the Emperor was washing his hands before supper and the Duchess was holding a towel for him, he dropped a large diamond at her feet – the Great Diamond of the Dukes of Burgundy. When she picked it up, Charles said that he could not take it away from such a beautiful hand, begging her to keep it for love of him. The tale seems unlikely – a letter written shortly after the visit, by an Imperial agent, says that Mme d'Etampes bore the Emperor deep ill will because of his 'icy' manner towards her. Another story is that the young M. d'Orléans, noted for his wild antics, jumped up behind the Emperor, shouting, 'You are my prisoner!' – without looking behind him Charles V spurred his horse into a frantic gallop. There was also the Chancellor Poyet, who managed to upset some logs on to the Emperor, knocking him to the ground and bruising him badly. No doubt Charles was only too glad to leave Paris, to visit the Constable de Montmorency at his magnificent château of Chantilly. However, Queen Eleanor, the Dauphin, and M. d'Orléans insisted on accompanying him to the frontier.

Henry VIII had been in a fine fright at the news of Aigues-Mortes, and with reason. In December 1538 Pope Paul finally excommunicated him. A crusade was proclaimed against 'the most cruel and abominable tyrant' – it was to include the Emperor and the Kings of France and Scotland. Early in 1539 Charles and François entered into a solemn pact against Henry Tudor. There were rumours of a vast invasion fleet which might sail from the Low Countries at any moment. Levies were mustered all over England, fortresses built along the south coast, beacons erected at look-out points. King Henry reviewed a march-past by 15,000 Londoners at Westminster. But Charles and François had too many problems to waste money and men on such an adventure. By 1540 François was again writing friendly letters to the English King – at Christmas he sent him three *pâtés* made from the biggest wild boar ever killed in France. Henry was saved.

No doubt Anne de Montmorency, always practical, had been against the English adventure. The Constable was all powerful. Not only did he possess the power which Cardinal Richelieu would one day wield, but he was also the King's dearest friend. A Venetian Ambassador wrote of him, 'He rules everything, for himself and just as he pleases.' Brantôme, who had often met him, says that he could make men tremble

Marguerite d'Angoulême c1527. She wears white
in mourning for her first husband, the Duc
d'Alençon.

'like leaves in the wind'. The new Chancellor, Guillaume Poyet, was one of Montmorency's creatures. (In 1538, on one of those interminable royal progresses, the
previous Chancellor, Antoine du Bourg, had been thrown from his mule in the
gateway of Laon where he was trampled to death.)

Montmorency's brutal hand was evident in the new policy towards Reformers.
Anne said his prayers every morning, but he was a bigot without imagination. The
army had a saying, 'Beware the Paternosters of M. le Conêtable!' Peace with the Emperor
had ended any need to placate Lutheran Germany. By 1539 severe measures were
again being ordered against heretics. They continued for the remainder of the reign.
François even approved an index of prohibited books which had been drawn up
by the Sorbonne.

Among the works proscribed were those of Clément Marot. His Psalms had been
published in 1539 and again in 1541. Furthermore, he had offended Mme d'Etampes
by an ill-timed witticism. In 1542 he again fled from France, just before the Sorbonne
condemned his works. At Geneva he was received with acclaim. However, Calvin
could make little of the frivolous poet. Eventually Clément, caught playing cards,
had to make his escape from the Protestant Rome. Poor and miserable, still hoping
to return to France, Marot died at Turin in 1544.

Calvin had been established at Geneva since 1541. Another of the books proscribed
by the Sorbonne was his *Institutes of the Christian Religion*. It was dedicated to François
– the author declaimed 'Through this work, Sire, I should like to serve France . . . in
confessing the faith of the persecuted believers.' For the Reformers persisted in
regarding the King as a secret ally. Many years later, Theodore de Bèze, Calvin's
lieutenant and biographer, wrote of 'this incomparable book' that 'had François
read it, a severe wound might even then have been inflicted on the Babylonish
harlot. The King, unlike those who succeeded him, was quite capable of forming
his own opinion and had already given proof of no small discernment. A patron of
learned men, he was not personally disaffected towards the Reformers'. The *Institutes*
have been described as a Protestant *Summa Theologica* – Bossuet called their author
'the second patriarch' of the Reformation. The book was both a confession of faith
and a plan of action. It united most of the various small groups of French Reformers
and re-orientated them, giving them a cohesion which they had hitherto lacked.
But the full force of the Calvinist offensive would not be felt in France until the next
reign. Meanwhile, burnings continued throughout the realm.

One measure introduced during Montmorency's 'ministry' was undeniably
constructive. In 1539 the Edict of Villers-Cotterêts ordered that all legal documents
must be drawn up in French instead of Latin. It meant the end of the langue d'oc, of
Gascon, of Béarnais, and Provençal – hitherto in much of southern France registers
had been kept in the language of the troubadours. It was an important step in the
unification of the realm. But the Edict was essentially legal in intention. Throughout
François's reign officials were riding the length and breadth of France, writing down
infinitely diverse laws and customs in an attempt to achieve a general codification.

La feu Royne de nauarre
marguerite

There was even a colonial enterprise. In 1541 Jacques Cartier made a third voyage to Canada. He was accompanied by the Sieur de Roberval, a party of colonists, and twelve priests. A settlement was made at Cap Rouge, nine miles north of Quebec. But this time the natives were less friendly. They were suspicious of Cartier because he had not brought back the Indians he had abducted in 1535. However the French found what looked like diamonds, as well as gold in minute quantities. After great hardships they sailed for home, taking the disillusioned settlers with them, in 1543. Alas, the 'diamonds' proved to be rock-crystal – for a long time after, the French called anything worthless 'a Canadian diamond'. By then a costly war had begun and François had no more money for further expeditions.

In 1542 Montmorency decided to complete the destruction of Admiral Chabot, who had been under a cloud since 1536. After the Semblançay affair and continuing revelations about how financiers made their fortunes, François was always ready to believe he was being robbed. Middle age made him still more distrustful. A favourite's surest road to ruin was to be caught mulcting the royal revenues. Undoubtedly Chabot was guilty of irregularities. In 1538 the King asked for a report on his conduct. Poyet, an enemy, was put in charge of the investigation. It was alleged that the Admiral had sold fishing rights and licences for maritime expeditions, had misappropriated moneys intended for the wars, and taken bribes from the Portugese Ambassador – including a tapestry worth 30,000 crowns. In February 1541 Chabot was arrested and found guilty. The sentence ordered that he be deprived of all his offices, that his goods be confiscated, that he pay an *amende* of 400,000 livres, and that he be banished. In the meantime he was imprisoned at Vincennes.

At the moment of his utter ruin, Chabot's luck turned. Mme d'Etampes pleaded with King François for her old friend and ally. Only a month after his condemnation Chabot was excused the *amende*. In June 1541 he was given new estates and offices. In March 1542 he was absolved of *lèse-majesté* and, shortly after, exonerated of all other charges.

For even Anne de Montmorency could be brought down. He had many powerful enemies, among them the King's sister as well as the King's mistress. Marguerite was particularly annoyed by his Navarrese policy – he would do nothing to regain her husband's lost lands. The Constable's chief supporters were the Dauphin and Diane de Poitiers, support far from pleasing to the King. His ruin became inevitable in October 1540 when Charles V gave Milan to his son, the future Philip II. Until then François had hoped that the Emperor would settle the Duchy on M. d'Orléans. There was an ominous incident at the wedding of Jeanne d'Albret, Marguerite's daughter, to the Duke of Cleves. The unwilling little bride complained that her golden crown and furred mantle were too heavy for her to walk whereupon the King ordered Montmorency to carry her up the aisle on his back – stoically the Constable obeyed. In the autumn of 1541 he retired to his country palaces.

Chancellor Poyet survived his patron by a year. He had his uses, as a *Parlementaire* who knew the law. No doubt he modelled himself upon Duprat. A keen implementer

Left Charles, Duc d'Orléans, from François's tomb at Saint-Denis. *Right* The Dauphin Henri, from the portrait of him as King of France by François Clouet.

EVERYTHING GOES ILL   227

of savage taxation, a radical reformer of the laws, a persecutor of heretics, there was no more thoroughgoing advocate of the royal prerogative. But Poyet remained a second-rate figure. In the summer of 1542 François was still conferring honours upon him – by the autumn the Chancellor stood arraigned of misappropriation and other crimes. When he was sentenced in 1545 the King blamed his judges for being too lenient. However Poyet was released from the Bastille after paying not only a fine of 100,000 livres but also a further 17,000 livres for the expenses of his trial.

Chabot would probably have succeeded Montmorency. But in 1542 he suffered a severe heart attack – when he died the following year, his funeral was attended by all Paris. The new Ministers were the Cardinal de Tournon and the Marshal d'Annebaut. François de Tournon, now in his mid-fifties, was a career Churchman, a skilled diplomat, and a patron of the arts who understood how to reassure the King. Claude d'Annebaut was simpler, hard working rather than ambitious, a brave soldier but a poor general. Like so many of François's favourites he had been taken prisoner at

Claude de France with her daughters and
daughter-in-law. From a posthumous miniature in
Catherine de Medici's Book of Hours.

Pavia. Later he had again been captured, in Picardy, whereupon the King insisted
on bearing the cost of his ransom. In 1544 François made him Admiral. Annebaut and
Tournon retained their influence for the rest of the reign. Cavalli noted that the King's
business was 'discharged almost entirely by the Cardinal de Tournon and by the
Admiral. He takes no decision and makes no reply without their advice. He accepts
their opinion in everything, and if ever he talks to some ambassador and agrees to
something which has not been approved by them, he repudiates or changes it.' Even
so, the Venetian believed that 'in great matters of state, those of peace or war, His
Majesty, tractable in everything else, requires that all obey him. In such cases no one
at court, however important, dares to do other than refer the matter to His Majesty.'

In fact, even the highest Ministers of François I in these last years were far from
all powerful. Tavannes wrote that 'Alexander the Great saw women when he had no
business – François attended to business when he had no more women . . . everywhere
the ladies had too much power.' Two women dominated the court – Anne d'Etampes
and Diane de Poitiers. The factions which followed them squabbled viciously.
François's apparent hesitancies, his sudden changes of mind, may often have been
due to the venomous currents of court intrigue. Mme d'Etampes was the most powerful person in France. Mary of Hungary, Regent of the Low Countries, wrote ironically
to her brother Charles V that 'the demoiselle', meaning François's mistress, 'does
exactly what she pleases and arranges everything, the reason indeed for matters
being so well conducted!' Like Mme de Pompadour in the eighteenth century, Mme
d'Etampes was unjustly accused of being an enemy agent. The surest testimony in
her favour is that she always retained the affection of Marguerite of Navarre.

There are two portraits of Anne extant. One is a drawing by François Clouet –
it shows a pretty, rather homely, girl with strong physical appeal. The other is a
small painting by Corneille de Lyon of the Duchess in her thirties, golden haired
with shrewd eyes and a firm mouth, overpoweringly elegant in black (*see* p. 141).
This was the slight, graceful woman who had enslaved François I. Marot, when she
was his friend, wrote that to her belonged the golden apple which Paris awarded to
Venus. Anne was as wilful as she was vivacious and intelligent, but though she
undoubtedly influenced the King's policies, one can only guess at her political views.
It is probably safe to say that at home she disliked any persecution of the Reformers,
that abroad she distrusted Charles V.

Her anti-Imperialism must have delighted Charles d'Orléans. Born in 1522 he had
grown into a most attractive young man, the best looking of all the King's sons –
smallpox had made him blind in one eye but it was not noticeable. Laughing, extravagant, frivolous, whimsical, he put many in mind of the youthful François I. His
father approved of his liveliness – he used to say that 'a true Frenchman ought to be
quick, active, lively and always alert'. M. d'Orléans was popular with everybody.
The Swiss Guard nicknamed him Abednago. The nobility would far rather have
had him as Dauphin than his surly brother. Charles was as fair in hair and complexion
as Henri was dark – the inevitable Venetian observer commented, 'they are in nature

Henri II by Primaticcio, much as he must have
looked at the close of François's reign – he turned
grey very young.

EVERYTHING GOES ILL   231

completely contrary'. Although François himself much preferred this sympathetic son, he would not give him Brittany. The Emperor had proposed giving Charles his daughter Marie with the Low Countries and Franche-Comté for her dowry, if François would settle Burgundy on them. As well as Orléans, Charles already possessed the Duchies of Angoulême, Bourbon, and Châtelherault. François was not prepared to make even his favourite child into another Charles the Bold. Understandably, Orléans hoped for another war in Italy which might win him Milan.

The other dominant feminine influence at François's court was Diane de Poitiers, widow of the Seneschal of Normandy. Born in the last year of the fifteenth century, she retained remarkable beauty until middle age. A blonde, her face was unmistakably masterful, with a high forehead, a strong nose, and a pursed mouth. She had a peculiarly fashionable figure, well suited to Mannerist art, with a small head and long legs. The likenesses of her which survive, such as Luca Penni's *Diane Chasseresse* or Jean Goujon's statue, must be idealized representations – no woman of fifty could have looked like this, not even a Mistinguette or a Marlene Dietrich. But the seventeenth-century historian, Eudes de Mezeray, went too far when he imagined 'a young prince adoring a face from which the colour had fled, full of lines, a greying head, eyes half dimmed and sometimes red and bleared, loving what in another woman he would have found distasteful'. Undoubtedly Diane was very lovely for her years. Brantôme saw her six months before she died at nearly seventy, 'still so beautiful that I think that even the heart of a rock would have been stirred by her!' Legend says that, to preserve her beauty, she drank essence of gold and bathed in asses' milk like Nero's wife, Poppaea. None the less, Mme la Seneschale was careful to observe proprieties, always dressing in black and white as a widow should – though some said she did so because these colours suited her best. The tale, immortalized by Victor Hugo in *Le Roi s'amuse*, that Diane saved her father from execution – he had been caught up in Bourbon's conspiracy – by giving herself to François is a gross libel. Marino Cavalli understood perfectly the relationship between her and Henri. The Dauphin, he wrote, 'has real affection for her, but people consider that there is nothing lustful in it, that it is more like that which exists between mother and son – they say she has taken it on herself to teach, correct and counsel the Dauphin and make him act in a way worthy of him'. But Diane was also possessive, and coldly ambitious. Her advantage over Mme d'Etampes lay in the fact that her day was in the future – when the Dauphin should succeed to the throne.

The future Henri II has been described as the King of France who looked most like a nobleman. Certainly, François Clouet gives him the air of a Proustian Duke in fancy-dress – tall, distinguished, and bored (*see* p. 227). Primaticcio's portrait shows a much more striking face, impossibly long and desperately sad; Henri's black hair is cut short, almost sculptured, his beard curiously trimmed, while his ornate armour makes him look like a paladin from Ariosto or Cervantes – a 'Knight of the Dolorous Countenance'. Cavalli was impressed by the Dauphin. 'His qualities promise France the finest King that she has had for two centuries', he wrote. 'At twenty-eight years, this prince is of a

Left Diana of Anet, a contemporary sculpture once ascribed to Jean Goujon, sometimes said to represent Diane de Poitiers, the Dauphin's mistress. *Right* Claude de Lorraine, Duc de Guise (1497–1550), from a portrait c1525–7.

very robust constitution, but somewhat melancholy in humour. He is very skilled in the use of arms. He is not a good conversationalist, but very clear and firm in his opinions – what he has once said, he holds to stubbornly. He is of mediocre intelligence, slow to react. Yet that sort of man is often the most successful, maturing late like autumn fruit which is frequently better and longer lasting than that of spring or summer.'

The chief supporters of Diane's faction were Montmorency and the Guise family. The latter were a younger branch of the House of Lorraine. Their head was Claude de Guise whom François had made a Duke. Claude's seven sons were all able, spirited young men and his daughter Marie was Queen of Scots. The eldest son, François d'Aumale, would be one of the most famous of sixteenth-century soldiers, the future 'M. de Guise le Grand'. Another son, the brilliant and ambitious Charles de Guise, became a Prince of the Church. Nor was their uncle a spent force – in 1540 Cardinal Jean de Lorraine was being spoken of as a possible candidate for the Papacy.

One person whom everyone ignored was Mme Catherine, the Dauphin's wife. She never complained. The Italians observed, 'she is very obedient'. Catherine could scarcely be otherwise because she was barren for the first ten years of her marriage. It was known that Henri might not be able to beget children – he seems to have suffered from hypospadias. But in 1539 the girl he had raped in Piedmont bore him a daughter. The birth put the stigma of barrenness squarely on Catherine. Nor was she of any diplomatic importance. Montmorency, still in power at·that time, discussed with the council the possibility of a divorce. The Duc de Guise hopefully suggested one of his own daughters as a replacement, the beautiful Mlle Louise. But Catherine knew how to manage François. Throwing herself at the King's feet, sobbing, she cried that she knew she was to be divorced – to spare himself the pain of telling her, would he please let her retire to a convent. François embraced her. 'My daughter', he said, 'God has ordained that you should be my daughter-in-law and the Dauphin's wife and I do not wish it otherwise. Perhaps God will answer your prayers and ours.' Catherine tried everything. She made pilgrimages, consulted doctors, astronomers, astrologers, alchemists, and magicians, and drank love-potions. She even refused to ride mules because they were infertile. In the spring of 1543, she at last found herself pregnant. On 16 January 1544 she bore a son, 'le petit Dauphin', the future François II and husband of Mary Queen of Scots. Catherine would bear another nine children. Yet Henri continued to ignore her – he was interested only in Diane.

The other women in François's life were his sister and his one remaining daughter. Queen Marguerite had become more retiring. She was working on her poems, to be published as *Les Marguerites de la Marguerite*, and on her book of stories which she began in 1542. The latter, modelled on Boccaccio – her secretary was translating *The Decameron* – was called the *Cent Nouvelles Nouvelles* and would be published after François's death as the *Heptaméron*. As always, Marguerite was suspected of heresy. She was too prone to ridicule priests and friars, to scoff at superstitious devotions, and too fond of mystical piety. (Brantôme alleges that she used her piety to seduce lovers, leading the conversation from divine love on to carnal love.) Her protégé, the scholar printer Etienne Dolet, was burnt in 1546 for denying the soul's immortality, while her former secretary, Bonaventure des Periers, was (as author of the anti-Christian *Cymbalum Mundi*) a reputed atheist, who committed suicide in 1544. Her only child, Jeanne d'Albret, was forced to marry the Duke of Cleves – the brother of Henry VIII's rejected Queen – despite piteous protests.

King François was more merciful to his own daughter, Marguerite, who did not marry the Duke of Savoy until after her father's death. Describing her at 'twenty-two and perhaps more', Cavalli says that although she has not yet found a husband 'she is worthy of the greatest princes in the world, such is her prudence, modesty, goodness and talent. And she is well versed in Latin, in Greek and even in Italian.' Brantôme refers to her a little differently in his *Lives of Gallant Ladies*. He had heard of 'a daughter of the Blood Royal' who having slept with a certain Chevalier 'acquired such a taste for making love that she kept the Chevalier a whole month in her dressing-room, feeding him with lusty soups and strong meats'.

In October 1541 Charles V sent a mighty armada against Algiers. It was struck by a terrible storm which lasted for three days – the Emperor lost most of his fleet and half his troops. In July 1542 Imperialist agents murdered two of François's diplomats who were on their way to negotiate an alliance with Sultan Suleiman. Conflict was inevitable. In any case the French would never abandon hope of recovering Milan. Later that month the King's declaration of war upon the Emperor, his *cri de guerre*, was read throughout France to the sound of trumpets.

'Le gran Roy françois', a contemporary drawing
of the King during his last years.

The Dauphin and Marshal d'Annebaut laid siege to Perpignan for six weeks. It was defended by the Duke of Alba and they had small success. In the north Charles d'Orléans was more successful and captured Luxemburg. Fearful that he would miss the glory at Perpignan, the foolish young man suddenly hurried south. His father angrily ordered him back but in the meantime Imperialists had retaken Luxemburg. Then news came that the French garrisons in Piedmont were beleaguered. The Dauphin

took his troops to their rescue. There were inconclusive campaigns throughout the autumn and the winter of 1542 and the early months of 1543.

In February 1543 Charles V brought Henry VIII out of the isolation in which he had languished for so long, with a secret treaty. In June the English declared war on France. Henry was no longer threatened by Scotland. In the previous year the Scots' rout at Solway Moss had been so humiliating that James V is said to have died of shame. In the winter of 1543–4 preparations were made for a joint Anglo-Imperial offensive, the 'Enterprise of Paris'. Henry was to invade France from Calais, Charles from the Low Countries – after joining forces both armies would march on Paris.

However, 1543 was not altogether a disheartening year for François I. In September he recaptured Luxemburg. He then fortified Landrecies. The Emperor, with a large army which included 5,000 English troops under Sir John Wallop, tried to take it. François skilfully reinforced the beleaguered town with fresh troops and provisions, whereupon Charles gave up, withdrawing to winter quarters. None the less, he had knocked François's only ally, the Duke of Cleves, out of the war, ravaging his little State and forcing him to make peace in September.

There was only one direction from which help might come. In Hungary Sultan Suleiman was conquering all before him. During the summer of 1543 Barbarossa, with a hundred galleys, burnt Reggio and then sailed for Marseilles. Here he was joined by a French fleet of forty vessels under the Comte d'Enghien. In October the joint Franco-Turkish armada sacked Nice, carrying off its inhabitants into slavery, although they failed to take the citadel. The Turks were then given Toulon as a base in which to winter – the port's citizens were evacuated, save for heads of households and crafts-men. The guests raided local villages for slaves and sold them openly in the streets. Toulon became a second Constantinople, so people said, where the infidels celebrated Ramadan. Barbarossa, waited on by two Pashas and an entourage clad in long robes of cloth of gold, presided over this outpost of Islam. He was incensed by the inactivity of the French and, according to Monluc, 'showed himself very angry and made acid and sneering remarks'. Eventually, in the spring of 1544, after exacting an enormous payment in gold from his hosts, the great corsair left Toulon and launched what has been described as the most dreadful raid which Italy has ever known. Even François must have been embarrassed by the news.

The one great French victory of the war was won in Piedmont during the spring of 1544. François d'Enghien – a Prince of the Blood and a cousin of the King – was in command, although only twenty-three years old. He had laid siege to the Imperialist fortress of Carignano. Charles V's governor in Lombardy, the Marquis del Vasto – the same officer who had commanded the Spanish *arquebusiers* at Pavia – decided to force a battle in order to relieve it. He had 18,000 infantry, 800 light horse, and 200 heavy cavalry. Enghien, young and keen, was only too anxious for a chance of fighting, though he had had difficulty in obtaining permission from the King. He mustered 13,000 foot, 600 light horse, and 900 heavy cavalry. After his experience at Pavia, del Vasto believed that his *arquebusiers* could always rout French *gendarmerie* – he was so confident that his baggage-train included wagon loads of fetters for the prisoners which he expected to take.

The two armies met near Ceresole d'Alba, a village about thirty miles from Turin, on 11 April – Easter Monday. The battle was remarkable for the employment by each side of completely new tactics. The French stationed *arquebusiers* behind their first rank of pikemen; they were meant to fire at the moment of collision, killing the enemy officers who fought in front. Unfortunately, the Imperialists had the same idea, placing pistol-eers behind their first rank. In consequence both front ranks were slaughtered with-out either side gaining an advantage. Eventually, on the right and in the centre, the

The Battle of Ceresole d'Alba, 11 April 1544, from
a contemporary German engraving.

French and Swiss infantry routed the Imperialists. On the left, the enemy were at first triumphant. Here Enghien's infantry broke and ran. The Count himself led the *gendarmerie* in three splendid but disastrous charges, losing more men each time. It seemed like Pavia all over again. In despair, Enghien 'cursed the hour that he was born' and tore off his gorget to cut his throat. Just as he was about to do so news came that elsewhere the Imperialists were running. Del Vasto managed to retreat, saving some troops, but lost more than 6,000 men and all his cannon.

François was then forced to recall most of the army of Piedmont, to repulse an Imperialist invasion from the Low Countries. The year 1544 was proving to be the most dangerous of François's reign – even worse than 1525. He had let Enghien fight in Italy only because he had hoped that it would make Charles V withdraw his troops from the north. Instead, in June the Emperor invaded Champagne with 30,000 Germans and 7,000 Spaniards. By July he had reached Saint-Dizier. The Dauphin and Annebaut

took up a position near Châlons – their forward troops were badly cut up on 23 July. Meanwhile 40,000 English soldiers, in blue doublets and blue and red hose, had been landing at Calais since June. Commanded by Henry VIII in person, they invested Boulogne on 19 July.

Saint-Dizier, under the gallant Comte de Sancerre, held out until early August. The Count only surrendered after receiving a letter from the Duc de Guise ordering him to do so. The letter was a forgery – the Imperialists had captured the cipher used by the French army. It is said that no reverse in any of his wars angered François so much as the taking of Saint-Dizier. Charles then marched on Paris, along the right bank of the Marne, burning villages and châteaux. He took Epernay and Château-Thierry which he reduced to ashes. A terrified mob of refugees fled before the Imperialist army.

The King fell ill at this desperate moment. He had to keep to his bed. Weeping, François prayed, 'Oh my God, you are making me pay very dear for a kingdom which I

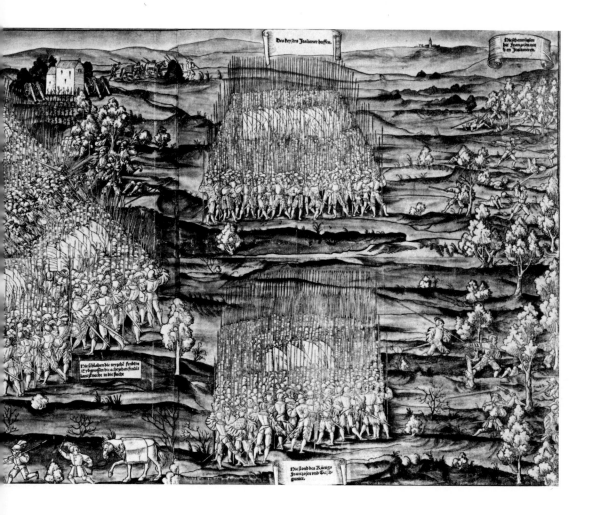

once thought you had given me freely enough. May your will be done!' He told Marguerite, who was nursing him, 'Ma mignonne, go to church at Compline and pray to God for me that, though his will is to love and cherish the Emperor more than I, he will at least ordain that I shall not see Charles entrenched before my capital.' François continued, 'I am determined to go out and meet him and fight – I pray God to give me death in battle rather than make me endure another captivity!'

Paris was in a state of wild panic. François wrote to its citizens that 'the enemy has been reduced to such straits that it is impossible for him to escape destruction'. He assured them, 'I will save you from harm – I do not know the meaning of fear.' On 10 December the King arrived to inspect his capital's defences. The Parisians were impressed neither by the royal communiqué nor by trenches being dug on the directions of an Italian engineer. The chronicler records that a procession of atonement to the shrine of St Geneviève could not pass through the streets, which were blocked by crowds fleeing with their goods in handcarts – 'for fear of the army of the Emperor which was drawing near'. Cellini believed that Charles could easily have taken the city.

Henry VIII saved Paris. Instead of marching to join the Emperor, his 'Enterprise of Paris' became the 'Enterprise of Boulogne'. The English preferred gaining another French port to a hazardous expedition inland. Charles grew desperate. The Dauphin had adopted a most effective scorched-earth policy, breaking down bridges and destroying any corn, wine, or other provisions which could not be removed. The Imperialist army, starving, grew mutinous and began to desert. Charles's strength lessened every day. Without English reinforcements he faced defeat. He retreated to Soissons. When Annebaut came to Charles's camp he found him surprisingly unwarlike. On 18 September the Peace of Crépy was signed between the Emperor and the King of France. The chief clauses were that François was to withdraw from Savoy and Piedmont and that Charles d'Orléans would marry either the Emperor's daughter or his niece – the dowry of one would be the Low Countries and Franche-Comté, of the other Milan. And, once again, His Most Christian Majesty swore an oath to fight the Turk.

Boulogne fell the day after Crépy was signed. King Henry returned to England, leaving Lord Lisle with 4,000 men to hold his new town. Soon the Dauphin and 30,000 men invested Boulogne. An attempt to take it by surprise failed miserably. A fort was built opposite the lost town. But the French were unable to recapture it. François decided to attack England. He had been laying the foundations of a French navy for many years. As long ago as 1517 he had founded a port for this purpose, Le Havre – originally called Franciscopolis. Here 200 sail assembled in August 1545, 'the most beautiful ships that ever eyes beheld' says Monluc. They included twenty-five galleys which had sailed up from the Mediterranean. Annebaut, in his capacity as Admiral of France, led this French armada across the Channel. The English fleet, with Henry VIII watching nervously from the shore, refused to leave the shelter of the Portsmouth batteries. The Admiral then made some feeble raids on the Isle of Wight and on the Sussex coast. After a desultory cannonade off Shoreham, the French, suffering from an outbreak of plague, were only too glad to go home. The only English

Left Jean Cauvin (1509–64) – Calvin – from a
portrait by Holbein. *Right* François Vatable
(d. 1547) the Hebraist, a Professor at François's
new Collège des Lecteurs Royaux. From a woodcut
of 1580.

loss was their great ship, the *Mary Rose*, which had capsized with all hands. The siege
of Boulogne dragged on. Peace was not made until June 1546. Even then, France only
regained Boulogne in the next reign.

Wars and patronage had exhausted the royal treasury. Desperate expedients were
tried to raise money. In 1539 François established a lottery – an Italian invention – in
Paris. In 1542 he borrowed massively from the merchants of Lyons, which for the
moment had ambitions of becoming a moneymarket after the fashion of Florence or
Augsburg. He was also borrowing heavily from foreign bankers. He continued to sell
offices and titles – the latter cost several hundred gold crowns each. The *rentes* were
levied in 1544, 1545, and 1546.

In 1542 the *gabelle* (salt tax) was levied in areas of south-western France which had
hitherto been exempt. There were armed uprisings, notably at La Rochelle. François
interrupted his campaigning to come and charm this rich port into submission. 'I
forgive and pardon you willingly (*de bon cœur*)' he told its angry citizens, 'and I hope
to win your hearts and assure you that you have won mine.' None the less, he installed
M. de Jarnac as Governor with a large garrison. Jarnac's martial law provoked fresh
uproar – the King had to recall him. In 1544 new taxes set off another conflict between
François and his 'faithful subjects' of La Rochelle.

Heresy was beyond control. The 'new religion' was particularly fashionable among

Woodcuts by Geoffroi Tory showing *left* heretics being executed and *right* as victims of a massacre.

intellectuals. Robert Estienne, François Vatable, Jean Goujon, and even Corneille de Lyon turned Protestant while the great Guillaume Budé seems to have died as one. François protected friends like Estienne but otherwise joined in a threefold alliance of King, Sorbonne, and Parlement. All over France faggots blazed and crackled to a chorus of agonized screams. The most spectacular fires were at Meaux in September 1546 where fourteen martyrs went to the stake together with their tongues cut out. The worst atrocity had already taken place. Small communities of Waldensian heretics, surviving from the Middle Ages, lived in remote valleys in the Alps – they might have been left in peace had they not publicly proclaimed their kinship with the Protestants. In 1540 the Parlement of Aix condemned seventeen citizens of the little hill town of Mérindol to be burnt. The King pardoned them, on condition they were converted to Catholicism. In 1545 he authorized the condemnation of five years before – it is probable he did not read what he was signing. The President of the Aix Parlement took 6,000 troops into the mountains. Mérindol, with two other little towns and thirty villages, was burnt to the ground and 2,000 Vaudois were butchered. 'In one church alone,' says an eyewitness, 'I saw nearly 500 women and children killed.' François was horrified when he learnt what had happened and ordered the punishment of those responsible.

Even at court François knew little peace. The Dauphin deeply resented the terms of Crépy. He considered that his father had jeopardized his future. Undoubtedly it was unwise to bequeath so much power to Orléans – contemporaries believed that the Emperor meant to use him as an ally against France when Henri II ascended the throne. The Dauphin protested publicly, at Fontainebleau in the presence of three Princes of the Blood. Meanwhile the factions of Mme d'Etampes and Mme la Seneschale continued to quarrel. There was also the affair of Jarnac and La Châtaigneraie.

Guy Chabot, later Baron de Jarnac, was the son of the Jarnac of La Rochelle and a cousin of Admiral Chabot. His mother was Mme d'Etampes's sister. 'Guichot', as François called him, was a slight, handsome fop whose sole occupation was love-affairs. Even by Renaissance standards he overdressed. One day the Dauphin asked him how he could afford it. Jarnac replied that it was through his stepmother's kindness. Henri misunderstood him. He had it put round the court that Jarnac slept with his stepmother. When Jarnac heard the libel he shouted, 'Whoever lies like this is evil and a coward!' The Dauphin's following had an obvious champion to avenge the insult, M. de La Châtaigneraie. 'My uncle', as Brantôme proudly refers to him, 'was much feared as he wielded a very good and a very quick sword. He was unusually strong, not too tall, not too short, a fine figure of a man, vigorous if a little fleshy.' Indeed, as a boy La Châtaigneraie's father had spiced his food with powdered gold, steel, and iron. Later he had studied under the greatest fencing masters in Italy, who at that time were the best swordsmen in Europe. He was also a famous wrestler. None the less, as a member of the old *noblesse chevaleresque* who still believed in trial by battle, he had qualms about fighting Jarnac. However, formal challenges were issued in July 1545. François, who must have known the truth from Mme d'Etampes refused to permit the duel. (It eventually took place in the next reign when, to everyone's surprise, Jarnac mortally wounded La Châtaigneraie.)

Potentially, the rivalry between the Dauphin and M. d'Orléans was the most dangerous. It solved itself in a peculiarly tragic fashion. In the autumn of 1545 Duke Charles was on his way to Boulogne where the French army was besieging the English. 'Plague' broke out – probably some sort of influenza – near his lodgings. 'It makes no difference – I'll stay here,' said Charles. 'No son of a King of France ever died of plague.' He went with the Dauphin to inspect some houses which were known to be infected. Laughing, Charles slashed a quilt with his sword, smothering himself and his brother with feathers. Soon after he was taken ill. He died on 9 September. Some thought he had been poisoned but most agreed it was the plague. François fainted at the news. An eyewitness (the Imperial Ambassador) says, 'he wept for a long time, crying loudly and shedding tears in great quantity'. The King moaned that God was punishing him for his sins. The whole court was in tears. The Emperor wrote a letter of condolence which so moved François that he replied in his own hand, 'praying God will be gracious to you so that you may never need such comfort nor feel what pain it is to lose a son'.

The King was very ill himself. In July he had burst a blood vessel in the groin and it had turned septic. The doctors were in despair but he recovered. However, at the beginning of 1546 he was attacked by a slow, recurring fever which culminated with an abscess which broke out in three places – it was feared his bladder was ulcerated.

A parade helmet of embossed and chiselled steel, probably commissioned by François. It was made in 1543 by Filippo Negroli of Milan.

He also suffered terrible fainting fits and it seemed unlikely he would live. This was the same malady from which he had suffered in 1539. None the less, he appeared to make a fair recovery.

The court was as fractious as ever. Guise's eldest son, François d'Aumale, an aspiring soldier, was fiercely jealous of Enghien, the hero of Ceresole. Although a brilliant military career lay before him, M. d'Aumale's chief distinction so far was his famous wound. He returned from fighting the English with a broken lance sticking through his head – it had entered between the nose and the right eye and come out between his ear and the nape of his neck. The great surgeon, Ambrose Paré, managed to extract it with a winch. Henceforth M. d'Aumale was known as 'le Balafré' – scarface.

In February 1546 when the King was at Roche-Guyon, 'the snow being very deep', some young courtiers began to play snowball. M. d'Enghien came out to see the fun – someone threw a coffer full of linen from a high window of the château which fell on to his head. He was dead within a week, scarcely twenty-seven years old. François was inconsolable. 'I have indeed offended God', he said, 'Who has taken two of my sons from me and after them someone whom I loved as my own child.' A Count Bentivoglio in the service of the Guise was suspected. However, the King decided it had been an accident and refused to allow any inquiry. It may even have been meant as a joke. Young courtiers often nearly strangled or drowned one another in brutal horseplay. Pitched battles in the streets were a favourite outlet for high spirits. Another amiable pastime was placing the obscene bodies of hanged criminals in the beds of ladies of the court.

Shortly after M. d'Orléans's death the King asked the Dauphin to preside over meetings of the Council, as it would be good experience for him. Ungraciously, Henri refused, 'because everything goes ill at present' and afterwards people might blame him for it.

The lake at Fontainebleau, from an engraving
of 1666 by Israel Silvestre.

243

Aged
and
Melancholic

In the summer of 1546 Mme la Dauphine presented François with a grand-daughter. This was Elizabeth de Valois, a future wife of Philip II of Spain. Henry VIII was asked to be the godfather. He sent a special envoy, Sir Thomas Cheyney, Knight of the Garter, to represent him at the christening. On 3 July, writing at Fontainebleau 'at 12 o'clock at night', Sir Thomas drew a charming vignette of François enjoying himself. 'And even now the King, the Dauphin, the Admiral and a great company of ladies came under my chamber window in three little galleons singing as sweetly as ever I heard, the King himself being one of them that sang. Such a triumph at a christening as I think was never seen or heard of as this is like to be!' (The lake on which the galleons sailed may still be seen at Fontainebleau.)

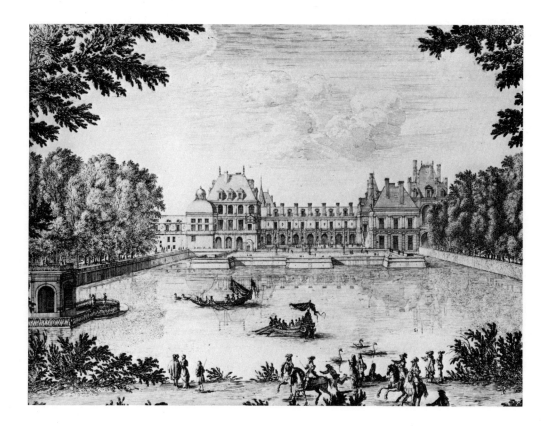

The year 1546 was the year when Cavalli reported how strong and well the King seemed. In September, Wooton – the resident English Ambassador – wrote from Beaune, 'He delights so much in the forest that he has been there four or five days hunting every day and will stay three or four days more!' (François once said that when he was old he would have himself carried after the hounds, that when he was dead he would hunt in his coffin.)

Yet the King was suffering strange tirednesses and attacks of melancholy. His face had become much too full and heavy, and he was losing his teeth. His hair was very thin and he wore his beard long which made him look much older. Monluc, who visited him about this time, says that, 'François was now grown aged and melancholic and did not caress men as he had once done.' Even for a confirmed nomad, the King was unusually restless, moving every few weeks from one beautiful palace or hunting-box to another. For years he had burnt the candle at both ends, yet he was always less strong than he looked. Besides his many illnesses he had also suffered a number of injuries. Like his parents and his children he was tubercular – by now he was riddled with the disease. But he continued to keep late hours, to indulge in violent exercise with his hounds by day and sleep with his mistresses by night. Marshal de Tavannes thought, 'ladies more than years caused his death'. It is worth remembering that of previous Kings of France only Louis XI had reached his sixties. Both Henry VIII and Charles V died in their mid-fifties. In 1546 François was fifty-two.

By Renaissance standards he was an old man. He looked back with despairing nostalgia to the one indisputable triumph of his reign – the victory of Marignano. Even now, François was contemplating a fresh attack on Charles V. His restless wanderings were largely along the frontier, from Savoy to Champagne, to inspect the fortifications which he had ordered to be built in case of war. He was engaged in constant negotiations with Henry VIII. He even seems to have told the English that he was about to renounce the Pope and would soon replace the Mass with a Protestant Communion Service. For François could never resign himself to losing his beautiful Milan, which, because of Orléans's death, would stay with the Habsburgs. His subjects were not so enthusiastic. Cavalli reported that people were saying that the King's wisdom was a matter of words rather than deeds, that all his wars had gone badly despite his fine speeches.

About this time the Dauphin, dining with his cronies, boasted what he would do when he was King. He named the men whom he would make Marshals of France and those who would take over the great offices of the household. Above all he would recall Montmorency. He did not notice Briandas, his jester, leaving the room. Briandas, who really was half mad, went straight to François. Instead of calling him 'King', the fool, in his cap and bells, began, 'God keep you, François de Valois!' 'What's this, Briandas?' demanded the King. 'Who taught you to speak like that?' *'Par le sang Dieu,'* answered Briandas, 'you are King no longer!' He told the household officers they had all been replaced – as Chamberlain he named Saint-André, a boon companion of the Dauphin whom François particularly disliked. *'Par la mordieu,'* ended the jester, 'you will soon see the Constable here, who will put you in prison where *you* will have to learn how to play the fool. Run away – you're a dead man!' After questioning Briandas, François summoned the Captain of the Scots Guard and forty archers and rushed to the Dauphin's room. However, the party had fled. The infuriated King vented his rage on the servants, striking at them with a halberd until they jumped out of the windows – he had the tables and chairs thrown after them. Henri had to stay away from court for a month. It was only with difficulty that François was persuaded to let him return.

Early in 1547, during a ball at Saint-Germain, the King received news that Henry VIII had died on 28 January. According to the Imperial Ambassador, François 'laughed loudly and joked with his ladies'. His mood changed when he remembered how the Englishman had recently reminded him that 'they were both mortal'. From then on François became 'more thoughtful than hitherto'. Martin du Bellay says that this was 'because he was nearly the same age as Henry and of the same constitution and was worried that he would soon follow him'. He ordered a great Requiem Mass to be sung at Notre-Dame for the repose of Henry's soul. That same night François fell ill. It was only a cold but shortly after he grew feverish. He took no notice. Each day his courtiers found him stranger and stranger. Having spent two or three days at Mme d'Etampes's château at Limours, he went on to Rochefort where he hunted every day. But each evening he had an attack of fever when he returned, so he decided to go to Saint-Germain, hunting as he went. By now he was being carried in a litter. 'Leaving Rochefort', says du Bellay, 'he came to lie at Rambouillet, intending to spend only a night there, but he found such good sport, both hunting and hawking, that he stayed for five or six days. Then the fever, which had long plagued him, gradually became unceasing and an abscess broke out. . . .' This was at the end of February. The abscess was so terrible that the doctors saw little hope of curing it.

By 20 March it was realized that the King's case was desperate. He confessed and received Communion. When his daughter Marguerite visited him he was unable to speak to her. By Tuesday, 29 March, François knew that he was dying. We know about his last moments from the despatches of the Imperial Ambassador, Dr Jean de Saint-Mauris. The King said, 'he knew it was all over with him and for that reason he would devote his mind to God and examine his conscience, ordering that no one should try to speak with him on matters of State'. He 'prayed long, blaming himself for his sins and asking pardon'. Among the sins, the King included the multitude of evils which he had brought upon his people and the many times when he had waged war to the detriment of all Christendom. François asked the Dauphin to keep Tournon and Annebaut as his Ministers and not to recall Montmorency. He also asked him to be kind to the Queen whom, he said, he had treated badly. 'Further, he spoke of Mme d'Etampes, beseeching him not to use her harshly, to have pity on her because she was a woman, but also exhorting him not to let himself be ruled by others as he had been by Mme d'Etampes.' After they gave the King the Holy Oils he took a crucifix in his hand and would not leave go of it.

François did not want his mistress near him. When he saw her come into his chamber he gestured with his hand for her to go away. Mme d'Etampes returned to her own chamber where she threw herself flat on the ground with a dreadful scream, shrieking, 'Earth swallow me!' Recovering, she called for her litter and left for Limours escorted by her brother, the Bishop of Condom.

The next day, Wednesday, the King felt a little better. He summoned some of his servants and asked God to forgive him any scandal which he might have caused them. By now he was half delirious. Pathetically, he begged four people to stay with him until the end. These were Tournon, Annebaut, Sourdis (his personal valet), and the Master of the Horse, M. de Boisy (son of Artus Gouffier). François said that he knew it was the custom for courtiers to leave their sovereigns when they were dying, abandoning them to strangers. The four stayed. The King told Boisy that he would die within the next twenty-four hours. That night he gave the Dauphin his blessing and embraced him. Henri fainted on the bed – François did not want to let go of him. Then the King picked up his crucifix again and said, '*In manus tuas, Domine, commendo spiritum meum!*' His last words were 'Jesus, Jesus!' When he lost the power of speech, it was seen that he was still praying – 'his hands were clasped, his eyes lifted towards heaven and sometimes he tried to cross himself. The Most Christian King died between one and two o'clock on the morning of 31 March 1547. When the doctors opened his body they found an abscess in the stomach, his kidneys shrivelled, his entrails putrefied, his throat corroded, and one of his lungs in shreds.

Henri II at once recalled Montmorency. He was more merciful to his father's mistress than might have been expected. Mme d'Etampes had remained at Limours 'in tears and continual lamentations', sending messages to court to beg her husband to be kind to her. She was terrified when both her chief henchman, M. de Longueval, and her steward were arrested. The mob wanted to stone her. However, apart from confiscating some of her goods, Henri left her alone. Queen Eleanor had to be content with chasing poor Marie de Canaples into a convent.

Marguerite had not seen her brother since February 1546. She had been staying in Navarre, tired and disillusioned, grieving for many friends who had died a hideous death. The news of François's illness filled her with dread. She dreamt that his ghost appeared to her, moaning, 'My sister! My sister!' No one dared tell her that he had died. At last she met a mad nun who was in tears. 'Why do you weep?' asked Marguerite. 'Alas!' cried the nun, 'I weep for your misfortune!' Then Marguerite knew that her brother was dead. 'You have tried to hide the death of the King from me,' she said reproachfully to her ladies, 'but God has told me through the mouth of this madwoman.' The last of the Trinity lingered on, inconsolable, her time devoted to mysticism and writing strange verse. She died, a good Catholic at the end, in December 1549.

François was given a funeral of which he would have approved. It was the most magnificent of any King of France hitherto. First, his body was taken to the country

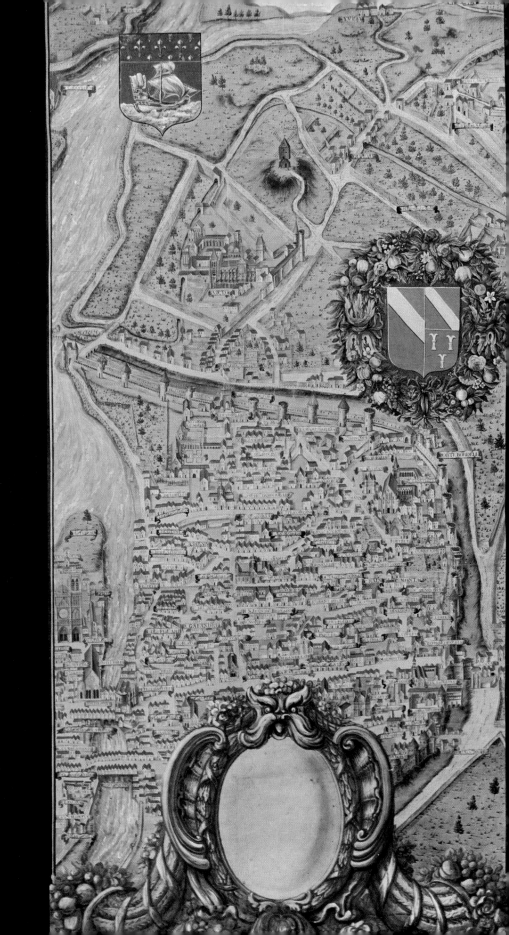

palace of the Bishop of Paris at Saint-Cloud. On Sunday, 24 April, a painted wood and wax statue of François was placed on a throne – its face had been modelled by François Clouet from the King's death-mask. The statue was dressed in François's own clothes. It had a shirt of fine linen bordered at the neck and cuffs with black silk, and a camisole of red satin lined with red taffetas and trimmed with silver. Over these were a tunic of white and crimson satin sewn with golden fleurs-de-lis and a royal mantle of violet velvet similarly embroidered with the lilies. It had boots of cloth of gold with crimson satin soles. On its head was the royal crown, in one hand the sceptre and in the other the *Main-de-Justice*. For eleven days meals were set before the statue at the accustomed times by the gentlemen of the household, each dish being ceremonially tasted by the Grand Master as though the King were still living. On 18 May Henri, wearing a violet velvet mantle with a train twenty feet long borne by five great lords, came and blessed his father's corpse with Holy Water. In theory he was still only Dauphin and not yet King. On 21 May François's coffin was taken to the church of Notre-Dame-des-Champs where the coffins of the two sons who had predeceased him were waiting.

On the morning of Monday, 22 May, the funeral cortège set out for Saint-Denis. First, through the crowded streets, came the archers, *arquebusiers* and crossbowmen of the town of Paris, clad in black, followed by friars of many Orders, by the parish priests of Paris carrying crosses, by 500 poor men in mourning carrying great wax tapers, and by the twenty-four town-criers of Paris, wearing the King's arms and ringing their bells. As they came to each cross road or square the latter all cried, 'Pray to God for the soul of the most high, most puissant and most mighty François, by the grace of God Most Christian King of France, first of his name, clement prince, father of the arts and sciences!' After them marched the watch, on foot and on horseback, all in black and after them the dignitaries of Paris – clergy and academics, lawyers and merchants. The royal household came next. First, the outriders and grooms, then the hundred *Suisses* (porters), then 200 gentlemen carrying poleaxes, and then all the other officers, every one in black – chaplains, squires, pages, valets, *maîtres d'hôtel*, controllers, treasurers, clerks, doctors, ushers, and even barbers and surgeons. The household was followed by the Grand Prior of the Temple, who was Premier Squire of the realm, carrying the Fanion or Banner of France.

At last, down the narrow muddy streets between the tall wooden houses, came the chariot which bore the King's coffin. It was draped in black velvet which swept the ground and was emblazoned with the arms of France. The chariot was drawn by six horses, two by two, each caparisoned in black velvet embroidered with a great white satin cross. Behind it rode the Squire de Noailles carrying the King's gauntlets, the Squire Poton carrying his helm, crowned and mantled with violet velvet sewn with lilies and furred with ermine, the Squire Chevalier carrying the royal shield bearing the arms of France, and the Squire Colvoisin carrying the King's surcoat. With them marched François's war-horse, caparisoned in violet velvet. The great lords and prelates of the realm followed – the Princes of the Blood, the Cardinals, the Bishop of Paris and thirty-three other Bishops in white mitres, and the Presidents of the Parlement. These were accompanied by the Ambassadors of the Pope, of the Emperor, of the Kings of England and Scotland, of the Dukes of Ferrara and Mantua, and of the Venetian Republic. The procession was brought up by the Chevaliers of Saint-Michel, the gentlemen of the bedchamber, and 400 archers of the Guard. In the dusk they found the Cathedral at Saint-Denis draped in black but illuminated by a myriad of candles.

At noon on the following day the long cortège, led by Admiral d'Annebaut in red from head to foot, again marched out to Saint-Denis. After the great Requiem had been sung by the Cardinal de Bourbon, the three coffins were lowered into the vault. A chosen company went down after them. In the vault the Grand Master laid down his staff of office, the Heralds their tabards, the Captains of the Guard their standards, and the Admiral the Banner of France. The Squires laid down the King's armour, his lance and sword. The Chevalier de Lorraine laid down the crown, the Duke of Lorraine the sceptre, and Orazio Farnese the *Main-de-Justice*. Then there was silence. It was broken by the Admiral crying, 'Le Roy est mort!' The words were repeated three times by the Heralds. After a pause, Annebaut took up the Banner of France and shouted, 'Vive le Roy Henri, deuxiéme de ce nom!' The cry was taken up by the Heralds, everyone present joining in. Finally, there was the funeral banquet – by custom it was regarded as constituting the late King's last act of hospitality. (Most of this account is taken from the relation by Guyenne King-at-Arms who was present.)

Henri II, who by tradition had not been allowed to attend his predecessor's obsequies, erected a splendid tomb at Saint-Denis. It was the work of Philibert de l'Orme, assisted by Pierre Bontemps. Below, François and Queen Claude are depicted in death. Above, they are shown as they were in life. They are flanked by their two sons while a daughter kneels behind them. Although François was only fifty-two his face – which is almost certainly a good likeness – is that of an old, weary man. It is none the less regal. (It may well have been modelled on the wooden funeral effigy – if so it is François Clouet's last portrait of the King.) Henri also commissioned Pierre Bontemps to make a monument to contain his father's heart. This is a strange but beautiful object, a stone casket with four legs standing upon a stone pillar.

Martin du Bellay ends his memoirs with a eulogy of François. 'This prince was much mourned both by his subjects and by foreigners, for he had excelled in every virtue.' Most contemporaries would have echoed his good opinion of the King. To them François appeared as the perfect Renaissance man, the personification of Castiglione's ideal. That is how Cavalli saw him. 'This prince is of a most sound judgement and of wide erudition; there is no matter, no science, no art, which he does not understand no less well than those who are specially trained in such things.' The Venetian continued that François, besides being skilled in all military matters, was 'well versed in hunting, in painting, in literature of every sort and of every language, and in all bodily accomplishments necessary for a true *cavaliere*'.

Below François I in death, from his tomb at Saint-Denis.
Overleaf left François I – a drawing for a fresco by Primaticcio. *Overleaf right* Map showing the kingdom of France and northern Italy at the close of François I's reign.

However, the Renaissance man went out of fashion. Since the eighteenth century such admiration of a King who was so obviously imperfect has puzzled historians. Writing in the 1760s William Robertson believed that 'the appellation of Father of Letters bestowed upon François, hath rendered his memory sacred among historians, and they seem to have regarded it as a sort of impiety to uncover his infirmities or to point out his defects'. The nineteenth century knew no such scruples. Between them, Victor Hugo and Michelet gave François I the reputation of a shallow profligate.

What is beyond question is François's love of beauty. Even Guizot, that stern Protestant bourgeois, admitted that the King loved everything which ennobles the mind, everything which expresses what is greatest in the human soul.[1] Today France is at last realizing how much she owes to François. There have been two exhibitions in Paris. One, at the Grand Palais, was on the School of Fontainebleau. The other, in the Salon Carré of the Louvre, reassembled as much of his collection as possible, bringing together again his Leonardos, his Raphaels, his Fra Bartolommeos, his Titians and other wonderful works. Everyone who saw them will recognize that within a few years François I transformed the cultural life of France to a degree unparalleled at any time in her history.

[1] *L'Histoire de France* (1876)

English Channel

Flanders

Calais
Guines
Ardres
Boulogne
Artois
Thérouanne
Tournai
Dourlens
Dieppe
Abbeville
Cambrai
Picardy
Amiens
Péronne

Le Havre
Mézières
Mouzon
Luxembourg
Rouen
Compiègne
Laon
Pagny
Chantilly
Soissons
Rheims
Normandy
Crépy
Roch-Guyon
St Denis
Villers-Cotterets
St Germain-en-Laye
Meaux
Epernay
Châlons-sur-Marne
St Cloud
Paris
Vincennes
Château Thierry
Rambouillet
Limours
St Dizier
Brittany
Alençon
Rennes
Etampes
Fontainebleau
Champagne
Orléannais
Sens
Châteaubriand
Vendôme
Orléans

Blois
Chambord
Plessis-les-Tours
Tours
Amboise
Romorantin
Burgundy
Besançon
Anjou
Loches
Berry
Poitou
Châtelherault
Franche Comté
Vienne
Bourbonnais
Moulins
Savoy
La Rochelle
Lyonnais
Rochefort
Angoulême
La Marche
Lyons
Chambéry
Bay of Biscay
Cognac
Angoulême
Auvergne
Vienne
Mont Cénis
Susa
Cognac
Turin
Bordeaux
Grenoble
Dauphiné
Mont Genèvre
Guyenne
Embrun
Albret
Dordogne
Cisteron
Garonne
Provence
Nérac
Avignon
Villeneuve de Marsin
Mérindol
Armagnac
Aix-en-Provence
Antibes
Dax
Languedoc
St Maximin
Fréjus
Bayonne
Toulouse
Arles
Marseilles
Hendaye
Navarre
Béarn
Aigues Mortes
Toulon
Pau
St Jean Pied-de-Port
Foix
Golfe du Lion
(Gulf of Lions)
Tarascon
Perpignan

Milan
Ticino
Marignano
Mont Cénis
Susa
Pavia
Grenoble
Turin
Po
Dauphiné
Mont Genèvre
Ceresole d'Alba
Piedmont
Embrun
Mediterranean Sea
Cisteron
Saluzzo
Durance
Col d'Agnel
Provence
Nice
St Maximin
Antibes
Marseilles
Fréjus
Toulon

On the same scale

0   50   100   150 Miles
0   50   100   150   200 Kilometres

Bibliography

FURTHER READING
There is no proper bibliography. The only over-all guide is still H. Hauser's *Les Sources de l'Histoire de France, XVIe siècle* (vol. II, Paris, 1907), which is inadequate. The chapter on François I in G. Dodu's *Les Valois* (Paris, 1934) contains a summary of the more important primary material. Anything by Baron de Ruble gives useful reference while M. François's *Le Cardinal de Tournon* has an impressive if limited list of sources.

DOCUMENTS
For French documents of the period see: *Catalogues des Actes de François Ier* (10 vols., Paris, 1887–1908); G. Ribier, *Lettres et Mémoires d'Estat des roys, princes, ambassadeurs sous les règnes de François Ier, Henry II et François II* (2 vols., Paris, 1666); and A. de Varillas, *Histoire de François Ier* (2 vols., Paris and La Haye, 1685–6).

There is no collection of François's letters and verse but the following are worth mentioning: *Poésies de François Ier, Louise de Savoie, Duchesse d'Angoulême, de Marguerite, Reine de Navarre, et correspondance intime du roi . . .* (ed. A. Champollion-Figeac, Paris, 1847); *Le captivité de François Ier* (ed. A. Champollion-Figeac, Paris, 1847); and *Lettres de François Ier à Louise de Savoie* (in *Les grands faits de l'Histoire de France racontés par les contemporains* (ed. L. E. Dussieux, 3 vols., Paris, 1874).

The most interesting collection of letters from the reign is that of his sister. See *Lettres de Marguerite d'Angoulême, sœur de François Ier* (ed. F. Génin, Paris, 1841); *Nouvelles Lettres . . .* (ed. F. Génin, Paris, 1842); and *Répertoire analytique et chronologique de la correspondance de Marguerite d'Angoulême . . .* (ed. P. Jourda, Paris, 1930). A good edition of her *Heptaméron* is that by M. François (Paris, 1950).

Among foreign collections the Venetian take first place: M. Sanuto, *I diarii* (Venice, 1879–); M. Tommaseo, *Relation des Ambassadeurs vénitiens sur les affaires de France* (2 vols., Paris, 1838); and R. Brown, *Calendar of State Papers, Venetian* (London, 1864–). For the English see *Letters and Papers, Foreign and Domestic, of the reign of Henry VIII . . .* (London, 1862–); and *State Papers of the reign of King Henry the Eighth* (London, 1830–). Among the Imperial are: *Papiers d'Etat du cardinal de Granvelle* (9 vols., Paris, 1841–52); *Correspondance du cardinal de Granvelle* (12 vols., Brussels, 1877–96); and *Correspondence of the Emperor Charles V and his Ambassadors at the Courts of England and France, 1519–1551* (ed. W. Bradford, London, 1850).

MEMOIRS
J. Barillon *Journal . . .* ed. P. de Vaissière, 2 vols., Paris, 1897–9

A. de Béatis *Voyage du Cardinal d'Aragon . . .* Paris, 1918

P. de Bourdeille de Brantôme *Œuvres Complètes . . .* 11 vols., Paris, 1864–82

G. & M. du Bellay *Mémoires de Martin et Guillaume du Bellay* ed. V. L. Bourilly and F. Vindry, Paris, 1908

B. Cellini *The Life of Benvenuto Cellini* (trans. J. A. Symonds) London, 1889

G. Guiffrey (ed.) *Chronique du roi François Ier . . .* Paris, 1860

G. de Jaligny *Histoire de Charles VIII, Roy de France* Paris, 1617

L. Lalanne (ed.) *Journal d'un Bourgeois de Paris sous François Ier* Paris, 1854

R. de la Marck, sieur de Fleurange *Mémoires . . .* Paris, 1913

Le Moine sans froc *Le Couronement du roy François premier de ce nom, voyage & conqueste de la duché de Millan, victoire et repulsion des exurpateurs d'icelle . . .* Paris, 1520

Louise de Savoie *Journal . . .* (in *Nouvelle collection des Mémoires pour servir à l'histoire de France*) ed. Michaud & Poujoulat, Paris, 1838

J. de Maille *La tres ioyeuse plaisante & recreative hystoire . . . de Bayart* Paris, 1527

G. de Marillac *Vie du connétable de Bourbon* (in *Choix de chroniques et mémoires sur l'histoire de France*) Paris, 1836

B. de Lasseran Massencome de Montluc *Commentaires . . .* Lyons, 1593

G. de Saulx de Tavannes *Mémoires . . .* Paris, 1829

F. de Scépeaux de Vieilleville *Mémoires . . .* (in *Mémoires pour servir à l'histoire de France*) Paris, 1827

GENERAL
There are few books in English on 16th-century France. Even in French there is comparatively little on the reign of François I and there is no definitive biography of the King.

The best introductions to the period remain H. Lemonnier's *La France sous Charles VIII, Louis XII et François Ier* and *La Lutte contre la maison d'Autriche: La France sous Henri II 1519–59* (parts 1 and 2 of vol. V of H. Lavisse's *Histoire de France,* Paris, 1903), Volumes V, VI, VII and VIII of Michelet's *Histoire de France – La Renaissance et la Réforme* (Paris, 1885) – are splendid if inaccurate stuff which make enjoyable reading.

BIOGRAPHIES OF THE KING
A. Bailly *François Ier, Restaurateur des Lettres et des Arts* Paris, 1954

A. Castan *La Mort de François Ier . . . d'après les dépêches secrètes de l'ambassadeur impérial Jean de Saint-Mauris* (in *Mémoires de la Société d'Emulation du Doubs*) Besançon, 1879

L. Cerf *L'Histoire vue par un médecin. Héritiers et bâtards de rois, les Valois* Paris, 1939

G. Dodu *Les Valois* Paris, 1934

Duc de Lévis Mirepoix (and others) *François Ier* Paris, 1967

L. Madelin *François Ier, le souverain politique* Paris, 1937

J. Michelet *François Ier et Charles Quint 1515–47* Paris, 1880

A. Mignet *Rivalité de François Ier et de Charles Quint* 2 vols., Paris, 1875

A. Paulin Paris *Etudes sur François Ier, roi de France . . .* 2 vols., Paris, 1885

J. Rey *Histoire de la captivité de François Ier* Paris, 1837

C. Terrasse *François Ier, le roi et le règne* 2 vols., Paris, 1943–8

LIVES
E. Armstrong *Robert Estienne, Royal Printer* Cambridge, 1954

P. Barocchi *Il Rosso Fiorentino* Rome, 1950

P. H. Bordeaux *La régente et le connétable* Paris, 1954

V. L. Bourilly *Guillaume du Bellay,*

seigneur de Langey, *1491–1543* Paris, 1905

K. Brandi *The Emperor Charles V* London, 1939; New York, 1965

A. Buisson *Le Chancelier Antoine Duprat* Paris, 1936

F. de Crue *Anne de Montmorency* 2 vols., Paris, 1885–9

F. Dimier *Le Primatice* Argenteuil, 1928

P. Erlanger *Diane de Poitiers* Paris, 1955

M. François *Le Cardinal François de Tournon* Paris, 1951

L. Goldscheider *Leonardo da Vinci* London, 1964

J. Héritier *Catherine de Médicis* Paris, 1940

P. Jourda *Marguerite d'Angoulême* 2 vols., Paris, 1930

P. Jourda *Marot* Paris, 1956

D. M. Mayer *The Great Regent, Louise of Savoy 1476–1531* London, 1966

J. Plattard *G. Budé . . .* Paris, 1923

L. Plattard *Vie de François Rabelais* Paris, 1928

A. F. Pollard *Henry VIII* London, 1951; New York, 1966

W. Robertson *The History of the Reign of the Emperor Charles V* 2 vols., Dublin, 1769

A. de Ruble *Le Mariage de Jeanne d'Albret* Paris, 1877

J. J. Scarisbrick *Henry VIII* London, 1968; California, 1968

A. Spont *Semblançay: le bourgeoisie financière du XVIe siécle* Paris, 1895

J. de Vandenesse *Journal des voyages de Charles Quint de 1514 à 1551* Brussels, 1874

LIFE AT COURT

L. Batiffol *Le Siècle de la Renaissance* Paris, 1909

G. Budé *Traité de la Vénerie . . .* (trans. into French by Loys le Roy) Paris, 1861

B. Castiglione *The Book of the Courtier* (trans. Sir T. Hoby) London, 1561

A. Denieul-Cormier *La France de la Renaissance* Paris, 1962; as *The Renaissance in France* (trans. A. & C. Freemantle) London, 1969

F. de Crue *La Cour de France et la société au XVIe siècle* Paris, 1888

J. du Fouilloux *La Vénerie et Fauconnerie* Paris, 1585

A. de Ruble *La Cour des Enfants de France sous François Ier* Paris, 1886

J. G. Russell *The Field of Cloth of Gold* London, 1969; New York, 1969

CHATEAUX OF FRANÇOIS I

J. Androuet du Cerceau *Les plus excellents bastiments de France* 2 vols., Paris, 1576–9

Sir R. Blomfield *History of French Architecture 1494–1661* 2 vols., London, 1911

P. de Cossé Brissac *Châteaux de France disparus* Paris, 1947

L. de Laborde *Les contes des Bâtiments du Roi 1528–71* 2 vols., Paris, 1877

Le père Dan *Le Trésor des merveilles de la maison royale de Fontainebleau* Paris, 1642

L. Dimier *Le château de Fontainebleau et la cour de François Ier* Paris, 1949

E. de Gancy *Châteaux de France* Paris, 1948–53

F. Herbet *Le château de Fontainbleau* Paris, 1937

F. & P. Lesueur *Le Château de Blois* Paris, 1914

THE ARTS

J. Adhémar *Le Dessin français au XVIe siècle* Lausanne, 1954

S. Béguin *L'Ecole de Fontainebleau – Le Maniérisme à la cour de France* Paris, 1960

A. Blum & P. Lauer *La Miniature française aux XVe et XVIe siècles* Paris, 1930

Sir A. Blunt *Art and Architecture in France 1500–1700* London, 1953; Baltimore, 1954

H. Bouchot *Les Artistes célèbres; Les Clouet et Corneille de Lyon* Paris, 1892

Lord Clark *The Nude* London, 1955; Princeton, 1955

La Collection de François Ier (Catalogue, *Edition de musées nationaux*) Paris, 1972

L. Dimier *Histoire de la peinture française des origines au retour de Vouet 1300–1627* Paris, 1928

L. Dimier *La Peinture française au XVIe siècle* Marseille, 1942

L. Dimier *Les portraits peints de François Ier* Paris, 1910

L'Ecole de Fontainebleau (Catalogue, *Edition des musées nationaux*) Paris, 1972

Inventaire de la librairie de Blois 1518 & 1544 (in *Anciens Inventaires et Catalogues de la Bibliothèque Nationale,* vol. I) Paris and Blois, 1908

J. Marquet de Vasselot *Les Emaux limousins de la fin du XVe siècle et de la première partie du XVIe* Paris, 1921

C. Maumené and L. d'Harcourt *Iconographie des rois de France* Paris, 1928 (vol. I)

P. Mellen *Jean Clouet* London, 1971; New York, 1971

Sir J. Pope-Hennessy *The Portrait in the Renaissance* London, 1967;

Princeton, 1967

J. Shearman *Mannerism* London, 1969; Baltimore, 1967

S. H. Steinberg *Five Hundred Years of Printing* London, 1955; Baltimore, 1956

G. Vasari *Le Vite de' più eccellenti pittori, scultori e architettori* 9 vols., Milan, 1962–6

R. A. Weigert *La Tapisserie française* Paris, 1956

H. Zerner *The School of Fontainebleau; etchings and engravings* London, 1969; New York, 1970

CONSTITUTIONAL AND ADMINISTRATIVE

R. Drouet *L'Etat des finances de 1523* Paris, 1923

C. de Seyssel *Le Monarchie de France* Paris, 1961

J. H. Shennan *The Parlement of Paris* London, 1968; Cornell, 1968

G. Zeller *Les Institutions de France* Paris, 1948

THE REFORMATION

H. Hauser *Etudes sur la Réforme française* Paris, 1909

L. Febvre *Au cœur religieux du 16e siècle* Paris, 1957

Illustrations and Acknowledgments

Page numbers in **bold type**
denote colour illustrations

Figures in **bold type** refer to colour plates; those in *italics* to black-and-white illustrations.

Index